Residential Landscaping II

Residential Landscaping II

PLANTING AND MAINTENANCE

Philip L. Carpenter

Professor of Horticulture
Purdue University

PDA Publishers Corporation
Mesa, Arizona

Cover photograph by A.E. Bye
Cover sketches and most sketches in this
book are by Cathy Lambert

copyright © 1983 by Philip L. Carpenter

Library of Congress Cataloging in Publication Data

Walker, Theodore D.
  Residential landscaping.

  Vol. 2: Residential landscaping : planting and
maintenance / Philip L. Carpenter.
  Vol. 2 published in Mesa, Ariz.
  Bibliography: v. 1, p.
  Includes indexes.
  1. Landscape gardening.   2. Landscape architecture.
I. Carpenter, Philip L. (Philip Lee), 1933-
SB473.W34   712'.6   81-18833
ISBN 0-914886-16-9 (v.1)
ISBN 0-914886-15-0 (pbk.)
ISBN 0-914886-21-5 (v. 2)
ISBN 0-914886-22-3 (pbk. : v. 2)

P D A PUBLISHERS CORPORATION
1725 E. Fountain
Mesa, Arizona 85203

Contents

Preface

PLANTS AND YOU

To most homeowners, plants represent the landscape. Even more narrow in thinking is the idea that "landscaping a home" just means planting trees and shrubs. Landscaping, if this is the right term, is much more. It means establishing the total environment of the home, office building, school, etc., and this includes, among many things, the use of a total plant community to provide an aesthetically pleasing setting on a year-round basis. The family living at a particular site is unique and different from every other family, so every landscape should be different and represent the needs of an individual family. The planting of a bluegrass lawn, a row of evergreens across the front of the home, and a shade tree in the front and back yard, just because every other home in the neighborhood has them, does not represent a total landscape that meets the needs of the individual family, and it certainly is not aesthetically pleasing.

The requirements of the family now and in the future must be considered when the site is being developed. Among the many choices to be made is the selection of the plant material. Too often the statement is made "I want something that is fast growing so that it will provide shade for the patio or house." There are many important considerations that must be made when selecting plant material for the landscape, but probably one of the least important is how fast it grows. You should consider whether 1) the plant's size and aesthetic quality fit the site and harmonize with the rest of the plants in the landscape; 2) whether the plant will accomplish the desired purpose; 3) if the plant will require low maintenance; 4) if it will provide year-round interest at the site; and 5) whether it is a plant that is really desired by the owner.

A plant should fit the site both aesthetically and physically. It is just common sense not to plant a large tree in a small courtyard or next to the home. The ultimate size of the plant must be considered. Too often that cute little evergreen in the container that is planted within a couple feet of the building, in a few short years is a green monster growing over the walls, windows, and walks. Also, the plant should blend into the total landscape and become part of the landsape not the entire landscape. A blue spruce (*Picea pungens glauca*) in the center of the front yard is an example of a plant that frequently dominates rather than blends into the total landscape.

Besides the aesthetics involved, the plants used at a site may serve many useful purposes, but nearly all of these purposes relate to environment modifications. Trees may be used to provide shade for a home, deck, or patio. This shade reduces summer temperatures and, in the case of homes and small buildings, reduces markedly the costs of air conditioning. Throughout many sections of the country, trees and shrubs have been used for windbreaks to reduce the harshness of an area. These windbreaks will reduce the winter heating bill as well as, making the site more hospitable during the winter months. Other uses of plantings to modify the environment include such things as erosion control, noise level reduction, visual screening, light screening, etc. All of these effects of plants in the landscape in their environment modification role make the site a more hospitable and pleasant place for man.

For most owners, the landscape plant material is just part of the total outside environment of their home. The plants do not represent a form of recreation and therefore, should be low maintenance. Plants that require special care or constant attention should be avoided. If you believe in a minimum use of pesticides, you should not use plants in your landscape that require frequent applications of pesticides to maintain them in a healthy condition. For example, the American elm (*Ulmus americana*) has been replaced in many locations by large plantings of honey locusts (*Gleditsia triacanthos*). This tree, in many sections of the country, requires several applications of insecticides during the summer to protect the tree from borers, mites, and mimosa webworm. Without the use of the insecticides the tree would be defoliated by midsummer and, if attacked by borers, killed.

Obviously this tree is not a low maintenance plant and when used in the landscape should only be used on sites where the application of insecticides is both acceptable and practical.

Maintenance that is bothersome may take another form besides the application of pesticides. Too often plants are selected that are not entirely winter hardy (low temperature sensitive) for a particular section of the country or the microclimate conditions found in a specific location on the site. This may require the construction of protective structures which, in the winter months, not only require time and expense, but also may be very unattractive. Unless one has gardening and plant interests, the use of plants requiring as little maintenance as possible is recommended.

If at all possible the plants used in a landscape should contribute on a year-round basis to that landscape. Often a plant is chosen only for its flowers or its attractive fall foliage. An example of this is the forsythia, which has beautiful yellow flowers early in the spring, but the rest of the year is just very ordinary in appearance. If this shrub is used, it should be integrated with the rest of the plant material. Too often it is used as a single specimen planting; for a very few days of flowering it

A combination of plants, water and rocks form an attractive landscape.

dominates, but after flowering it adds very little to the site.

Many evergreens, because they are always green, contribute to the site on a year-round basis. But if the entire landscape's plant material is composed of evergreens the site can be boring and uninteresting. For interest, consider plants that change with the seasons. Flowering dogwood (*Cornus florida*) is a prime example of a plant that provides continuous interest. Obviously this plant is spectacular in flower, but also consider it at other times of the year. Following the flowering in the spring the plant's branching habit and fine foliage add beauty to the landscape. In the fall the foliage will turn a rich red to maroon color, and, when the foliage falls, there is left on the tree the brilliant red fruit which attracts birds during the winter. Also, the bark and winter form are attractive. This plant contributes year-round to the landscape, and there are many other species that do likewise. Determine what each plant will look like every month of the year in your landscape, and use, as much as possible, those plants that contribute totally to the design.

The hardest factor to discuss is the selection of plants based on the owner's likes and dislikes. Yet this aspect is of prime importance because it controls the ultimate criteria for selecting the plant, which is: "Does the client like the plant?" The above mentioned factors should be considered in plant selection, but, even if the plant meets the other criteria, personal taste will dictate the final decision.

Plants are the backbone of the landscape in that they are living biological systems that constantly change and contribute to the site. They will modify the environment of a site and, if used properly, contribute greatly to the overall quality of human life.

ABOUT THIS BOOK

In this book and in the first volume, *Residential Landscaping I* (by Theodore D. Walker) we provide an in-depth view of the three phases in the development of residential and small area landscape sites. First, the landscape site should have a design prepared before any construction starts or, if the site is partially landscaped, a design should be prepared for an orderly and sound future development. Then, once the design has been prepared to the satisfaction of the owner, the construction of the landscape site should be done. This includes the installation of the plant material as well as the building of landscape features such as fences, decks, patios, walks, etc.

Following the installation the site must be maintained if it is to develop to its fullest potential through the growth of the landscape plant material.

There is a chapter on the plants used in the landscape with emphasis on how the plant's environment will affect its growth and development. In another chapter the terminology of the nursery industry is covered to aid the reader in buying quality landscape plant material.

Once the plans are prepared and the contracts signed, the installation of the landscape is ready to begin. The planting of the plant material is covered in three chapters on how to plant trees and shrubs, the planting of herbaceous plants such as annual and perennial flowers, bulbs, ground covers, and turf installation. Details are given on methods of coping with the adverse conditions found at some sites, as well as planting on sites with good growing conditions. There is also a chapter on planting a vegetable and fruit garden.

Maintaining the plant material growing on the site is covered in the last chapters of the book. Pest control as well as the physical care of the plants is examined in detail. The safe use of pesticides, and the proper methods of fertilizing, watering, and pruning are the main subjects of these chapters. The scheduling of maintenance practices and the use of various tools and equipment for maintaining the home landscape are discussed in other chapters of the section.

A well landscaped site increases in value, but more importantly, it becomes a more pleasant and desirable place to live or work. Plants are an essential part of the landscape and understanding how to select plants that are suitable for a particular use in the landscape is very important. Plants should fit the site, serve the purpose for which they were installed, require little maintenance, be suited for the environment found at the site, and above all, be liked by the person owning the site.

LaPorte County Landscaping
Plants improve the appearance of a railroad tie retaining wall.

1

Starting Out Right

Plants are complex biological systems that require specific conditions to attain their optimum growth. To have and maintain a successful landscape, you must understand these environmental requirements and use plants that will adapt to the conditions of the site. Each site, no matter how large or how small, has within it certain microclimate conditions that affect plant growth. It is important to be aware of how these factors influence plant growth and what modifications might be necessary to make the soil more receptive to plant growth and development. You can then select plants that will thrive in these conditions. Grow exotic and unusual specimens only if you are willing to spend the time and effort necessary to provide satisfactory growing conditions. Factors to consider are those that involve climate, such as light and temperature and atmospheric conditions, and those that involve the root environment, such as soil structure, drainage, and nutrients.

CLIMATIC FACTORS

Plant growth is affected by the macroclimate (general environmental conditions over a large geographic area) and the microclimate (conditions prevailing within a small area). Many macroclimate effects are obvious: tropical plants, those that will not tolerate low temperatures, cannot be used as outdoor landscape plants in northern parts of the country where temperatures go below freezing, and plants that need moist, boggy conditions cannot be used in the arid desert areas of the southwest. To a large extent, macroclimate conditions determine which plants can be used in the landscape.

More subtle are the microclimate plants. Three examples of microclimates that might occur in a residential landscape site are the increased wind velocity around the corners of a home, the possible increase in temperature from a light-colored reflective surface, or the drastic change in soil conditions where sand or trash from the construction is dumped. Other microclimate factors are light, temperature, and atmospheric conditions and these will be discussed in detail.

Light. Light is the energy source for all plant growth. Together with water, fertilizer, oxygen, carbon dioxide, and other factors, light in the visible spectrum is essential for growth. The three most important characteristics of light are *quantity, quality,* and *duration.*

Quantity. The quantity (intensity) of light greatly influences the rate of photosynthesis, which is the process whereby light energy is converted to chemical energy that plants can use. There are five factors that influence the quantity of light which reaches the leaf surfaces of plants: (1) the atmosphere, which determines the amount of light transmitted to the earth's surface; (2) gases, which absorb small quantities of certain wavelengths, and clouds, which may reduce the light to only four percent of its normal intensity; (3) solid pollutants like dust and smoke, which in certain locations can reduce light and which may settle on foliage and further reduce the light available for photosynthesis; (4) the angle at which the sun strikes the earth's surface (this accounts for the seasonal variation in light intensity); and (5) the latitude of the site, southern sites have less variation than northern sites.

In your landscape you must plan for the amount of light that will pass through the various layers of foliage: high trees, plants under the trees, and ground covers. In forests, only the tallest trees receive full sunlight, and the same will be true in your landscape if the site has plantings underneath shade trees. In a dense forest, only about one percent of the light will reach the understory plants. In most home landscapes about 20 percent of the light that strikes the trees will reach the plants that are growing beneath them. Thus, you must select plants that grow under less-than-optimum light conditions. For example, a bluegrass lawn cannot become established or thrive under a dense shade tree like a Norway maple (*Acer platanoides*) because bluegrass requires high light intensity. At low light intensities the bluegrass will not thrive; in fact, in a relatively short time it will actually decline to a point where individual plants die out or become so weakened that they cannot compete with other plants trying to become established in the lawn.

Some plants need full sun to really thrive but can tolerate shade or lower light intensities. Such shade-tolerant plants can be used in areas that do not receive full sunlight, such as the north sides of buildings and homes. Yews *(Taxus* sp.) and flowering dogwood *(Cornus florida)* are examples of such plants. Other plants require lower light intensities (shade) to grow to their best; these plants are generally classified as shade-requiring (Table 1-1). Some ferns and many of the tropical foliage plants fall into this category.

A.E. Bye and Associates

Fig. 1.1 *Light filtering through overstory trees to the understory plants such as turf and ground covers.*

Fig. 1.2 *Flowering Dogwood (Cornus florida) as an understory species in the landscape and a shade-tolerant ground cover. Myrtle (Vinca minor) is growing under both the overstory and understory trees.*

1.2

Fig. 1.3 *The ferns require shade. Will thrive in dense shade.*

Table 1-2 lists many shade-tolerant shrubs and trees; when selecting plants for the shade areas in your landscape, follow this information. Very few shrubs require shaded conditions in which to grow, but some shrubs can withstand them. The deeper the shade, the more difficult it is for the shrubs to grow. Most plants will not flower and fruit nearly as well in shade as in full sunlight, and the deeper the shade, the fewer the flowers produced. Table 1-1 includes those plants that actually require shaded conditions to grow well and those that will withstand shaded growing conditions better than most other plants.

Table 1-1 continued

Botanical	Common name
Rhododendron obtusum	Hiryu Azalea
Rhododendron smirnowii	Smirnow Rhododendron
Rhododendron yakusimanum	Yakusima Rhododendron
Rhododendron yedoense	Yodogawa Azalea
Sarcococca spp.	Sarcococcas
Skimmia spp.	Skimmias
Stewartia spp.	Stewartias
Trachelospermum spp.	Star-jasmines
Tsuga spp.	Hemlocks
Vinca spp.	Periwinkles, Myrtles

Table 1-1 Plants that require shade in summer.

Botanical	Common name
Acer pensylvanicum	Striped Maple, Moosewood
Acer spicatum	Mountain Maple
Ajuga spp.	Bugleweeds
Ardisia spp.	Ardisias
Berberis spp.	Barberries
Chimonanthus praecox	Wintersweet
Clematis florida	Cream Clematis
Clematis lanuginosa	Ningpo Clematis
Clematis macropetala	Bigpetal Clematis, Downy Clematis
Clematis montana	Anemone Clematis
Clematis patens	Lilac Clematis
Convallaria majalis	Lily-of-the-Valley
Cornus alternifolia	Pagoda Dogwood
Cornus florida	Flowering Dogwood
Cornus nuttallii	Pacific Dogwood
Euonymus japonica	Japanese Euonymus, Evergreen Euonymus
Gardenia jasminoides	Gardenia, Cape-jasmine
Gaultheria spp.	Wintergreens
Hosta spp.	Plantain Lilies
Ilex aquifolium	English Holly
Ilex crenata	Japanese Holly
Ilex latifolia	Lusterleaf Holly
Leucothoe spp.	Leucothoes
Pachysandra spp.	Pachysandras
Paxistima spp.	Pachistimas
Podocarpus macrophyllus	Yew Pine, Yew Podocarpus
Rhododendron austrinum	Florida Azalea
Rhododendron calendulaceum	Flame Azalea
Rhododendron carolinianum	Carolina Rhododendron
Rhododendron catawbiense	Catawba Rhododendron
Rhododendron dauricum	Dahurian Rhododendron
Rhododendron Xgandavense	Ghent Azalea
Rhododendron indicum	Indian Azalea
Rhododendron kaempferi	Torch Azalea
Rhododendron kiusianum	Kyushu Azalea
Rhododendron luteum	Pontic Azalea, Sweet Azalea
Rhododendron maximum	Rosebay Rhododendron
Rhododendron mucronatum	Snow Azalea
Rhododendron mucronulatum	Korean Rhododendron

Table 1-2 Plants that tolerate full shade in summer.

Botanical	Common name
Acer circinatum	Vine Maple
Actinidia arguta	Bower Actinidia
Arundinaria spp.	Bamboos (some)
Asarum spp.	Wild Gingers
Aspidistra elatior	Cast-iron Plant
Bambusa glaucescens	Hedge Bamboo
Celastrus spp.	Bittersweets
Cornus amomum	Silky Dogwood
Cornus mas	Cornelian Cherry
Cornus officinalis	Japanese Cornel
Cyrtomium falcata	Holly Fern
Daphne spp. (evergreen spp.)	Daphnes
Epimedium spp.	Barrenworts
Euonymus fortunei	Wintercreeper
Fatsia japonica	Japanese Fatsia
Ficus spp.	Figs
Hamamelis virginiana	Common Witch-hazel
Hydrangea anomala	Climbing Hydrangea
Hydrangea quercifolia	Oakleaf Hydrangea
Liriope spp.	Lilyturfs, Liriopes
Lonicera henryi	Henry Honeysuckle
Lonicera japonica	Japanese Honeysuckle
Ophiopogon japonicus	Mondo Grass, Dwarf Lilyturf
Pachysandra spp.	Pachysandras
Parthenocissus spp.	Creepers
Phyllostachys spp.	Bamboos (some)
Podocarpus macrophyllus	Yew Pine, Yew Podocarpus
Sasa spp.	Bamboos (some)
Skimmia spp.	Skimmias
Taxus spp.	Yews
Trachelospermum spp.	Star-jasmines
Tsuga spp.	Hemlocks
Vaccinium spp.	Blueberries, Cranberries, Huckleberries
Viburnum dentatum	Arrowwood
Vinca spp.	Periwinkles, Myrtles

Table 1-3 lists plants that need high light intensity. These plants, if they are to grow at an optimum rate, should receive at least a half day of full sunlight. Lower light intensities will reduce the growth rate of these plants, and, under some extreme conditions, the plants could decline and eventually die from lack of light. The quantity of light available at a landscape site must be taken into account by the landscape designer; for example, unusual microclimate conditions of low light intensities on the north side of structures, courtyards, and understory plantings require specially chosen plant selections.

Table 1-3 Plants that require full sun in summer.

Botanical	Common name
Aesculus glabra	Ohio Buckeye
Ailanthus altissima	Tree-of-heaven
Albizia julibrissin	Silk Tree, Mimosa
Antigonon leptopus	Coralvine, Rosa de Montana
Bumelia lanuginosa	Chittinwood, Wooly Buckthorn
Callistemon citrinus	Lemon Bottlebrush Red Bottlebrush
Caragana spp.	Pea-trees, Pea-shrubs
Carya spp.	Hickories
Caryopteris spp.	Bluebeards, Blue Spireas
Castanea spp.	Chestnuts
Ceanothus spp.	Ceanothus
Celtis spp.	Hackberries
Cinnamomum camphora	Camphor Tree
Cistus spp.	Rockroses
Coronilla varia	Crown Vitch
Corylus spp.	Filberts, Hazelnuts
Cotoneaster spp.	Cotoneaster
Crataegus spp.	Hawthorns
Cytisus spp.	Brooms
Elaeagnus spp.	Elaeagnus
Eucalyptus spp.	Eucalyptus, Gums
Fraxinus pennsylvanica	Green Ash, Red Ash
Fraxinus velutina	Velvet Ash
Genista spp.	Woodwaxens, Brooms
Ginkgo biloba	Ginkgo, Maidenhair Tree
Gleditsia triacanthos	Honey-locust
Gymnocladus dioica	Kentucky Coffee-tree
Helianthemum nummularium	Sunrose
Juniperus spp.	Junipers
Lagerstroemia indica	Crape Myrtle
Laurus nobilis	Grecian Laurel, Sweet Bay
Leucophyllum frutescens	Ceniza, Texas Ranger
Lotus corniculatus	Birdsfoot Trefoil
Maackia spp.	Maackias
Malus angustifolia	Southern Crabapple
Malus coronaria	Sweet Crabapple
Malus ioensis	Prairie Crabapple
Melia azedarach	Chinaberry
Myrtus communis	Myrtle
Nerium oleander	Oleander
Parkinsonia aculeata	Jerusalem Thorn Mexican Palo Verde

Table 1-3 continued

Botanical	Common name
Passiflora spp.	Passionflowers
Phellodendron spp.	Corktrees
Picea engelmannii	Engelmann Spruce
Picea glauca	White Spruce
Picea omorika	Serbian Spruce
Picea orientalis	Oriental Spruce
Pinus aristata	Bristlecone Pine
Pinus banksiana	Jack Pine
Pinus bungeana	Lacebark Pine
Pinus cembra	Swiss Stone Pine
Pinus contorta	Lodgepole Pine, Shore Pine
Pinus echinata	Shortleaf Pine
Pinus edulis	Pinyon Pine
Pinus elliottii	Slash Pine
Pinus flexilis	Limber Pine
Pinus halepensis	Aleppo Pine
Pinus jeffreyi	Jeffrey Pine
Pinus palustris	Longleaf Pine
Pinus ponderosa	Ponderosa Pine, Western Yellow Pine
Pinus sylvestris	Scots Pine
Pinus taeda	Loblolly Pine
Pinus virginiana	Srub Pine, Virginia Pine
Populus spp.	Aspens, Cottonwoods, Poplars
Potentilla spp.	Cinquefoils
Prunus spp.	Almonds, Apricots Cherries, Peaches, Plums, etc.
Punica granatum	Pomegranate
Pyrus spp.	Pears
Quercus spp.	Oaks
Rhus spp.	Sumacs
Robinia pseudoacacia	Black Locust
Rosa spp.	Roses
Sabal minor	Dwarf Palmetto
Salix spp.	Willows
Santolina spp.	Lavendar-cottons
Sapium sebiferum	Chinese Tallow-tree
Sassafras albidum	Sassafras
Sciadopitys verticillata	Japanese Umbrella-pine
Sequoiadendron giganteaum	Giant Sequoia, Giant Redwood
Serenoa repens	Saw Palmetto
Shepherdia spp.	Buffalo Berries
Sophora spp.	Sophoras, Pagodatree
Sorbus spp.	Mountain-ashes
Syringa spp.	Lilacs
Tamarix spp.	Tamarisks
Umbellularia californica	California Bay, California Laurel
Vaccinium vitis-idaea	Cowberry, Mountain Cranberry
Wisteria spp.	Wisterias
Yucca spp.	Yuccas

Quality. The quality of light refers to the wavelengths present. Natural light possesses all the essential wavelengths; the greatest photosynthetic activity occurs in the red and blue wavelengths. Chlorophyll reflects green light, which is why foliage appears green. In most outdoor landscape light quality is not too important, unless artificial light is used frequently for illumination.

However, the quality of light is important in interior landscapes. Any artificial lights used should contain a broad spectrum of wavelengths, including a strong input of red light. Avoid predominantly green light because it reduces plant growth and vigor. Fluorescent lights should have cool white bulbs so that a broad spectrum of wavelengths is available for plant growth and development. Figure 1-4 shows the wavelengths produced by the sun and those utilized by the plant. With certain types of light, more than one source is needed to achieve satisfactory growth. Figure 1-5 shows the differences in wavelengths produced by light from various sources.

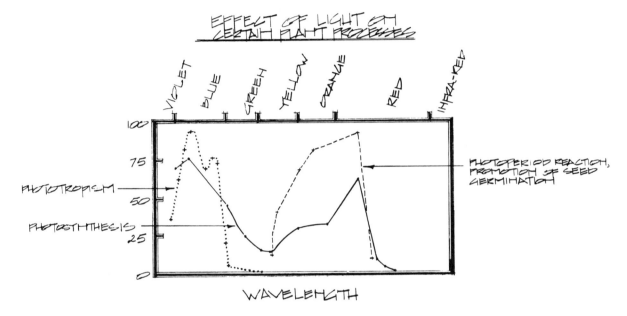

Fig. 1.4 *The visible light spectrum and some of the plant processes affected by light.*

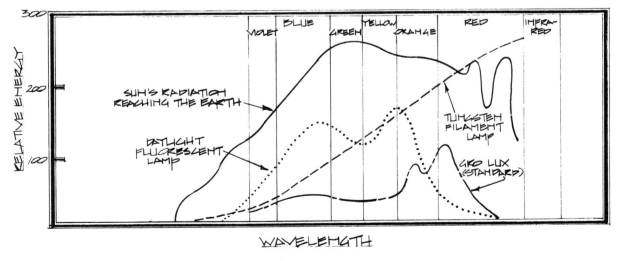

Fig. 1.5 *Light produced from various sources provides different wavelengths. A combination of sources may be necessary to obtain good growth of interior landscape plantings.*

Duration (Photoperiod). Many of the seasonable changes in plant growth, flowering, leaf fall, dormancy, hardiness, leaf size, development of pigments, germination, are controlled by the duration of the light (more correctly, the length of the dark period). There is a classification of plants based on their flowering response to photoperiodism. Plants that flower only under short photoperiods (usually less than 12 hours light, or, more precisely, more than 12 hours of continuous darkness) are called short-day plants. The chrysanthemum is a short-day plant. Plants that require long periods (14 hours or more) of light for flowering (short dark periods) are classified as long-day plants. An example of a long-day plant is Rose-of-Sharon *(Hibiscus syriacus).* Plants that do not respond to photoperiods are considered day neutral.

In addition to flowering, photoperiodism also influences the cold-hardening process that is necessary for plants in many areas of the country to survive the low winter temperatures. As days grow shorter in the fall, growth ceases, and plants enter a dormant state. When plants are dormant, they stop growing and deciduous plants lose their leaves; dormant plants are more resistant to low-temperature injury than when they are actively growing. Plants have adapted genetically over time to the photoperiod of a particular geographic area. Plants of a particular species from the south may not go into dormancy rapidly enough if they are moved to a northern site. The same species growing in the north will respond to the shortening of the day length and go into dormancy before the low temperatures set in. The point is that a plant, even though it is of the same species as native plants of that same species, may not be hardy in a particular section of the country. More detail on the hardiness of plants is given in the section on temperature.

Red wavelengths influence photo-periodism and therefore the development of dormancy and hardiness. Artificial light sources such as streetlights and other relatively high intensity lights near or in the landscape may affect plants' photoperiod. In most cases the amount of red light from these sources is low, and thus there is no influence on the development of dormancy. It has been suspected that sodium vapor lamps, which produce orange-colored light, might emit enough red light to prevent landscape plants from developing dormancy and thus make plants susceptible to low-temperature injury in the fall. However, so far, research evidence has not supported this theory.

Temperature. The temperature effects on plant growth are threefold. Most familiar are the low-temperature effects of an extremely bad winter or killing frosts. High-temperature injury to plants usually occurs in artificial conditions rather than in the natural environment. The third effect of temperature is on the growth processes of plants. For plant growth to be near optimum, temperature must be in a relatively narrow range. Above and below this optimum temperature growth slows down, and eventually, as divergences from the optimum increase, growth ceases. However, permanent injury to plants does not occur until temperature extremes are reached. Each plant species has its own optimum temperature range for growth as well as temperature limits beyond which it will be injured. Here we are mainly concerned with low-temperature injury because this is usually the most important effect of temperature on landscape plants.

Low-Temperature Injury. Extremely low temperatures injure or even kill certain plant species. The temperature at which this occurs varies according to the species, the growth stage, and the rapidity of temperature decline. Tropical foliage plants from Florida are not hardy in the northern areas of the country; they cannot survive the winters, and some will be injured if exposed for even a very short period (sometimes only a few seconds) to low temperatures. Be careful to protect tropical plants from temperatures near freezing and below when transporting and installing them in the home in the winter months.

Landscape plants vary greatly in their hardiness. The system of temperature zones helps define the areas of the country in which certain plants are hardy. These zones are indicated on a plant hardiness map (Figure 1-6). The numbers reference the average low temperatures in the zone; each zone represents a 10°F difference. The smaller the number, the colder the area. For example, zone 4 has an average annual minimum temperature of -30°F to -20°F. Thus, a plant species that survives in hardiness zone 4 but not in 3 is said to be winter

Fig. 1.6 *United States Department of Agriculture hardiness zone map showing the various plant hardiness zones in the United States. These zones are based on the average annual minimum temperatures recorded in that area. Do not use any plants that are not cold hardy in the particular hardiness zone of your landscape site.*

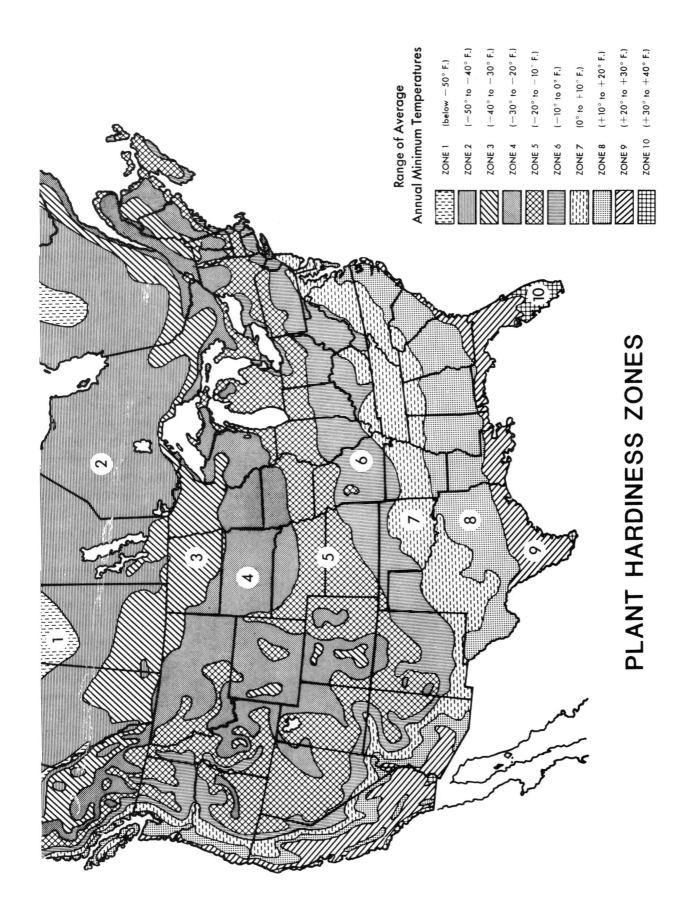

Range of Average
Annual Minimum Temperatures

ZONE 1   (below —50° F.)
ZONE 2   (—50° to —40° F.)
ZONE 3   (—40° to —30° F.)
ZONE 4   (—30° to —20° F.)
ZONE 5   (—20° to —10° F.)
ZONE 6   (—10° to 0° F.)
ZONE 7   (0° to +10° F.)
ZONE 8   (+10° to +20° F.)
ZONE 9   (+20° to +30° F.)
ZONE 10 (+30° to +40° F.)

PLANT HARDINESS ZONES

hardy to zone 4. Plants classified as having a hardiness to a certain zone should not be used beyond that zone. To be absolutely successful, do not use plants that give even the slightest hint of hardiness problems in a particular area. In other words, if you live in zone 6, use plants that are reported hardy to at least zone 6. Give yourself a one-zone safety factor for those unusually hard winters that occur occasionally. Exceptions are for protected microclimates on your site, in which case more "tender" species such as the Japanese Maple (Acer palmatum) might be used successfully.

Low-temperature injury can hit dormant plants or plants going into dormancy at the beginning of fall. As temperatures drop, two things may injure plants that are normally hardy. First, if too-low temperatures occur in a relatively short time, such as a drop from warm temperatures of 60 to 70°F to 5 to 10°F, in a few hours before hardiness has developed, there may be severe cold injury. Hardiness has several stages and develops from a gradual decline in temperatures over many days or weeks. If this adaptation never has a chance to take place, the plant plunges into extremely cold temperatures without protection.

LaPorte County Landscaping

Fig. 1.7 *A protected microclimate, where more tender species such as the Japanese Maple* (Acer palmatum), *might be used.*

This type of injury may also occur in the early spring. If temperatures warm up for only, say, 48 hours, plants rapidly lose their hardiness and become susceptible to cold injury as temperatures drop again. Landscape plants are particularly susceptible to this type of injury after the so-called January thaw that often occurs in the northern section of the country, when there are warm temperatures for several days and then extremely low temperatures return. There is very little that can be done to protect plants from this type of injury, but, fortunately, extensive damage from these unusual conditions is rare.

The second type of low-temperature injury occurs when the temperature on the plant's surfaces (trunk, or foliage if evergreen) declines rapidly, say 10 to 20°F per minute, for several minutes. When this happens, smooth-barked, nearly planted trees are often susceptible to *sun scald* and *frost cracks*. Sun scald can occur on evergreens particularly broad-leaved evergreens. On bright, clear, but very cold days, the sun will heat the surface of the bark or foliage to several degrees above freezing, perhaps to as much as 75 to 80°F. If the sun suddenly is covered by clouds or goes behind a building, or a shadow is cast on plants, there is a very rapid decline in the temperature (10 to 20°F per minute) on the plant surfaces, and ice cyrstals form in the plant cells. The crystals cause an interruption in the biochemical processes of the cell. This can cause the death of tissue, hence the sun scald.

Frost cracks or bark splitting involves the same rapid decline in temperature as in sun scald, but in this case the tree trunk, including the bark, first expands in the warm temperature and then contracts rapidly as the temperature declines. The wood does not cool and contract as quickly as the bark, so the bark splits open. Sun scald and frost cracks always occur on the south or southwest side of trees.

You can prevent or at least reduce the risks of sun scald and frost cracks by taking precautionary steps during the planting operation and subsequent care of the plants. Each fall, wrap the trunks of newly planted trees with burlap strips until the trees are well established and have developed substantial top growth. Limbs of established trees will shade the trunk, and rough bark provides its own shade. Remove this wrapping each spring and replace it in the fall as needed. Fruit tree trunks are sometimes painted white to reflect the light, so that there is less chance of temperature buildup. However, painting tree trunks white is not an acceptable practice for trees in the landscape

Fig. 1.8 *Wrapping a tree trunk to reduce the chances of sun scald and/or frost cracks.*

Table 1-4 Plants that require shade in winter.

Botanical	Common name
Arctostaphylos spp.	Bearberries Kinnikinnick, Manzanitas
Ardisia spp.	Ardisias
Aspidistra elatior	Cast-iron Plant
Berberis spp. (evergreen spp.)	Barberries
Buxus spp.	Boxwoods
Calluna vulgaris	Heather
Camellia spp.	Camellias
Chamaecyparis lawsoniana	Lawson False-cypress, Port Orford Cedar
Cyrtomium falcatum	Holly Fern
Daphne spp.	Daphnes
Erica spp.	Heaths
Euonymus fortunei	Wintercreeper
Fatsia japonica	Japanese Fatsia
Hedera spp.	Ivies
Ilex Xaltaclarensis	Altaclara Holly
Ilex aquifolium	English Holly
Ilex latifolia	Lusterleaf Holly
Ilex Xmeserveae	Meserve Holly, Blue Holly
Ilex opaca	American Holly
Ilex pedunculosa	Longstalk Holly
Kalmia latifolia	Mountain Laurel
Leucothoe spp.	Leucothoes
Mahonia spp.	Mahonias
Pachysandra spp.	Pachysandras
Paxistima spp.	Pachistimas
Pieris spp.	Pieris, Andromedas
Podocarpus macrophyllus	Yew Pine, Yew Podocarpus
Rhododendron carolinianum	Carolina Rhododendron
Rhododendron catawbiense	Catawba Rhododendron
Rhododendron impeditum	Cloudland Rhododendron
Rhododendron indicum	Indian Azalea
Rhododendron kaempferi	Torch Azalea
Rhododendron kiusianum	Kyushu Azalea
Rhododendron maximum	Rosebay Rhododendron
Rhododendron mucronatum	Snow Azalea
Rhododendron obtusum	Hiryu Azalea
Rhododendron smirnowii	Smirnow Rhododendron
Rhododendron yakusimanum	Yakusima Rhododendron
Sarcococca spp.	Sarcococcas
Sciadopitys verticillata	Japanese Umbrella-pine
Sequoia sempervirens	Coastal Redwood
Sequoiadendron giganteum	Giant Sequoia, Giant Redwood
Skimmia spp.	Skimmias
Taxus spp.	Yews
Viburnum davidii	David Viburnum
Viburnum japonicum	Japanese Viburnum
Viburnum odoratissimum	Sweet Viburnum
Viburnum rhytidophyllum	Leatherleaf Viburnum
Viburnum suspensum	Sandankwa Viburnum
Vinca spp.	Periwinkles, Myrtles

because of its undesirable appearance. Before transplanting a large specimen tree, mark its north side so that you may plant it with the same orientation in your landscape. In that way, the protective shade patterns of its limbs will help prevent sun scald and frost cracks. Finally, plant certain broad-leaved evergreens so that they are protected from the winter sun; that is, plant them on the north sides of homes, behind fences, and in similar areas.Table 1-4 lists plants that need winter shade.

The root system of some plant species are also sensitive to low-temperature injury. For example, the tops of Cranberry Contoneaster (*Cotoneaster apiculata*) can, when properly hardened, withstand a low temperature of -10° to -20°F, yet the roots are severely injured if the air temperature reaches 22°F or below. The critical low temperature for root injury varies greatly, depending on the plant species (see Table 1-5).

The soil temperature in the root zone of trees and shrubs grown in the ground is usually well above the critical temperature. However, container-grown plants have their soil mass and roots exposed to the air on top and on the sides. This dual exposure lowers the soil temperature inside the container; if a container is relatively small, the temperature could drop critically, injuring plant roots. You must therefore protect the container in the winter: store the plants in an unheated building where low temperatures are moderated (heat would promote growth, and the plants would not winter correctly). This technique is used by those who grow bonsai plants.

The last type of low-temperature injury causes indirect harm. This is desiccation; it especially affects broad-leaved evergreens. Winter burn occurs on bright, sunny days when the soil has frozen to depths that includes most

Table 1-5a Root killing temperatures of immature roots

Botanical	Killing temperature	Common names
Buxus sempervirens	26.6	Common Boxwood
Cotoneaster microphylla	24.8	Littleleaf or Rockspray Cotoneaster
Ilex cornuta 'Dazzler'	24.8	Dazzler Chinese Holly
Pyracantha coccinea 'Lalandei'	24.8	Lelande Scarlet Firethorn
Mahonia bealei	24.8	Leatherleaf Mahonia
Cotoneaster dammeri	23	Bearberry Cotoneaster
Ilex crenata 'Helleri'	23	Heller Japanese Holly
Ilex 'Nellie Stevens'	23	Nellie Stevens Holly
Ilex opaca	23	American Holly
Cornus florida	21.2	Flowering Dogwood
Euonymus kiautshovica	21.2	Spreading Euonymus
Ilex 'San Jose'	21.2	San Jose Holly
Magnolia stellata	21.2	Star Magnolia
Leucothoe fontanesiana	19.4	Drooping Leucothoe
Viburnum plicatum f. tomentosum	19.4	Doublefile Viburnum
Euonymus alata 'Compacta'	19.4	Compact Winged Euonymus
Taxus x media 'Hicksii'	17.6	Hicks Yew
Koelreuteria paniculata	15.8	Goldenrain Tree
Kalmia latifolia	15.8	Mountain Laurel
Pieris japonica	15.8	Japanese Andromeda
Rhodonendron 'Purple Gem'	15.8	Purple Gem Rhododendron
Rhododendron schlippenbachii	15.8	Royal Azalea
Juniperus conferta	12.2	Shore Juniper
Juniperus horizontalis 'Plumosa'	12.2	Andorra Juniper
Juniperus squamata 'Meyeri'	12.2	Meyer Juniper

Table 1-5b Root killing temperatures of mature roots

Botanical	Killing temperature	Common names
Magnolia x soulangiana	23	Saucer Magnolia
Magnolia stellata	17	Star Magnolia
Cornus florida	19.9	Flowering Dogwood
Ilex crenata 'Convexa'	19.9	Clonvexleaf Japanese Holly
Ilex crenata 'Hetzi'	19.9	Hetz Japanese Holly
Ilex opaca	19.9	American Holly
Pyracantha coccinea	17.9	Scarlet Firethorn
Ilex cornuta 'Dazzler'	17.6	Dazzler Chinese Holly
Cryptomeria japonica	16	Japanese Cryptomeria
Cotoneaster horizontalis	15	Rock or Rockespray Cotoneaster
Viburnum carlesii	15	Korean Spice Viburnum
Pieris japonica 'Compacta'	15	Compact Japanese Andromeda
Acer palmatum 'Atropurpureum'	14	Redleaf Japanese Maple
Ilex 'Nellie Stevens'	14	Nellie Stevens Holly
Mahonia bealei	12.2	Leatherleaf Mahonia
Rhododendron 'Hinodegiri'	10	Hinodegiri Azalea
Cotoneaster microphylla	8.6	Littleleaf or Rockspray Cotoneaster
Euonymus alata 'Compacta'	6.8	Compact Winged Euonymus
Leucothoe fontanesiana	5	Drooping Leucothoe
Juniperus squamata 'Meyeri'	-0.4	Meyer Juniper
Juniperus horizontalis 'Plumosa'	0	Andorra Juniper
Rhododendron carolinianum	0	Carolina Rhododendron
Rhododendron catawbiense	0	Catawba Rhododendron
Koelreuteria paniculata	-4	Goldenrain Tree
Taxus x media 'Hicksii'	-4	Hicks Yew
Juniperus conferta	-9.4	Shore Juniper
Rhododendron 'P.J.M. Hybrids'	-10	P.J.M. Hybrid Rhododendrons

From:

1. Havis, J.R. 1976. "Root hardiness of woody ornamentals." *HortScience* 11:385-386.
2. Studer, E.J., P.L. Steponkus, G.L. Good, and S.C. West. 1978. "Root hardiness of container grown ornamentals." *HortScience* 13:172-174.
3. Published in *Plants and The Landscape*, Vol. 4, No. 4, Autumn 1981.

of the plant's root mass. The sun warms the foliage surfaces to well above freezing, and the foliage loses water by transpiration. However, the roots cannot take up water because the soil is frozen. Thus the result is marked loss of water; if this occurs for any period of time, the tissues of a plant will dry out and it will die. Shallow-rooted broad-leaved evergreens such as the evergreen rhododendrons and English ivy (Hedera helix) are especially susceptible to winter burn.

To reduce the effects of winter burn, make sure you place susceptible plants in areas of winter shade, and not in open windy areas or on the sides of structures that face the prevailing winter winds (see Table 1-6). Also, apply a 2-to 3-inch-deep mulch to reduce the depth to which the soil freezes. This increases the roots' chances of being able to take up water in the winter. Continue a watering program into the fall (when inadequate rainfall occurs) so there is sufficient moisture for the winter months. If you cannot devote much time to maintaining your landscape, do not use plants that have special moisture requirements.

Table 1-6 Plants that tolerate little wind.

Botanical	Common name
Acer circinatum	Vine Maple
Acer japonicum	Full-moon Maple
Acer palmatum	Japanese Maple
Arctostaphylos spp.	Bearberries, Kinnikinnick, Manzanitas
Ardisia spp.	Ardisias
Arundinaria spp.	Bamboos (some)
Aspidistra elatior	Cast-iron Plant
Aucuba japonica	Japanese Aucuba, Gold-dust Plant
Bambusa glaucescens	Hedge Bamboo
Berberis spp.	Barberries
Buxus spp.	Boxwoods
Calocedrus decurrens	California Incense Cedar
Camellia spp.	Camellias
Chamaecyparis lawsoniana	Lawson False-cypress, Port Orford Cedar
Clerodendrum spp.	Glory-bowers
Cornus florida	Flowering Dogwood
Cornus kousa	Japanese or Chinese Dogwood
Corylopsis spp.	Winterhazels
Cotoneaster frigidus	Himalayan Cotoneaster
Cotoneaster lacteus	Parney Cotoneaster
Cotoneaster salicifolius	Willowleaf Cotoneaster
Cryptomeria japonica	Japanese Cryptomeria
Cyrtomium falcata	Holly Fern
Cytisus spp.	Brooms
Daphne spp.	Daphnes
Epimedium spp.	Barrenworts

Table 1-6 Continued

Botanical	Common name
Fatsia japonica	Japanese Fatsia
Ficus spp.	Rubber Plant, Figs
Firmiana simplex	Japanese Parasol Tree
Franklinia alatamaha	Franklinia
Fuchsia magellanica	Magellan Fuchsia
Hibiscus spp.	Hibiscus
Hosta spp.	Plantain Lilies
Hydrangea spp.	Hydrangeas
Ilex spp.	Hollies
Laburnum spp.	Laburnums
Leucothoe spp.	Leucothoes
Magnolia acuminata	Cucumber Tree
Magnolia macrophylla	Bigleaf Magnolia
Magnolia tripetala	Umbrella Magnolia
Mahonia spp.	Mahonias
Oxydendrum arboreum	Sorrel Tree, Sourwood
Pachysandra spp.	Pachysandras
Paeonia spp.	Peonies
Pieris spp.	Pieris, Andromedas
Pinus wallichiana	Himalayan White Pine
Podocarpus macrophyllus	Yew Pine, Yew Podocarpus
Rhododendron spp.	Rhododendrons, Azaleas
Sasa spp.	Bamboos (some)
Sciadopitys verticillata	Japanese Umbrella-pine
Sequoia sempervirens	Coastal Redwood
Sequoiadendron giganteum	Giant Sequoia, Giant Redwood
Skimmia spp.	Skimmias
Stewartia spp.	Stewartias
Symplocos spp.	Sweetleafs
Taxus spp.	Yews
Thuja spp.	Arborvitaes
Tsuga spp.	Hemlocks
Viburnum davidii	David Viburnum
Viburnum japonicum	Japanese Viburnum
Viburnum odoratissimum	Sweet Viburnum
Viburnum plicatum	Japanese Snowball Viburnum Doublefile Viburnum
Viburnum rhytidophyllum	Leatherleaf Viburnum
Viburnum sieboldii	Siebold Viburnum
Viburnum suspensum	Sandankwa Viburnum
Viburnum tinus	Laurestinus Viburnum
Vinca spp.	Periwinkles
Vitis spp.	Grapes
Wisteria spp.	Wisterias

High-Temperature Injury. High-temperature injury that occurs on very hot days is caused by plantings losing excessive amounts of water or by receiving too much reflected heat. If reflected temperatures build up to 130°F or higher for an hour or more, plant tissues may die. If you are growing plants near white surfaces or in areas such as courtyards where white reflective surfaces are present, use only plants that will tolerate extremely warm temperatures.

Atmospheric Conditions. *Pollution.* Pollution, of both air and soil, often damages plants. A serious air pollution problem results from drifting herbicides (weed killers). If not used properly, a weed killer can drift for fairly great distances: two or three city lots away or farther. The injury symptoms are abnormal growth, such as foliage twisting and curling. Except for extremely sensitive species like tomatoes, the injury is rarely permanent. The disfigured plants will return to their normal growth habits the same season, or at least by the next growth season. However, to reduce chance of injury, use the proper techniques for applying lawn herbicides discussed in Chapter 8.

Soil Pollution. Of a more serious nature are soil pollutants. Dumping waste products in the soil on the landscape site during the building process can create extremely difficult conditions for plant growth. Cement, sand stone, and lumber all can change the soil characteristics to a point where plant growth may be difficult, if not impossible. The best solution is for you or the contractor to remove all excessive waste materials and dispose of them in an approved site. If this is not possible, bury the materials deeply enough so that they will not cause a problem.

There has been an increasing number of pesticide and herbicide spills or accidents caused by homeowners not applying the material according to the label recommendations or, even worse, by using the wrong herbicide. For example, a powerful soil sterilant that kills all vegetation along a fence row may result in the death of nearby trees under the fence. You must use all pesticides and herbicides according to label recommendations. Never use any material from an unlabeled container, and never borrow from a friend or neighbor without reading about how to use the product. If you have an accident with an herbicide and valuable vegetation is threatened, contact your local county agricultural agent for help.

Occasionally fuel-oil spills, gas-line leaks, and industrial runoff problems pollute the soil, but these accidents are relatively rare, and there is little that you can do to prevent them. If they do happen, clean up the area and replant any damaged plants once you are sure the cleanup is complete.

Salt pollution occurs from using salt to melt snow and ice. The salt desiccates plants' tops and roots, and it degrades the soil structure by adding excess sodium. If you live in an area where salt injury is a possibility, follow these precautions. First, use as little salt as possible to melt snow and ice. Second, use salt only around driveways and curbs, not in other landscape plantings. Third, design the landscape bed so that water flow is away from the bed. Finally, use only plants which can tolerate unspecified salt sources and soil-borne salt (Table 1-7).

Table 1-7 Tolerance of woody landscape plants to highway de-icing salt.

Plant names	Unspecified Salt source	salt spray	Soil-borne salt
Abies balsamea Balsam Fir	M,S	M	S
Abies concolor White Fir	—	T	—
Acer campestre Hedge Maple	—	T,M	—
Acer ginnala Amur Maple	M	M,S,	—
Acer negundo Box-elder	M,S	M,S	M
Acer palmatum Japanese Maple	—	S	—
Acer platanoides Norway Maple	T,M T		T,M
Acer pseudoplatanus Sycamore Maple	S	T	S
Acer rubrum Red Maple	S	M,S	S
Acer saccharinum Silver Maple	M,S	T,M	S
Acer saccharum Sugar Maple	M,S	M,S	S
Acer tataricum Tatarian Maple	S	S	—
Aesculus hippocastanum Horse Chestnut	—	T	T
Ailanthus altissima Tree-of-heaven	—	T	—
Alnus glutinosa European Alder, Black Alder	M,S	T,M,S	S
Alnus incana Speckled Alder, White Alder	S	M	S
Alnus rugosa Speckled Alder, Hazel Alder	S	M	—
Amelanchier x grandiflora Apple Serviceberry	—	S	—
Amelanchier laevis Allegany Serviceberry	—	S	—
Berberis species Barberry	S	M,S	S
Betula alleghaniensis Yellow Birch	T	—	—

KEY
T = tolerant
M = intermediate
S = sensitive

From: Roadside De-Icing Salts and Ornamental Plants *by Ruth Kvaalen, Horticulture Department, Purdue University.*

Plant names	Unspecified salt source	salt spray	Soil-borne salt
Betula davurica Dahurian Birch	S	—	—
Betula lenta Cherry Birch, Sweet Birch	T	—	—
Betula nigra River Birch	—	—	S
Betula papyrifera Canoe Birch, Paper Birch	T,M,S	M	—
Betula pendula (Betula alba, B. verrucosa) European White Birch	—	M	—
Betula populifolia Gray Birch	T	M	—
Buxus sempervirens Common Boxwood	S	—	S
Caragana arborescens Siberian Pea-shrub	T	T	—
Carpinus betulus European Hornbeam	S	S	S
Carpinus caroliniana American Hornbeam, Blue Beech	S	—	—
Carya glabra Pignut Hickory	—	S	T,S
Carya ovata Shagbark Hickory	S	T,M	—
Carya species Hickory	S	—	—
Catalpa speciosa Northern or Western Catalpa	—	M	—
Celtis occidentalis Hackberry	M,S	S	—
Cerccis canadensis Eastern Redbud	—	S	—
Chaenomeles speciosa Flowering Quince	—	M,S	—
Chamaecyparis pisifera Sawara False-cypress	—	S	—
Cladrastis lutea American Yellowwood	—	M	—
Cornus alba Tatarian Dogwood	—	S	—
Cornus mas Cornelian Cherry	—	S	—
Cornus racemosa Gray Dogwood	—	S	—
Cornus sericea (Cornus stolonifera) Red Osier Dogwood	S	S	—
Corylus avellana European Filbert	S	S	S
Crataegus crus-galli Cockspur Hawthorn	S	S	—
Crataegus laevigata (Crataegus oxyacantha) English Hawthorn	—	S	—
Crataegus species Hawthorn	T	M,S	M
Elaeagnus angustifolia Russian Olive	T	T	T,M
Elaeagnus umbellata Autumn Olive	—	S	—
Euonymus alata Winged Euonymus	S	M	S
Euonymus europaea European Spindletree	—	S	—
Fagus grandifolia American Beech	S	M,S	—
Fagus sylvatica European Beech	S	S	S
Forsythia x intermedia Showy Border Forsythia	—	M	—
Fraxinus americana White Ash	T,M	M	S
Fraxinus excelsior European Ash	—	T	—
Fraxinus pennsylvanica Green Ash	T,M	M	T,M
Ginkgo biloba Maidenhair Tree	—	M	—
Gleditsia triacanthos Honey Locust	T	T,S	T
Gymnocladus dioica Kentucky Coffee Tree	—	T	—
Halimodendron halodendron Salt Tree	—	T	—
Hippophae rhamnoides Sea-buckthorn	T	T,M	T
Juglans nigra Black Walnut	S	M	S
Juglans regia Carpathian Walnut, English Walnut	—	M	—
Juniperus chinensis 'Pfitzerana' Pfitzer Juniper	—	—	T
Juniperus horizontalis 'Plumosa' Andorra Juniper	—	—	T
Juniperus species Juniper	—	T,M	—
Juniperus virginiana Eastern Red-cedar	T,M	T,M	M
Kolwitzia amabilis Beauty Bush	—	S	—
Larix decidua European Larch	—	T	—
Larix species Larch	S	T	—
Ligustrum species Privet	—	M,S	—
Ligustrum vulgare Common Privet	S	M,S	S
Liriodendron tulipifera Tulip Tree, Yellow-poplar	—	S	—

Plant names	Unspecified salt source	salt spray	Soil-borne salt
Lonicera japonica Japanese Honeysuckle, and Hall's Honeysuckle	M	—	M
Lonicera species Honeysuckle	—	S	—
Lonicera tataricum 'Zabelii' Zabel Honeysuckle	T,S	M,S	—
Lonicera xylosteum European Fly Honeysuckle	T	T,M	—
Lycium species Matrimony Vine	T	T	T
Malus baccata Siberian Crabapple	M	—	—
Malus species and cultivars Apple, Crabapple	M,S	S	—
Metasequoia glyptostroboides spp. Dawn Redwood	—	S	—
Morus alba White Mulberry	T	M,S	—
Morus species Mulberry	T	S	—
Parthenocissus quinquefolia Virginia Creeper, Woodbine	T	T	—
Physocarpus opulifolius var. *intermedius* Dwarf Eastern Ninebark	M,S	—	—
Picea abies Norway Spruce	—	M,S	S
Picea glauca White Spruce	M,S	T,S	M
Picea glauca 'Densata' Black Hills Spruce	T	—	—
Picea pungens Colorado Spruce	—	—	M,S
Picea pungens 'Glauca' Blue Colorado Spruce	T,M	T	—
Pinus banksiana Jack Pine	—	T	—
Pinus cembra Swiss Stone Pine	—	S	—
Pinus mugo Mugho Pine	—	T	T
Pinus nigra Austrian Pine, Black Pine	T,M	T	—
Pinus ponderosa Ponderosa Pine	T,M	—	M
Pinus resinosa Norway Pine, Red Pine	S	S	S
Pinus strobus Eastern White Pine	S	S	S
Pinus sylvestris Scotch Pine	T,M,S	M,S	—
Pinus thunbergiana (*Pinus thunbergii*) Japanese Black Pine	—	T	—
Plantanus x acerifolia London Plane Tree	—	S	—
Plantanus occidentalis American Sycamore	—	S	S
Populus alba White Poplar	T	T,M	T,M
Populus canescens Gray Poplar	T	T	T
Populus deltoides Eatern Cottonwood	T,M,S	T	T,S
Populus grandidentata Bigtooth Aspen	T	T,M	—
Populus laurifolia Laurel Poplar	S	—	S
Populus nigra 'Italica' Lombardy Poplar	T,S	T,M	S
Populus tremuloides Quaking Aspen	T,M,S	T,M	T
Potentilla fruitcosa 'Jackmanii' Jackman Shrubby Cinquefoil	T	—	—
Prunus armeniaca Apricot	T	—	—
Prunus avium Mazzard Cherry	—	M	—
Prunus padus European Bird Cherry	—	T,M	T
Prunus persica Peach	—	S	—
Prunus serotina Black Cherry	T,S	S	—
Prunus serrulata 'Kwanzan' Kwanzan Flowering Cherry	—	S	—
Prunus virginiana Chokecherry	—	T,M	—
Pseudotsuga menziesii Douglas-fir	M,S	M,S	M,S
Pyracantha coccinea Scarlet Firethorn	M	S	—
Pyrus species Pear	—	T,M	—
Quercus alba White Oak	T	M,S	T
Quercus bicolor Swamp White Oak	—	S	—
Quercus coccinea Scarlet Oak	—	S	—
Quercus macrocarpa Bur Oak	T,M	M	T
Quercus muehlenbergii Chinkapin Oak Yellow Chestnut Oak	—	S	—
Quercus palustris Pin Oak	S	S	—
Quercus robur English Oak	T	S	T
Quercus rubra Northern Red Oak	T	M,S	T
Quercus velutina Black Oak	—	—	T

Plant names	Unspecified salt source	salt spray	Soil-borne salt
Rhamnus cathartica Common Buckthorn	—	M	—
Rhamnus davurica Dahurian Buckthorn	—	T	—
Rhamnus frangula Alder Buckthorn	—	M	—
Rhus glabra Smooth Sumac	M	—	—
Rhus trilobata Skunkbush, Squawbush	T	—	T
Rhus typhina Staghorn Sumac	—	T	—
Ribes alpinum Alpine Currant	T	T	—
Ribes nigrum Black Currant	T,M	T	—
Robina pseudoacacia Black Locust	T	T	T
Rosa canina Dog Brier Rose	S	S	—
Rosa multiflora Japanese Rose, Multiflora Rose	S	—	S
Rosa rugosa Rugosa Rose	T	T,S	—
Rosa virginiana Virginia Rose	—	S	—
Salix alba White Willow	M	T,M,S,	—
Salix alba 'Tristis' Golden Weeping Willow	T	S	T
Salix alba 'Vitellina' Golden Willow	T,M	M,S	T,M
Salix caprea Goat Willow	M	M	—
Salix fragilis Crack Willow	T	T	T
Salix nigra Black Willow	—	M	—
Salix pentandra Laurel Willow	M	M	—
Salix purpurea Purple Osier Willow	T	—	T,M
Salix purpurea 'Nana' Dwarf Arctic Willow	S	—	S
Sambucus species Elderberry	—	S	—
Shepherdia argentea Buffalo Berry	T	T,M	
Sophora japonica Japanese Pagoda-tree	—	S	—
Sorbus aucuparia European Mountain-ash	S	M,S	—
Spiraea x bumalda Bumalda Spirea	M	S	—
Spiraea x vanhouttei Vanhoutte Spirea	T	—	S
Symphoricarpos albus Snowberry	T	T,M	—
Symphoricarpos orbiculatus Coralberry	S	S	—
Syringa reticulata (*Syringa amurensis* var. *japonica*) Japanese Tree Lilac	—	M	—
Syringa vulgaris Common Lilac	M	M,S	—
Tamarix species Tamarisk	T	T	T
Taxus baccata English Yew	—	S	—
Taxus cuspidata Japanese Yew	T	M,S	—
Thuja occidentalis American Arborvitae	T,M	M,S	M
Tilia americana American Linden, Basswood	S	M	S
Tilia cordata Littleleaf Linden	M,S	T,S	T,M,S
Tilia x euchlora Crimean Linden	—	S	—
Tilia platyphyllos Largeleaved Linden	—	T	—
Tsuga canadensis Canada or Eastern Hemlock	S	S	S
Ulmus americana American Elm	T,M,S	M	T,M,S,
Ulmus carpinifolia Smoothleaf Elm	—	M,S	T
Ulmus glabra Scotch Elm	T	T	M
Ulmus pumila Siberian Elm	T	M,S	T
Viburnum species	S	S	—

Injured

Normal

Fig. 1.9 *Dicamba injury on Taxus spp. Injury occurred from careless application of the herbicide on a nearby lawn.*

ROOT ENVIRONMENT

Soil Structure. During the construction of homes the soil structure of the site is frequently destroyed. Thus, before you can plant the landscape, you will probably have to modify the soil so plants can grow properly. Specific planting techniques for lawns, trees, shrubs, ground covers, and flowers are discussed in the following chapters; here the more general changes that are necessary are covered.

Soil is a living system that is specifically suited to the plants native to an area. Any nonnatural changes can greatly alter the character of a soil at a site and therefore affect the soil's ability to support the satisfactory growth of landscape plants.

The upper layers of a soil are the most fertile, containing a very active microflora and microfauna that greatly influence plant growth. These productive layers are generally very fragile and often destroyed by construction. In other instances, farming practices and erosion may reduce or completely eliminate the top layer.

The four major components of soil are (1) minerals, (2) organic matter, (3) water, and (4) air. A soil that is satisfactory for the growth of landscape plants has a proper balance of these four components. The ratio will depend on the soil type for the particular area in which the landscape is located.

The native soil habitat of trees and shrubs used in the landscape often contains all the layers and is rich in organic matter. As the plants grow, the soil furnishes nutrients and holds water. At the same time, the plants are trapping energy from the sun and converting carbon dioxide and water to carbohydrates, which are used as building blocks for their growth. When leaves are shed in the fall, the organic matter is utilized as an energy source by soil microorganisms. Thus the whole process begins again.

But consider the soil at many home sites. The topsoil has often been removed or so drastically disturbed that it has lost most of its productivity. The remaining subsoil generally has very little, if any, organic matter, and microorganism activity is minor. Drainage and aeration are poor. Plants placed in these hostile or very nearly sterile conditions will have a difficult time and certainly will not grow at an optimum rate.

You must take care when planting trees and shrubs in poor soils (special planting techniques for problem soils are discussed in Chapter 3). A cosmetic covering of a few inches

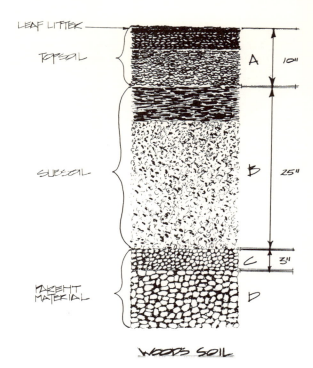

Fig. 1.10 *A soil profile of a forest soil. The drastically disturbed soil at most construction sites completely destroys the productive A and B layers.*

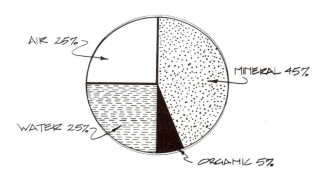

Fig. 1.11 *Physical components of a model silt loam soil when the small pores are filled with water and the large pores contain air. This is an ideal condition.*

of topsoil does *not* solve the problem and in some instances may even be detrimental to plants' establishment. A more serious problem may be the development of an artificial or *perched* water table: when the more porous, better drained topsoil is added on top of the poorer, often compacted subsoil, the water drains through the topsoil and stops at the interface between the added soil and the subsoil. In periods of heavy rainfall, the water collects at the interface, and the added soil soon becomes waterlogged. The plants' roots can be damaged from a lack of oxygen, and plants sensitive to waterlogged soils can die.

Minerals. The size and amount of the mineral particles affects a soil's texture. There are three particle classifications based on size: sand, silt, and clay. Sand has the largest particles, and the air spaces between particles improve aeration. However, this also means that it holds little moisture and few nutrients, so if your soil is excessively sandy, the site will have a tendency to be droughty. You will have to use special planting techniques and give attention to moisture needs after planting. Use drought-tolerant plants.

Silt particles are smaller than those of sand but larger than those in clay. This means that silt has an increased moisture-holding capacity, but its ability to retain nutrients is still poor.

Clay has the smallest and is the most chemically active of the three soils; it is responsible for almost all the nutrient capacity of the soil. Soils high in clay content have poor drainage and aeration and tend to become easily waterlogged. Use special planting techniques when planting in clay soils and buy plants that tolerate the heavy and tight clay soils. Two notes of caution here: plants that thrive in moist, highly organic soils such as bogs and marshes rarely do well in heavy clay soils. Also, plant lists for moist soils often include plants that will not tolerate heavy clay soils.

Terms such as loam, silt loam, and sandy loam refer to the soil texture as determined by the amounts of sand, silt, and clay present in the soil. As an example, a loam soil contains approximately 40 percent sand, 40 percent silt, and 20 percent clay. A sandy loam has 65 percent sand, 25 percent silt, and only 10 percent clay. A clay soil has 55 percent or more clay and drains very poorly.

Organic Matter. Organic matter contributes to the nutrient-holding capacity of a soil, and soil must contain sufficient quantities for plants to grow at an optimum rate. Generally, organic matter is present in only small quantities (3 to 5 percent) in most soils. Organic matter, such as manure, plant remains, decaying plants, peat moss, leaves, help keep soil loose and porous and helps aerate the soil, particularly clay soil. Because of its large and small pores, organic matter is like a sponge: it helps improve the mositure-holding capacity of sandy soils. Perhaps one of its most important functions is to provide an energy source for microorganisms in the soil; microorganisms in turn help contribute available nitrogen to plants and make other nutrients available to plants. Soils deficient in organic matter have essentially no microorganism activity. Methods of returning such soils to some degree of self-sufficient productivity (maintaining a stand of plants without adding fertilizer) are discussed later.

Water. Water in the soil is absolutely essential for plant growth and development. But too much water can be as detrimental as too little water. A soil that has all its pore spaces filled with water is saturated. Aeration is low, so only those plant species that can tolerate saturated soils survive for very long. Water normally drains from the soil by gravity, and the larger pore spaces fill with air until drainage stops. At this time the soil is at field capacity, which is the optimum amount of water for plant growth. But as the soil loses more water to evaporation or to plant use, the amount of water declines until the plants wilt from lack of water. Water plants before wilting occurs to avoid injury from water deficiency.

A good soil for plant growth has the right balance between large and small pores. Water drains rapidly from sandy soils because of the over-abundance of large pores, and clay soils get waterlogged because pores are too small. The basics of watering are covered in Chapter 9.

Soil Air. The composition of soil air is somewhat different than atmospheric air: oxygen levels decrease, and carbon dioxide builds up in the soil. Roots require oxygen for respiration and growth, so if the level of oxygen is depleted to the point where respiration cannot occur, roots are damaged and plants may die. The oxygen requirements of plants vary. For example, rhododendrons need a well-aerated soil (high oxygen content), but sycamores *(Platanus occidentalis)* grow in wet soils with relatively low oxygen levels.

Waterlogging, paving over tree roots, or compacting the soils all reduce the amount of oxygen available to tree roots. Many established trees die because fill soil has been placed over their roots during and after construction; the fill reduces the oxygen levels. Trees such as sugar maple *(Acer saccharum)*, beech *(Fagus sp.)*, and certain oaks *(Quercus* sp.) do not tolerate any fill soil or soil compacted over their roots. Good (not excessive) soil aeration is essential not only for newly planted landscape plants but for large, well-established plants.

Protecting Existing Plants. Too often a site is purchased for its large trees, but the trees are killed during construction of the home. The same unfortunate situation can happen during the course of individual projects, so homeowners should know about protecting existing plants.

The greatest danger to large trees is root damage, which can occur in a number of ways. Shallow-rooted trees such as beech may have their roots damaged by the traffic of construction equipment. It causes soil compaction. Another danger is that the addition of fill soil will change the moisture and aeration around the roots. The roots are part of a delicate biological system, and changing the oxygen levels by filling around them can seriously injure or even kill them. Installing patio or driveway paving over a root system can also be harmful, as can change in surface drainage or a rise in the water table. Finally, cutting off a large number of roots to install underground power, water, or gas lines, or to lower the grade can cause serious damage to trees.

Dry Well. A dry well can be constructed to protect trees from fill soil injury. This must be done before fill soil is added; it is too late after the trees have shown symptoms of decline, such as premature foliage dropping and brown, dried leaf edges. Some trees will tolerate up to 8 inches of fill, but others, such as beech, oak, and sugar maple, will not tolerate any fill unless a tree well is constructed. Even piling soil temporarily over a root system can kill a tree. Do not stockpile soil, except in open areas.

The construction of a tree well is much more complex than simply building a wall around a tree trunk. The first step is to remove the sod, leaves, and debris from around the tree to 3 feet beyond the drip line or maximum spread of the limbs. Broadcast (scatter) 1 pound of 12-12-12 fertilizer per inch trunk diameter over the stripped area. Work in the fertilizer to a depth of 2 to 3 inches, being careful not to damage any shallow roots during the process.

Install a high quality 4-inch drain tile system. Lay the tiles in the spoked-wheel pattern shown in Figure 1-13. This is the most commonly used system; the outlet should be tied into an existing storm sewer. If no sewer exists, construct a sump to drain the water. The tiles should slope 1/8 inch per foot. The joints in the tile should be tight, and cover the tiles with a fiberglass mat to prevent entry of roots and soil into the tiles. The outer perimeter of tiles should be at the drip line of the tree; install vertical tiles so that air will reach the root system.

Now build the dry well large enough to permit the future growth of the tree. The wall, which should taper slightly away from the tree trunk, can be made of stone, brick, or even cement blocks. A well made of cement blocks and faced with bricks blends in well with most

Fig. 1.12 *A large tree that has had fill soil and pavement placed over its root system. A tree well was constructed in an attempt to save the tree.*

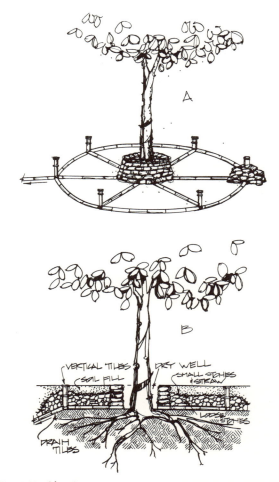

Fig. 1.13 a&b *The correct way to install a tree well to protect a tree's roots from injury by the addition of fill soil.*

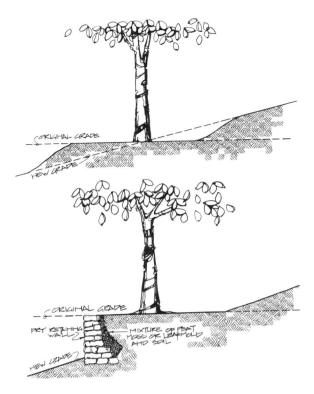

Fig. 1.14 *Use this method to reduce root loss when lowering grades at a landscape site.*

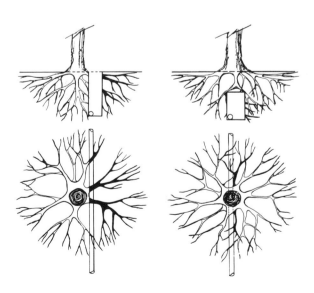

Fig. 1.15 *Tunnel toward the trunk of a tree to keep root loss at a minimum when installing power, gas, and water lines. Of course if possible, put lines outside of the drip line.*

landscapes. The height of the wall should be to the level of the fill soil to be added. You may want to fill the well with 2 to 3 inch stone to reduce the maintenance problem of removing debris that will otherwise accumulate in the well.

After the well is built and the tile system installed, place 3 to 6 inch stone 8 to 12 inches deep over the area. Cover the top of the stone with straw or a fiberglass mat to prevent soil from filtering into the air spaces between the stones, and add fill soil to the proper depth. Be careful not to crush any tiles during the placement of the stones or the addition of the fill soil.

If only one side of a tree is to be surrounded by fill, you can build half a dry well system. The drain outlet will be to the area of the original grade, and retaining walls will be necessary.

Soil Level. Lowering the soil level, if that operation involves cutting off roots, can cause the part of the tree fed by those roots to die; in fact, the entire tree may die. Establish a retaining wall at the drip line to protect as many tree roots as possible.

Trenching. Trenching near tree trunks cuts off just as many roots as making a deep grade change on one side of the tree. Because the tree roots radiate from the center, trench directly toward the tree trunk, and then tunnel under the trunk. This will destroy the least number of roots.

Equipment Injury. When heavy equipment such as bulldozers is being used, trees need protection from mechanical injury. The best method is to build a temporary protective fence at the drip line. This not only prevents equipment from running into the trunks but prevents soil compaction damage to the trees' roots. If a tree has a large spread, it may not be possible to construct a fence at the drip line; instead, build a triangular fence. A third method protects the trunk from bark wounds: wire planks firmly in place around the trunk to absorb the blows from equipment. Remove the planks when construction is completed.

Modification of Existing Soil Structure. The soil structure may have been drastically changed by construction. Before you plant, consider modifying the existing soil after construction to make it more satisfactory. The modifications for the entire site are discussed here; special planting techniques for individual plants or small areas are described in detail in Chapters 3 through 5.

19

Adding Organic Material. If soil has too much clay and drains poorly, there are three things that can be done to improve plant growth conditions. Ideally, organic matter should be added to the soil prior to planting; this will improve aeration, drainage, and microorganism activity. The benefit will be worth the time and expense.

One immediate method is to add large quantities (several inches) of well-rotted animal manure, preferably cattle or horse manure, that has an adequate amount of bedding material such as straw mixed in. The manure adds very few nutrients, but it does improve the soil structure. The manure should be plowed under immediately when it is applied. The three disadvantages of using manure are: (1) quantities may not be readily available, (2) the quality of the material varies greatly, and (3) weed seed is often introduced into the soil.

Another method is to add a topsoil that has a good organic matter content, at least 3 to 5 percent. Plan to add a total of 6 to 9 inches in two applications. First thoroughly work a 2-to 3-inch layer into the existing soil by plowing or deep tilling. Then add and work in a second layer. This technique helps prevent formation of a perched or artifical water table. The obvious advantage of this method is that the site is immediately ready to plant. Also, the thorough working of soil helps prepare a good bed for planting turf. However, it is difficult to maintain any degree of quality control over topsoil, and applying the soil satisfactorily to help prevent the formation of a perched water table costs more than just adding topsoil and smoothing the surface. Finally, if you are adding a lot of topsoil, the cost can be prohibitive. For example, to apply 6 inches of topsoil over a 1/2-acre lot requires almost 400 cubic yards; each cubic yard costs several dollars.

Additional improvement in a heavy soil structure with poor drainage can be obtained by adding at least 2 inches of sand and working it into the subsoil with a rototiller (plowing alone is not satisfactory). Sand is expensive if large quantities are required.

Preserving Original Soil. Rebuilding the soil at a landscape site is costly, and care has to be taken to preserve the basic structure of the soil. At most sites, it's a good idea to save and stockpile a 6- to 12-inch layer of the topsoil before beginning any type of construction or landscape work. When site modification has been completed, the topsoil should be properly replaced, as described above. It is the responsibility of the site owner, whether

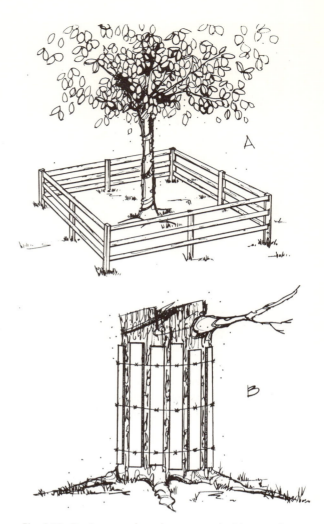

Fig. 1.16 *Barriers to reduce damage to valuable trees during construction.*

homeowner or developer, to ensure that the process is properly carried out.

Drainage. *Surface Drainage.* Good soil involves two types of drainage: surface and internal. Surface drainage is the movement of water on the surface of the soil.

Internal Drainage. To a large degree, the soil texture controls the internal drainage of a site: The more clay in a soil, the poorer the drainage. To obtain top productivity from tight clay soils, you can install an internal drainage system. But to be effective, the system must have an outlet, such as a storm sewer system or drainage lagoon.

Fig. 1.17 *Drain roofs and paved areas away from plant beds if soil in your area is poorly drained.*

Unfortunately, you cannot automatically install a system; local laws require that individual lots tie into the main sewer system. Contact the Soil Conservation Service (SCS) for data on how to install such a system. The added cost of providing good drainage in a site is minor in comparison to future rewards, so evaluate the drainage characteristics before you buy the site. If a septic system is required, careful evaluation of drainage characteristics is even more vital. If the site has poor drainage characteristics, consider installing an internal system before attempting to install the landscape plants.

Soil Nutrients and Testing. Soil is the source of the essential minerals and elements required for plant growth. These minerals enter plants through their roots, so if the soil lacks certain elements, you have to add them in the form of fertilizer.

The availability of minerals and other nutrients in soil is controlled to a large extent by the soil's pH, its acidity (sourness) or alkalinity (sweetness). The pH scale ranges from 1 to 14; 7 is neutral. The acidic side of the scale is from 1 to 7; the smaller the number the greater the acidity. The common pH range for soils is from 4.5 to 8.0; the best pH for most landscape plants is from 6.0 to 6.5, slightly on the acidic side. There are exceptions; members of the ericaceous family, for example (rhododendrons and azaleas) prefer a pH range of 4.5 to 5.0

Before starting to plant, test the soil. Your county agriculture extension service can provide invaluable information on how to take the soil samples and where to send them for analysis. Usually the cost is relatively low. If tests determine that a pH change is necessary for good plant growth, make the change prior to planting because once an area is planted it is more difficult to change its pH, particularly to lower it (make it more acid).

There are various soil test kits available from garden centers or by mail order (through advertisements in garden magazines or seed catalogs). If you are preparing a site for landscaping but are not an avid gardener, you should rely on professionally done soil tests. However, if you have a hobby greenhouse or extensive gardens with plants that have differing soil requirements, a soil test kit might be useful. Test only for pH and the major nutrients; the so-called minor elements are required in such small quantities that it is virtually impossible to make accurate determinations without complex and expensive testing equipment.

The materials for changing the pH are more effective if they are mixed into the soil. Sulfur is used to lower the pH; lime is used to raise it. Years ago farmers used to add lime to their soils to improve productivity. The results were good, primarily because the soils had very low pH's (very acid). Unfortunately, in some areas of the country it is still a common practice to add lime to the soils prior to planting landscape plants (including turf) without checking to determine not only if the soil pH should be raised, but if it should be, how much lime should be added. Some soils already have an optimum or too-high (alkaline) pH for plant growth, so adding lime could actually harm plants.

It is easier and cheaper to raise the soil pH than to lower it. If you do add lime, the amount necessary will depend on the amount of pH change desired, the type of soil, and the type of lime used. For the most long-lasting change, use agricultural limestone (calcium carbonate). If the soil lacks magnesium, adding dolomitic limestone (calcium carbonate and magnesium carbonate) will help solve the problem. You can get more rapid pH changes by using slaked lime (calcium oxide), but it costs more than limestone, and its effect will not last as long. Do

Table 1-8 Pounds of limestone needed to change soil reaction, by soil type.

Change in pH desired in plow-depth layer	Pounds of limestone per acre of soil					
	Sand	Sandy loam	loam	Silt loam	Clay loam	Muck
4.0 to 6.5	2,600	5,000	7,000	8,400	10,000	19,000
4.5 to 6.5	2,200	4,200	5,800	7,000	8,400	16,200
5.0 to 6.5	1,800	3,400	4,600	5,600	6,600	12,600
5.5 to 6.5	1,200	2,600	3,400	4,000	4,600	8,600
6.0 to 6.5	600	1,400	1,800	2,200	2,400	4,400

Source: Knott, J.E., 1980. *Handbook for Vegetable Growers,* New York: Wiley.

not use hydrated lime (calcium hydroxide). Table 1-8 provides the amounts of lime to add, based on soil type and amount of pH change desired. Be sure to obtain a starting pH as determined by soil tests.

Lowering the soil pH requires the addition of an acid-forming material like soil surfur. Sulfur is expensive if you are using large quantities, so you should acidify only those areas that are to be used for plants that absolutely require a lower pH. Use plants more tolerant of higher pH's in other areas. Do not use aluminum sulfate because some plants are injured by excessive aluminum in the soil. The amount of sulfur to add depends on the amount of pH change required and the soil type; see Table 1-9. Again, obtain a starting pH by soil tests.

Table 1-9 Pounds of soil sulfur (99 percent) needed to change soil reaction, by soil type.

Change in pH desired	Pounds of sulfur per acre of soil		
	Sandy	Loamy	Clay
8.5 to 6.5	2,000	2,500	3,000
8.0 to 6.5	1,200	1,500	2,000
7.5 to 6.5	500	800	1,000
7.0 to 6.5	100	150	300

Source: Knott, J.E., 1980. *Handbook for Vegetable Growers.* New York: Wiley.

You can also use sulfur applied to the surface to lower the pH under established turf if you take the proper precautions. Add the sulfur only when temperatures are below 80°F and during periods of relatively low humidities. The addition of sulfur when temperatures are above 80°F can cause serious foliar burn, which takes several weeks to clear up. The surface addition of sulfur will not affect the soil pH more than 1 to 2 inches down and therefore cannot influence the soil that surrounds tree and shrub roots.

It is important to add phosphorus before planting because this element is nearly immobile in soil. Phosphorus applied to the surface after a site has been planted will never reach most tree and shrub roots in sufficient quantities to be beneficial. Add the recommended amounts and work the phosphorus deep into the soil by tilling or plowing. If the soil is deficient of other elements, add them prior to planting if possible, or at planting time. Elements such as nitrogen and potassium move down into the soil with rainfall or irrigation. In some sections of the country soils are deficient in minor elements such as boron or manganese. Add only the minor elements based on recommendations from soil test results.

Before starting to plant or even preparing your planting design, study the site and evaluate the environmental conditions found at the site. Have the appropriate soil tests run. And then select the plants and the planting techniques best suited for the site so that you will be successful in developing your landcape.

Source for most tables in this chapter:

Flint, Harrison. 1983, *Landscape Plants for Eastern North America: Exclusive of Florida and Immediate Gulf Coast.* John Wiley & Sons, New York.

2

What You Need to Know When Buying Landscape Plants

The nursery industry uses its own unique terminology as well as scientific and common names to describe plant materials. You should understand all the terminology, especially that associated with root condition, size, quality and so on, so you can intelligently discuss plants with nursery personnel and buy exactly what you want and need. In this chapter root condition is stressed because it determines the time of year plants are sold, their price, and, to some extent, planting success. Shrubs and trees are sold as *balled and burlapped, container-grown, bare root,* or as some modification of one of these three conditions.

The American Association of Nurseymen (AAN) has developed a set of standards for nursery stock sold in this country. These standards are guidelines only; no governmental agency regulates the plant standards of the nursery industry. But there is really very little need for standards to be controlled by the federal government because the industry does a good job of regulating itself. As long as you understand the terms and methods used to judge the size and quality of the nursery plants you are buying, you should not have any problems.

Besides the terms of the nursery industry, you should also know the scientific names of plants and the general horticultural classification of plants. Using the scientific names for plants will eliminate some of the confusion which results when you rely solely on common names. For example, you often hear the names "pine" or "spruce" used to refer to any conifer tree. The person who asks for a pine or spruce probably has a specific plant species in mind, but to the nurserymen selling the plant this could mean any of several dozen different species. Similarly a jade plant or jade tree may mean *Crassula agentea* Thunb., which is a succulent house plant or a shrub in northern California; Silver Jade Plant (*Crassula arborescens* (Mill.)) Willd., a semi-arid shrub; or the jade vine, *Strongylodon macrobatus* A. Gray., which grows up to 30 feet in length. To help you understand and use the correct names, we present information here from Arthur H. Westing (Chapter 2) in *Horticultural Science* by Jules Janick (San Francisco: W.H. Freeman, 1975). The information provided here will give you the confidence and ability to select and buy plants for your landscape planting.

PLANT CLASSIFICATIONS.

A general classification for landscape plants puts plants into two categories: woody or herbaceous. Woody plants are those that develop hard, woodlike stems and trunks; herbaceous plants have soft, succulent stems and trunks. The woody plants are subdivided into trees or shrubs, based on their growing habit and size. Herbaceous plants (herbs) usually include flowers, some of the ground covers, and bulbous plants. Self-supporting or upright growth is a requirement for trees, shrubs, and herbs. Plants with a climbing or trailing growth habit are called *vines* if they are herbaceous, but *lianas* if they are woody.

Certain terms have a common usage that is not the same as the correct horticultural usage. For instance, nurserymen use the term *vine*, rather than *liana*, for all plants that have a climbing or trailing growth habit. *Herb* commonly refers to a small group of herbaceous plants used to season foods or for medicinal purposes, but horticulturists generally use the more specific terms of flower, bulb, etc.

Another classification is based on whether the plant retains its foliage throughout the entire year. Plants that lose their foliage during a portion of the year — usually winter — are called *deciduous;* examples are maples and forsythias. Plants that retain their foliage are called *evergreens.* The evergreens also lose their foliage, but not all at once. New foliage grows before the old is dropped, so the loss is not noticed. Evergreens are subdivided into broad-leaved and narrow-leaved varieties. Broad-leaved evergreens, English Ivy for example, have foliage that looks like that of deciduous plants; narrow-leaved evergreens such as pines and junipers have needle or scale-like foliage.

Another classification is based on the life span of the plants. Plants that complete a life cycle in one year or one growing season are

Fig. 2.1a *A deciduous plant loses its leaves in the fall.*

Fig. 2.1b *A combination of a narrow-leaved evergreen (Taxus* sp. *or Yew) and a broad-leaved evergreen (Hedera helix* or *English ivy).*

Fig. 2.2 *Petunias, an annual flower, being grown in decorative container.*

called *annuals.* In the nursery and landscape industries, the term generally refers to annual flowers planted in flower beds. The term *bedding plants* is derived from the practice of planting flowers in beds. Generally bedding plants are annuals.

A *biennial* is a plant that requires two growing seasons to complete its life cycle. In the first season it produces vegetative growth, often with the flower bud being formed. Low temperatures are required for the development

Fig. 2.3 *An herbaceous perennial such as a lily offers color and longevity to a landscape planting.*

Fig. 2.4 *Tropical foliage in a natural setting in a subtropical area of the United States.*

of the seed stalk which is produced during the second year. Cabbage is a typical biennial. Professionals in the nursery industry usually refer to biennials as herbaceous plants or bedding plants.

Plants that grow year after year are *perennials.* Almost all woody plants are perennial, as are many herbaceous plants, such as the peony. Perennials may take a short time to reach an age that allows flowering, or they may take many years to reach maturity. Generally, they do not die after flowering the first time. Trees and shrubs are woody perennials; many iris (rhizomes) and bulbs are herbaceous perennials. A perennial is a herbaceous plant that may be used in a bed or as an individual plant in the landscape.

Plants from warmer climates are called either *foliage plants* or *tropicals.* A foliage plant is used primarily for the beauty of its foliage and may or may not be a plant from the tropics. A tropical plant is usually a foliage plant whose native habitat is in warmer climates, such as southern Florida or California.

A final classification is based on a plant's tolerance to low temperatures. A plant that will withstand low temperatures in a particular region is called *hardy.* If it is susceptible to low-temperature injury, the plant is *tender;* however, this term is rarely used in reference to landscape plants. Plants are hardy or not depending on their tolerance to the low temperatures of the area in which they are grown.

Horticultural Plant Classification. The three major horticultural categories are *fruits, vegetables,* and *ornamentals.* Ornamentals are grown and used for aesthetic purposes with a subclassification of nursery plants and flowers. Nursery plants, often called woody ornamentals, include trees and shrubs, ground covers, vines and, to some extent, turf; they are produced primarily for landscaping purposes. The term *flowers* includes those plants produced by florists, such as pot plants and cut flowers; and bedding plants, which, as described, are most often herbaceous flowering annuals, biennials, or perennials planted in landscape beds.

Ground cover can be any plant used to cover large areas of a landscape, including turf grasses. A more common and restricted use of the term refers to those plants that are relatively low-growing — 15 inches or under and used in place of turf. Such ground covers are either herbaceous or woody perennials.

Scientific Classification. The use of the scientific (Latin) names of plants is not as common a practice here as it is in other countries, such as Great Britain. Even the landscape industry often uses common names rather than the more precise scientific names. This can lead to confusion because the same plant may have more than one common name. Learning scientific names is not difficult; if everyone used them, they would soon replace the less satisfactory common names.

All living things are divided into two kingdoms: animal and plant. The plant kingdom is divided into major and minor categories. The classifications from kingdom to family are major; genus and below are minor:

Major:
    Kingdom
       Division
          Class
             Order
                Family

Minor:
    Genus
       Species
          Variety
             Form
                Individual

Class names do not appear in the scientific names of plants. Classes of interest are *gymnosperms* and *angiosperms*. The gymnosperms are divided into three orders: Cycadales, Ginkgoales, and Coniferales. Cycadales are primitive plants, some of which are used in landscapes in certain tropical areas, such as southern Florida. The Ginkgoales contain only one family *(Ginkgoaceae)*, one genus *(Ginkgo)*, and one species *(Biloba)*. The maidenhair or ginkgo tree *(Ginkgo biloba* L.) is used in many landscapes. The conifers (narrow-leaved evergreens) are members of the order Coniferales. Plants of the angiosperms represent a majority of the food- and fiber-producing plants of the world. There are two major subclasses: monocots and dicots. The monocots number about 50,000 species; the dicots have about 200,000 species.

The family is generally the only one of the major classification of plants that is of interest to the landscape industry. Plants within a family often have similar enough characteristics to be of interest from a design or use point of view.

A binomial system is used to identify plants: genus and species names. Plants of a particular genus are very similar in structure, and, more importantly, the genus name is the first used in the binomial naming system. Examples of genus names are *Rosa* (roses), *Quercus* (oaks), and *Pinus* (pines). The genus is always capitalized and then followed by the species name.

Taxonomists consider the species grouping the basic unit of the system. Plants of the same genus and species can be very similar or even nearly identical. As an example, the scientific name of white oak is *Quercus alba.* All *Querus alba* have nearly the same growth habit, identical foliage, and flower parts. However, the subclassifications under species are very important. The variety (var.) is a definitive botanical subclassification of a species. For example, flowering dogwood with white flowers is *Cornus florida,* but *Cornus florida* var. *rubra.* is a pink flowering dogwood. The only difference between the two plants is the flower color. There is also a special type of horticultural variety, called a cultivar which is short for "cultivated variety." The botanical variety occurs naturally, whereas the cultivar is a variety that is grown in cultivation only. To carry the dogwood example a step further, the cultivar 'Cherokee Chief' would be added to the name as follows: *Cornus florida* var. *ruba* 'Cherokee Chief'. The cultivar name is written with single quotation marks or preceded by the abbreviation cv. In the landscape industry the botanical variety *rubra* may not be used since those familiar with the plants will know the cultivar has pink flowers. The name would thus appear as *Cornus florida* 'Cherokee Chief'.

Fig. 2.5   *The flowers of a pink flowered dogwood – Cornus florida var. rubra.*

Scientific genus and species names are written in italics; the cultivar name is in roman type. Occasionally an abbreviation appears at the end of the name; this denotes the authority who named the plant: *Quercus alba* L. was named by Linnaeus.

It is best to use scientific names. Many people are uncertain about how to pronounce the Latin names, but in most cases even the more difficult ones can be pronounced so that the plant can be recognized or the names can be written down on paper. It is better to correctly identify the plant you want than to use a common name that might apply to any one of several different plant species.

Fig. 2.6 *Balled and burlapped junipers that are ready for sale. Note the use of the twine to hold the burlap in place and help support the soil ball.*

NURSERY INDUSTRY TERMINOLOGY

Balled and Burlapped. For many years balled and burlapped plants have been considered the best way to buy plants, because they can be transplanted easily from the nursery to the landscape site with minimal losses. The term *balled and burlapped*, abbreviated B & B or b & b, describes how the plant is prepared in the nursery for sale. The plant is dug carefully, either by hand or with a machine, with an intact soil ball that contains most of the plant's roots. The soil ball must be of the proper size for the plant being dug and must not be broken or damaged or the root system will be injured. A damaged or broken soil ball greatly reduces the chances of the plant's survival at transplanting. Too small of

a ball markedly reduces the size of the root system that is moved with the plant, thus reducing the chances of successfully establishing the plant on your landscape site. The AAN has standards for the size of soil ball in relation to the size of the plant. These standards define not only the diameter of the soil ball but also the depth. They also differentiate beween plants grown in nurseries or plantations and those collected.

Nursery-grown plants are produced in a nursery, possibly transplanted several times, and root pruned. The plants are carefully developed and shaped, and kept as pest-free as possible. The soil ball size may be smaller on nursery stock because in many instances this stock has been root pruned one or more times during the time in the nursery. In the root pruning process the roots are mechanically cut, forcing branching and the development of a more fibrous root system. When the plant is balled and burlapped, it is possible to obtain more of the root system in the smaller soil ball.

Plantation-produced plants, such as the pines planted for Christmas trees, are grown in field conditions, but the care they receive after the initial planting is usually minimal. These trees are not root pruned and should have a larger soil ball than the same size tree grown in a nursery.

Collected nursery stock are plants removed from their natural environment, such as forests or wooded areas. These plants have never been transplanted, root pruned, shaped, or protected from pests. Their root systems may be very coarse, and sparse and transplant shock is severe because there is much root damage during the transplanting process. As with plantation-produced plants, collected plants should have larger ball sizes than nursery grown plants. Also, be aware that the chances for losing collected plants is greater. Finally, the shape and quality of collected plants are often not as satisfactory as that of nursery plants.

To reduce the chances of damaging the soil ball and to facilitate shipping, the soil ball is tightly wrapped in burlap. The burlap should be left intact at planting time since it will decompose rapidly in the planting hole. The burlap is held in place by lacing it with twine, by pinning it with special nails, or by using a combination of twine and nails. Plastic burlap is being used by a few nurseries, but often this material does not break down rapidly enough, and the roots will not penetrate the burlap. Consequently the plant may die in dry weather.

How large a plant can be moved? Size is limited only by the equipment available for handling the plant. It is relatively common to move b & b trees with 12 to 14 inch trunk diameters. Generally, all larger sized plants must be balled and burlapped for moving since they must be field grown to attain the desired size.

When you select balled and burlapped plants, inspect both the soil ball and the top of the plant. Do not buy plants with cracked, flattened, or misshapened soil balls or plants whose stem or trunk is loose in the soil ball. You or your landscape architect or landscape contractor should also carefully inspect the soil balls when the plants are delivered to your landscape site. Reject any damaged plants or those with questionable soil ball conditions. If b & b plants are to be held for extended periods of time, the soil balls must be mulched.

Balled and Potted. Balled and burlapped plants are expensive because of the labor involved in readying the plants: wrapping the burlap around the soil ball takes nearly as long as digging out the plant itself. For this reason a faster and cheaper method to protect the soil ball has been developed. The plant is dug out in much the same manner as for balling and burlapping but is placed in a papier-mâché container instead of being wrapped in burlap.

Fig. 2.8   A group of field dug and potted broad-leaved evergreens ready for sale.

Fig. 2.9   A large block of container-grown plants at a Florida nursery.

Fig. 2.7   A large deciduous tree that is balled and burlapped and ready for transplanting.

Plants prepared this way generally can be shipped with less damage to the soil ball because the container affords sturdier protection than the burlap wrap; moreover, balled and potted plants are easier to care for once they are dug because the rim of the pot will hold water and thus facilitate watering. In addition, no mulching of the soil ball is necessary.

However, balled and potted plants have some disadvantages. Only smaller plants can be placed in papier-mâché pots because there is a

28

Fig. 2.10 *A container-grown plant with a girdling root that could cause trouble in future years.*

Fig. 2.11 *Bare root plants lose much of their root system during digging.*

limit to the size of containers that can be formed. Also, a soil ball can be cracked at the time of digging, but some nursery personnel may still place the plant in a pot. It is difficult to detect this type of soil ball damage, so you may buy the plant, only to have it not prove satisfactory because of injury to the root system. Finally, as with balled and burlapped plants where the burlap is left on the plant at planting, the papier-mâché container is left on at the time of planting, but under certain conditions, such as dry, sandy soils, the papier-mâché does not decompose rapidly enough to permit good root penetration through the pot. Thus the plant's growth and development may not be satisfactory.

Container-Grown. Container-grown plants are grown for an extended period of time in the container, in some instances growing from a very small plant to a landscape-size plant. Containers are usually made of a permanent material such as metal or plastic and must be removed at planting time. Often the growing medium in the container is a very light and porous artificial mix (soil-less).

Container-grown nursery stock is sold year-round because no field digging is required. Also, you can plant container plants over a much longer season since the plants do not suffer transplanting shock by the disturbance of the entire root mass during the moving operation.

Several difficulties do occur when you use container-grown plants in your landscape. First, the size of the plant that can be produced in a container is limited by the size of the container. It is not practical to produce very large plants in a container because the root mass is restricted by the container's size. And when plants grown in a porous, artificial medium are transplanted to heavy and/or compacted, poorly drained soil, the root ball can become water logged during heavy rainfall because the water cannot drain fast enough into the heavy soil. Root damage occurs, and the plant is injured or dies.

Another problem with container-grown stock is that the root system sometimes becomes restricted and starts to grow in circles around the inside of the container. When the plant is transplanted, the roots may not grow outward, resulting in a plant that does not grow to its fullest potential. When roots grow circularly, girdling roots may develop around the base of the trunk, eventually strangling the top by cutting off moisture and nutrients. When planting container-grown trees, use the special planting techniques discussed in Chapter 3.

Bare Root Plants. As the term implies, bare root plants are plants that have all the soil removed during the digging process in the nursery. Bare root trees and shrubs are usually dug in the fall and stored bare root over the winter, with 100 percent humidity as protection for the roots. Temperatures are kept low, but above freezing. Bare root plants are usually the least expensive to purchase, but because of the relatively harsh root damage the plants receive in the digging process, the chances of these plants surviving and developing in the landscape are lower than with b & b, potted, or container-grown plants. However, if handled properly during shipment and during the planting process, bare root plants can be a good investment, particularly if you are going to use a large number of plants.

The most commonly sold bare root plants are roses, fruit trees, and deciduous shrubs. *Seedings* of conifers such as blue spruce *(Picea pungens)*, white pine *(Pinus strobus)*, Scots pine *(Pinus sylvestris)*, and similar plants are also sold bare root.

There is a strict size limitation for both bare root trees and bare root shrubs. Large bare root specimens cannot be moved successfully, and certain species cannot be transplanted bare root with any guarantee of success. Larger bare root conifers are particularly difficult to transplant, and must always be transplanted as container-grown, balled and potted, or balled and burlapped plants. Be extra careful when transplanting bare root plants because the roots may have been damaged, and in most instances bare root plants can be planted only in the early spring, before growth starts. Be sure to study the planting techniques for bare root plants in Chapter 3.

In recent years a process that extends the planting season of bare root plants has been developed called peat balling. During the winter nursery personnel remove plants from their bare root storage, and use a machine to press moist peat moss around the root system. This "peat ball" is enclosed in a plastic bag. When spring comes, the plants start to grow and develop; these plants can be planted until early summer without great risk of plant loss.

There are some disadvantages to using peat balled plants. The root system is wrapped in a very porous, organic medium (peat moss), which is ideal under some conditions. However, if the plant is transplanted into heavy soils, the plant root system can become waterlogged from too much rainfall or overwatering because the peat ball is a sump that collects excess moisture. Also, if you forget to remove the plastic wrapping or bag at planting time, the plants may die in mid-summer because the roots cannot become established in the soil.

NURSERY STOCK TERMINOLOGY

The nursery industry uses terminology that describes the quality and size of stock it produces. A general undersanding of the terms will be helpful when dealing with the landscape contractor or when purchasing landscape plant materials. The following information is a guide, but if you have specific questions concerning the plants you are purchasing, particularly large expensive specimen plants, you should obtain additional information from other sources such as other nurserymen or the local agriculture extention service.

The nursery industry uses the term *specimen* (spec.) to indicate plants of exceptionally good quality; those that have more branches (are heavier) and are very well shaped are also sometimes designated specimen plants. In some nursery catalogs, the letters, X, XX, or XXX are used to indicate a specimen plant, with the best quality designated XXX. Specimen plants cost more than others of the same type.

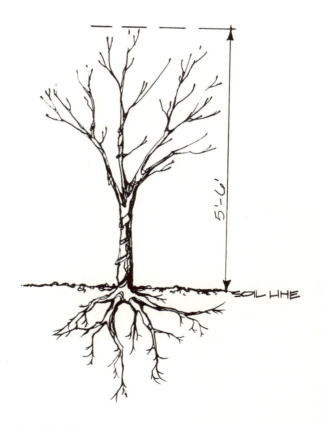

Fig. 2.12 *A bare root tree probably will be measured by its height from the soil line to the top.*

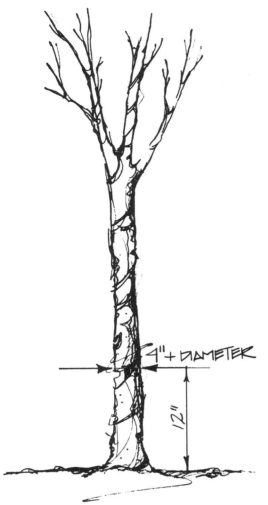
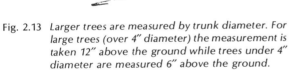

Fig. 2.13 *Larger trees are measured by trunk diameter. For large trees (over 4" diameter) the measurement is taken 12" above the ground while trees under 4" diameter are measured 6" above the ground.*

Shade Trees. Shade trees are measured by either height or caliper. Bare root trees are measured by height, up to 8 feet. As an example, an *Acer rubrum* (red maple) may be sold as a tree 5 to 6 feet in height. This means the tree is no less than 5 feet in height from the soil line to the top of the tree.

Larger trees are measured by calipers; in other words, the trunk diameter is measured 6 inches above the ground for trees with trunk diameters of 4 inches or less. For large trees (trunk diameter over 4 inches), the measurement is taken 12 inches above the ground. Thus, a *Quercus alba* (white oak) listed as a 5-1/2-inch tree has a trunk diameter of 5-1/2 inches 12 inches above the ground. The height of the tree varies as to species, area of the country where it is being grown, and the method of production.

Trees that are grown widely apart in a nursery tend to have a heavier trunk in relation to their height. Some trees that are collected in the forest do not have a very heavy trunk in relation to the top height; these trees are not of as good a quality as nursery grown trees. Trees crowded in a forest are deprived of light and have a tendency to grow tall and spindly.

Small Trees. There are two general types of small trees: small upright, and small spreading. These types are sized according to their height or as measured by caliper. The same general measuring rules as for the large shade trees hold for caliper measurements.

For a tree to be grown in a container you must know its size as well as the size of the container. It is important that the tree is grown in the container long enough to develop a root system that will hold the soil ball together when the container is removed, yet the trees should not be grown in the container so long that roots grow circularly, which could cause the development of girdling roots.

Deciduous Shrubs. Most decidous shrubs are sold on the basis of their height and spread. When you buy several shrubs of a given size, be sure their overall size is an average between the low and high measurements. As an example, five *Viburnum dentatum* 4- to 5-feet high will average 4-1/2 feet in overall height. None should be smaller than 4 feet.

A container-grown shrub should be grown long enough in a container so that a new fibrous root system develops enabling the root mass to hold the soil together and retain its shape when the plant is removed from the container. The container should be strong enough to retain the shape of the root mass and protect it from damage during shipment. The size of the plant in the container depends on the size of the container, but both the plant size and the container size should be given. For example, a 1-gallon plant does *not* indicate the shrub size, but a 15- to 18-inch *Cotoneaster divaricata* in a 1-gallon container tells you exactly how large the plant is.

Narrow-leaved Coniferous Evergreens. There are several types of evergreens. In fact, the AAN lists six types of conifers, ranging from the creeping prostrate types to the columnar types, with all gradations in between. The plants are sized according to their growth habits. For example, a spreading, low-growing evergreen shrub is sized by its spread. Intervals of measurement are established in much the same manner as for deciduous plants, and should be based on the measurement of the main part of the plant, not the maximum spread of the plant. Remember that as with deciduous shrubs the overall size of a group of narrow-leaved evergreens should be the average of the various sizes of each plant. For example, five *Taxus media* 'Hicks' 3- to 4-feet high should average 3-1/2 feet. The specifications for ball size depends on the size of plants and where the plant was grown. Balled and potted plants should have the same size ball as if burlap were used.

Container-grown conifers are measured in the same manner as balled and burlapped plants, except the size of the container is used as well as the size of the spread or height of the plant.

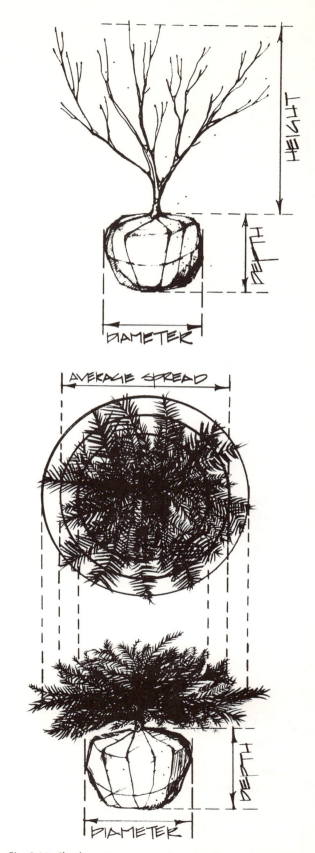

Fig. 2.14 *Shrubs are measured in height or spread depending on growth habit.*

Broad-leaved Evergreens. The same basic methods are involved in grading and sizing broad-leaved evergreens as with narrow-leaved coniferous evergreens.

Vines and Ground Covers. The AAN recognizes size types of plants as vines or ground covers. Vines and ground covers are sold on the basis of age, plant size or container size. If you are purchasing large quantities of ground covers, you should examine samples before buying so that you are certain of the size and quality of the plants.

Vines in pots or containers are generally sold by pot size. A 2-1/2-inch plant means the plant is growing in a 2-1/2-inch pot. The number of runners and length of the runners depends on the species of plants. For example, *Hedera helix* (English Ivy) might have a minimum number of two runners that would be at least 10 inches in length and is potted in a 3-inch pot.

Lining Out Stock. This term refers to small nursery plants that are sold to other nurseries for planting in rows (lined out in rows) in the nursery for further growth and sales. Generally, lining out stock is of interest only to other nurseries that will grow larger plants for the landscape industry or clients. However, some of the terms associated with lining out stock are important when evaluating plants in mail order nursery catalogs:

Age - The number of years since propagated or — in the case of seedlings — since growth started.

Transplanted - The number of times transplanted is represented by the letter T.

Seedling - Represented by the letter S.

Cuttings - Represented by the letter C.

Grafted - Represented by the letter G.

Size - Given in accordance with the intervals recommended for each plant class.

An example using the various terms described above is:

Picea pungens 'glauca' cv. Koster, Koster Spruce G 6-8 in., 4 yr. TT means Koster Spruce graft, 6 to 8 inches high, 4 years old and twice transplanted.

Standards for Other Plant Classifications. There are also set standards for other types of nursery stock, such as roses, fruit trees, small fruits, seedling trees and shrubs, bulbs, corms, and tubers. If you buy quantities of plants in these categories, make certain that you know what size and quality you are purchasing, particularly if ordering from a mail order house since the plants may be smaller than you expect.

WHERE SHOULD YOU BUY NURSERY PLANTS?

There are three basic sources of landscape plant materials: the landscape contractor, the garden center or retail nursery, and the mail order nursery. A landscape contractor will supply the plant material as described on your landscape plan. You may be involved in the selection of the individual plants, particularly the specimen plants that might be used, or you may depend on the landscape contractor to make all the selections. A landscape architect will help assist in the selection of the plant material and may inspect the plants to make certain they meet the standards required for the project.

If you are installing your own landscape plants, you will probably purchase most of your plants from a garden center or retail nursery. A retail nursery grows some of its own plant material, whereas a garden center is a merchandising center for plants. You can pick individual plants of high quality by keeping the following points in mind. Check for insect, disease, and physical damage such as broken branches, wounds on tree trunks and other disfiguration. Avoid plants with damaged or misshapened soil balls. Plants should show evidence of being well cared for and properly watered. Plants that have been allowed to dry out may be permanently injured. The leaves will be scorched (brown, dry edges) or wilted. Generally it is best to buy plants from a garden center or nursery that operates year-round. Also, unless you are well qualified to judge the quality of plants, buy from a garden center or nursery that has trained and experienced personnel who can answer your questions. Ask your friends where they obtained satisfactory plant material and service. If you have been dealing with a particular garden center or nursery and have been satisfied, continue to buy your plants from them.

The same general suggestions hold true for ordering from mail order nurseries. Remember that plants from a mail order nursery will be smaller, and in many instances, bare root due to the expense and difficulty of shipping large plants or plants in large containers or b & b plants. Beware of so-called "miracle" plants or new improved selection of poor quality plants like *Ulmus pumila* (Chinese elm or Siberian elm). The high pressure advertising tactics used in some newspaper supplements may not provide accurate information on the performance of the species or be representative of the landscape quality of the plant. If you have any doubts concerning plants advertised for mail order sale, check with your county agriculture agent. There are many excellent mail order nurseries in the country that will provide accurate information on a plant's growth habits and characteristics as a landscape plant.

Many mail order nurseries give complete guarantees that their plants will grow for one season. Read the guarantees for the nursery you are ordering from. Also remember that a mail order nursery will replace a plant during the proper planting season. If you plant a plant in the spring and it dies, it may not be replaced until spring, so be patient. Contact the company concerning your loss and they will probably notify you as to the date when you can expect a replacement.

Landscape contractors, garden centers, and retail nurseries will also have guaranteed policies on their plant material. The terms of these guarantees vary greatly, so make sure you fully understand the details of the guarantee. The firms you do business with will honor the terms of their guarantees, but in some cases it may be your obligation to take proper care of the plant material. The guarantee will be void if you do not. In most cases the guarantee offered by the firm provides good protection for you.

3

Planting Trees and Shrubs

Using proper planting techniques is as important as selecting and buying plants for your landscape. Taking the time and spending the money to establish plants correctly will pay off in landscape plants that grow well, require less maintenance, and develop to their fullest potential. Plant growth and development are largely controlled by the preparation of the soil at the planting site. There is much more involved in establishing a good root environment than just digging a hole in the ground. The root zones should possess as nearly as possible the same characteristics as the soils found in the native habitat of the plants. True, it is not possible to exactly duplicate the soil of a woodland, meadow, or desert, but important characteristics such as good aeration, moisture-holding capacity, proper nutrient balance, and adequate levels of organic matter should be available.

To achieve a satisfactory soil structure and the proper or correct nutrient levels for plants require specific planting methods based on conditions at your landscape site. This chapter discusses such planting methods and how to improve heavy, poorly aerated and drained soil or one that is droughty and high in sand content with the use of organic and inorganic soil addititives. It will be up to you to determine your soil conditions and use proper planting techniques. A plant sold with a guarantee for 1 year does not mean that it will be thriving 10 years after planting. It must be properly planted and maintained.

SOIL ADDITIVES

The first factors to consider are soil additives, such as peat mosses, which are used to improve planting sites. To have the greatest effect, soil additives should be mixed with the soil prior to planting. It is nearly impossible to change the physical characteristics of a soil once the site is planted without taking out the plant material and starting over. Obviously, this is very expensive and not necessary if the site is properly prepared prior to or at planting time. But on the other hand, nutrient needs, in the form of fertilizers, can be easily added long after planting.

Peat Mosses. There are three types of peat moss: sphagnum, hypnum, and reed or sedge. The best grade is sphagnum peat, which is imported primarily from Canada. It is the least decomposed of the various peats and thus will have the longest-lasting effect as a soil additive. Generally, the pH range for sphagnum peat moss is 4.0 to 5.5, so it is an excellent soil amendment for acid-requiring plants like azaleas and rhododendrons. It is relatively free of disease-causing organisms and weed seed and is generally more uniform in texture and content. Sphagnum peat moss is also the most expensive. It is sold in compressed bales, usually measured by the number of cubic feet in the bale after compression. A 6-cubic foot bale of sphagnum peat, when loosened, will yield 9 to

12 cubic feet of peat. You can roughly estimate that three 6-cubic foot bales will yield 1 cubic yard of loose peat moss. Sphagnum peat moss is available in several grades. Use a horticultural grade which provides the best particle size for soil amending.

The next-best quality peat moss is hypnum, found in bogs in some of the northern states. This moss is generally much more decomposed than sphagnum peat moss and does not compress well. Therefore, it is sold in bags that may hold up to 3 cubic feet. This moss cannot be fluffed up or loosened to increase its volume, so when calculating the amount to use as a soil amendment, you should consider the quantity given on the bag as the final volume. For example, it takes nine 3-cubic foot bags to provide enough for 1 cubic yard of soil additive. In certain localities the hypnum peats can be purchased in bulk.

Hypnum peat is usually sold as "native" peat moss; rarely does the name "hypnum" appear on the bag. Hypnum is cheaper than sphagnum, but it is not always free of weed seed and is not considered as free of disease-causing organisms a sphagnum peat moss; moreover, its variation in texture and pH is greater than the sphagnum, depending on the source. You should require a pH test if you are buying large quantities of hypnum peat, and you should inspect the peat to be sure that it is not too decomposed and that the particle size is not too small to make it a good soil amendment.

The poorest type of peat moss is reed or sedge, and it should be avoided for most planting purposes. It is generally very decomposed, with quite small particles, and consequently adds very little to the soil texture. Reed or sedge peat is not long-lasting in the soil because it rapidly breaks down into humus. This peat moss is sold in bulk or is bagged since it cannot be compressed. It is generally not weed free and is not free of disease-causing organisms. It may lack uniformity in texture and pH, so definitely run a pH test before using this material in large quantities.

Agricultural and Wood By-Products. Such materials as shredded hardwood and pine barks, ground corncobs, sawdust, and other agricultural by-products can be added to the soil, although they are not as good as peat mosses. Materials such as corncobs and sawdust have a high amount of cellulose, which breaks down rapidly and does not have a long-lasting effect on soil structure. Also, the micro-organisms that decompose cellulose deplete soil nitrogen. Plants grown in a soil amended with these materials will suffer severe nitrogen deficiencies unless a substantial amount of nitrogen is added to it, and additional amounts of nitrogen may be needed as decomposition occurs. Do not use high cellulose materials unless they are very inexpensive and you add supplemental nitrogen when planting and during the following months.

Shredded hardwood and pine barks are by-products of the lumber and paper industries. These barks are better used as mulches than as soil additives, but if you have access to a large quantity of material to improve the structure of a heavy soil, consider using shredded barks. Do not use large quantities of walnut and hickory barks because they may contain substances toxic to certain plant species. The barks should be ground finely enough so that smooth grading of the site is possible after they have been mixed into the soil. You do not have to add nitrogen unless a fair amount of sawdust or wood chips are mixed with the bark. Bark is considerably cheaper than sphagnum peat moss.

Manure. In many plantings manure is recommended as a soil amendment. However, this material is greatly overrated. Some of its basic properties are beneficial to the soil, but the disadvantages outweigh the advantages. The primary problem with manures is their lack of uniformity in both physical and nutrient content. The amount and degree of decomposition of manure depends on what bedding material was used and how much. Large numbers of weed seeds can be introduced into the landscape planting by manure, thus its use can make weed control exceedingly difficult. The length of time the manure has aged also determines its value as a soil additive. Fresh manure is too "hot" to be used as a nutrient source and may injure plants; well-rotted and aged manures may be too far decomposed to add any significant quantities of nutrients. If you have never used manure, or if you are doing a new landscaping project, it is better to not use manure as a soil additive.

Inorganic Additives. Inorganic soil amendments, such as sand, perlite, and vermiculite, improve soil aeration, but supply no energy to soil micro-organisms when used by themselves. Also, perlite and vermiculite are too expensive to use in quantities, and vermiculite tends to break down structually over time. Perlite can be used where weight is a problem, for example in planters, because it is very light. If its particle size is coarse enough, sand can be used to improve aeration and drainage. One

36

problem with sand is that its pH varies, depending on its origin. For example, throughout the midwest much of the sand has a high pH (7.8 to 8.0); when this sand is used with peat moss as a soil amendment, acid-loving plants such as azaleas and rhododendrons do not thrive because the reaction will quickly override the effect of the peat moss' acid pH.

Chemical Fertilizers. A fertilizer is a chemical mixture that adds mineral nutrients to the soil. There are many different fertilizers on the market, and selecting one for plant installation or the maintenance of a landscape requires careful consideration. But before these factors are examined, a brief discussion of the general types of fertilizers and their contents follow below.

The general analysis of a fertilizer is on its bag; a more detailed analysis is given on a small label attached to the bag. The detailed analysis results from a state's tests to determine whether the fertilizer meets the concentration listed on the bag. The numbers refer to the percentage of each of three major elements essential for plant growth: nitrogen, phosphorus, and potassium. The analysis will always contain these three percentages, always in the order just given. Thus, a 5-10-5 analysis means that the fertilizer contains 5 percent nitrogen, 10 percent phosphorus (P_2O_5), and 5 percent potassium (K_2O). Even if one or more of the major elements is not present, the analysis will still give three percentages: 0-20-0 means the fertilizer contains zero percent nitrogen, 20 percent phosophorus, and zero percent potassium. A fertilizer with all three elements present is sometimes called a complete fertilizer.

The label also indicates the form of the fertilizer nutrients, particularly nitrogen: it can be readily available for uptake by the plants or it can be slowly available to the plants. A fertilizer may contain all readily available nitrogen, all slow-release forms, or a combination of both.

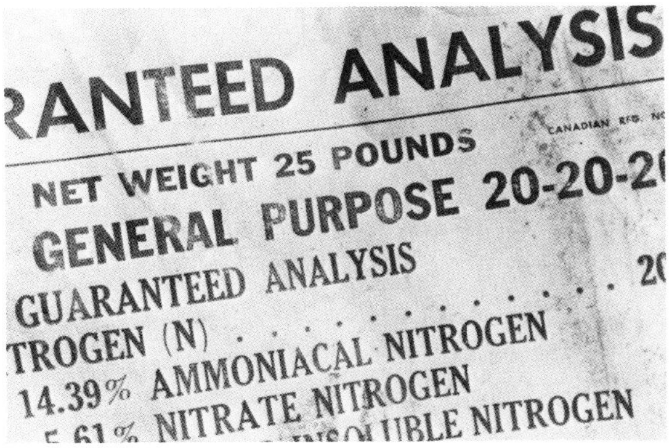

Some fertilizers have minor element supplements. The amount and type of the minor element must be given on the label along with the analysis of the three major elements. The label also gives the amount of inert material present. In many states a material must contain a total analysis of at least 20 percent of the three major elements (nitrogen, phosphorus and potassium) to be called fertilizer. So-called "miracle" soil additives and "secret" plant growth formulas cannot be legally sold as fertilizers.

Fertilizers can be placed in several categories, depending on their water solubility or source of materials. Here we consider soluable fertilizer and slow-release fertilizer.

Soluble Fertilizers. Soluble fertilizers dissolve in water and are immediately available to the plant for use in the growth processes. These fertilizers are available in three forms: (1) granular forms that are applied dry, (2) water-soluble salts that are dissolved in water and applied as a solution, and (3) liquids that may be applied in the concentrated form but usually are first diluted in water. No form is any more available than the other. In other words, a dry granular fertilizer is available to a tree or shrub in approximately the same amount of time as a water-soluble salt. Most granular fertilizers are readily available, usually the least expensive, and quite satisfactory for most landscape purposes. The dry forms are easier to mix in the backfill used around the roots when planting. Sometimes newly-planted trees and shrubs are watered with a fertilizer solution. In this case the water soluble salts or liquid should be diluted with water.

The soluble fertilizer may be neutral in reaction. That is, it will not affect the soil's pH. For most uses in the landcape, the neutral-reacting fertilizer is the most desirable. Most granular dry fertilizers are neutral, or nearly so, in reaction. However, plants that require soils with a lower pH (4.5 to 5.5) — rhododendrons and azaleas, for example — should be fertilized with an acidic-reacting fertilizer such as ammonium sulfate and ammonium phosphate. Aluminum sulfate is sometimes used to lower soil pH and is not really a fertilizer at all. (In some instances aluminum can be toxic to plant growth, so aluminum sulfate is not recommended to lower soil pH). The use of ammonium sulfate will help maintain a low soil

Fig. 3.1 *A sample label from a fertilizer bag showing the analysis of the major elements – nitrogen, phosphorus, and potassium.*

pH and at the same time supply some nitrogen to plants. There are several azelea and rhododendron fertilizers on the market; all should be acidic in reaction.

The fertilizers that dissolve in water and are applied as a solution have some advantages over the dry granular forms. First, if you follow directions on the label, it is impossible to overfertilize the plants because the concentration in the solution never increases. That is, the rate is controlled by the amount in the water; as this solution is added to the soil, the concentration never exceeds what is dissolved in the water. Another advantage is that because the fertilizer is concentrated, you can store sufficient quantities in a minimum of space. The big disadvantage is the cost. Based on the amount of plant food received per unit, water-soluble fertilizers are very expensive when compared to the price of dry granular fertilizer.

Slow Release Fertilizers. The most economical and generally satisfactory fertilizers for use in landscaping are the dry granular types, but there are some disadvantages to using them. Because nearly all the available nutrients are released at once when the fertilizer salts dissolve in the soil solution, the amounts available to the plant decline rapidly. For most landscape plants this is of no great importance, but turf needs a more continuous supply of nutrients. There are now several types of chemical fertilizers that release their nutrients gradually over time. Prior to their development, organic fertilizer was used (and often still is) to achieve a slow release of nutrients.

Organic fertilizers are often considered superior to the chemical fertilizers, although both types supply the same basic nutrients. One advantage of organic fertilizer is that there is less chance of fertilizer burn from overapplication than when a chemical fertilizer is used.

However, not all organic fertilizers are slow release, and injury from overapplication can occur with fresh manures high in ammonia content. The synthetic organic material urea is often considered slow release, but is actually very soluble and can cause severe injury if applied at excessive rates. The organic slow-release fertilizers include blood, tankage, castor bean pomace, and bone meal. They are very expensive as plant food and so are not recommended for your landscaping purposes.

The slow-release property of a chemical fertilizer is achieved by its low solubility in water, the particle size, or a coating. Low soluble slow-release fertilizers can be affected by the amount of moisture already in the soil, rainfall or irrigation, or by micro-organism activity. The second way a fertilizer may be slow release is by particle size. The larger its particles, the slower it will dissolve; thus, some materials can be available for even longer periods of time if they are manufactured in coarser grades. Finally, the coatings on granular or liquid fertilizer act as membranes through which the nutrients move gradually. The amount of water in the soil controls the rate of release.

Most slow-release fertilizers cost more than dry granular fertilizers. Their advantage is

Fig. 3.2   *Wood chips used as a mulch to provide weed control and a texture change from the turf.*

Fig. 3.3   *Stone mulch used to reduce maintenance around a tree and at the base of a wall.*

38

that only one application may be necessary. For your planting operations the dry soluble fertilizers are satisfactory. Also, remember that there are no miracle fertilizers which last for years, and fertilizer alone cannot cure environmental problems such as low light intensity, poor drainage, insects and disease. Fertilizer will only help improve plant growth, and healthy plants must have adequate nutrients to survive adverse site conditions.

MULCHES

The use of mulches, either organic or inorganic, is recommended for many landscape plants. In most instances the organic mulches are more pleasing in the landscape because they blend in with the surrounding plants and soil, and any structures. Shredded hardwood and pine barks, wood chips, bark chips, redwood bark, Douglas fir bark, and cocoa bean hulls are all examples of organic mulches. Inorganic mulches are usually stones of various sizes, colors, and types. In some instances by-products of various manufacturing operations are used for mulches.

Mulches have five purposes: (1) They provide a more satisfactory root environment for new plant growth and for certain established landscape plants, such as rhododendrons. (2) They help keep the soil moisture uniform by reducing the surface loss of water. (3) In winter mulches reduce the depth at which the soil freezes by acting as insulation. This added protection will often lessen the dessication injury that occurs among some broadleaf evergreens. (4) Mulches offer very good weed control, especially against annual weeds (see the section on weed control in Chapter 8). (5) Finally, mulches often improve the appearance of the site.

Apply organic mulches to a depth of 2 to 3 inches. If you try to save money by spreading a mulch too thin, it will not provide satisfactory weed control; a mulch that is too deep may not permit adequate air movement down to the roots. Also, the decaying of moist mulches may further reduce the oxygen available to the plant roots near the soil surface. Many organic mulches, such as shredded hardwood bark, decompose at such a rate that you have to add more mulch every 2 to 3 years. One cubic yard of mulch will cover 162 square feet of a landscape bed 2 inches deep.

The mulch should be coarse in texture to facilitate rapid drying of the surface. This drying helps prevent weed seeds that have blown onto the surface of the mulch from germinating. Also,

the dry surface breaks the capillary action of the soil, thus reducing water loss. Do not use peat moss as a mulch becaue it is an excellent seed germination medium: weed seeds that blow into it will thrive.

Inorganic mulches such as stone are nearly permanent. Use a depth of 2 to 4 inches to provide effective weed control. The type of stone should blend well into the site rather than stand out, so do not use brightly colored stone. Remember that stone is very heavy, and 1 ton of stone will cover only 108 square feet (1-1/2 tons/cubic yard) of a landscape bed 2 inches deep.

You can use plastic under mulches to eliminate weeds. This requires special care during the planting process to ensure that the water movement is away from the plant, not into the planting pit. Use black construction grade polyethylene 3 to 4 mils (0.003 to 0.004 inches) thick. There is a fiberglass mat available that is placed under the mulch to control weeds, but because it is not very effective against perennial weeds, do not use it. Techniques for installing plastic are discussed later in this chapter.

PLANTING IN GOOD SOIL

Even though soil conditions may be satisfactory for good growth, care is required when planting trees and shrubs because faulty planting techniques can jeopardize the future development of the plant. Proper planting helps ensure the future of the plant and the total development of the landscape.

Save the top soil if it is present when digging a hole. Good top soil is usually more friable (loose) and can be used as fill around the roots. The most convenient way of saving the top soil (and for mixing peat moss into the soil) is to place the soil on a sheet of plastic spread next to the hole. This is particularly helpful when planting a tree or shrub in a turf area: the plastic helps protect the turf from damage that can occur if the soil is placed directly on the turf.

Mix the top soil and subsoil thoroughly with sphagnum peat moss before putting it into the hole. Do not add any fertilizer to the soil mix, since it can burn the new, tender roots that are developing, slow down the establishment of the plant, or even kill it. Place 6 to 7 inches of the mix in the bottom of the hole. Firm the soil in the bottom of the hole gently by hand, but do not compact it. Next, carefully place the plant in the hole. If the plant is balled and burlapped or container-grown, handle the plant by its soil ball rather than by its trunk or stem. If a plant is bare root, support the plant with your hand and begin to fill soil in around the roots. Make sure the roots are spread evenly throughout the hole. Regardless of whether the plant is balled and burlapped, container-grown, or bare root, set it in the hole so that it is at the same depth as it was when it was growing; especially be careful to never plant deeper.

Once the plant is set at the proper depth, add more soil to the hole, firming gently by hand as you do so. For bare root plants, thoroughly work the mixture around the roots and eliminate air pockets as much as possible. When the hole is approximately three-fourths filled with soil, fill the hole to the top with water to settle the soil and help eliminate air pockets around the roots. After the water drains away, straighten the plant and continue to add soil until the hole is completely filled. Gently firm the added soil, but do not compact it.

After you complete the filling operation, construct a ring of soil 2 to 3 inches high around the edge of the planting hole to form a water basin. Water the plant with a fertilizer-water solution. The amount of fertilizer depends on the analysis; use a water-soluble fertilizer, and carefully follow the directions on the bag or label. Generally, if the fertilizer contains approximately 20 percent nitrogen, use a rate of 2 level tablespoons per gallon for watering newly planted plants.

CARE IMMEDIATELY AFTER PLANTING

The establishment of the plant in the landscape is not greatly influenced during the first year by the amount of nutrients in the soil; water is the key element.

If you are planting many trees or shrubs, one large basin around the entire area may be more satisfactory. Fill the basin with 2 or 3 inches of mulch. After you complete the planting, coat tree trunks with an insecticide to reduce the chances of attack by borers. These insects are a very real threat to newly planted trees, and the removal from the market of many effective insecticides has made borer control even more difficult. Several treatments per season may be necessary if the tree is attacked by borers. Check with the nursery or your county agricultural agent for recommendations for borer insecticides. Next, wrap the tree trunks with a tree kraft paper or burlap strips. Some experts prefer burlap strips since they allow the tree trunk to "breath."

The tree wrapping protects trunks from harsh environmental elements that might injure them, and it reduces moisture loss by the trunks throughout their establishment period. Even

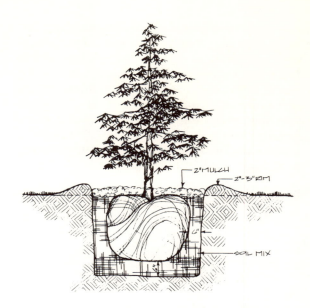

Fig. 3.4   *A guide for planting a small balled and burlapped tree.*

Fig. 3.5   *Apply tree wrapping to newly planted trees in the fall to protect them from sun scald and frost crack injury.*

more important, tree wrapping prevents trunk sun scald and frost cracks in the winter.

Pruning. You should prune nearly all newly planted trees and shrubs. The degree of pruning depends on the type of plant. For balled and burlapped, field grown, potted, and container-grown plants, remove only broken and damaged branches, and do any necessary shaping. Bare root stock requires much heavier pruning to reduce the leaf area in order to compensate for the massive loss of roots that occurred at the time of digging. To reduce the water demand by the top of the plant, remove 1/3 to 1/2 of the leaf area by thinning the branches and reducing their length. Do not ruin the natural shape of the tree or shrub; prune it in its natural growth habit. Never cut out the central leader or remove the top of newly planted trees, since this will destroy their natural growth habit. The pruning of trees and shrubs is discussed in detail in Chapter 9.

Supporting. If properly planted, shrubs do not have to be supported. However, oversized shrubs moved from one site to another occasionally do need some support. You can use the same techniques for both shrubs and trees. For most plants, the supports can be removed within one year after planting.

Provide support for all bare root trees and peat balled trees over 8 feet high. Smaller balled and burlapped, field grown-potted, and container-grown trees usually do not need support. A contractor who installs specimen trees over 4 inches in diameter should provide support.

There are several methods that can be used to support smaller trees during the establishment phase; height of the plant dictates

Fig. 3.6 *Prune newly planted material, particularly bare root plants, to reduce their leaf area. Prune to a natural shape.*

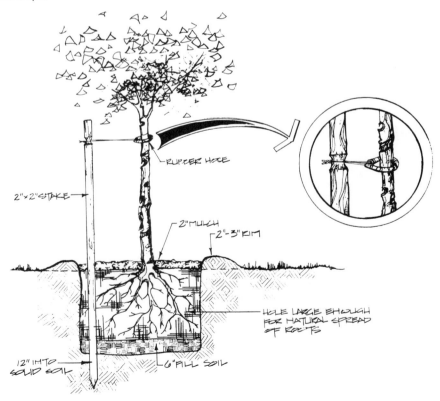

Fig. 3.7 *The single-stake method of staking a small bare root tree.*

which method is used. For smaller bare root trees, use a single stake that is approximately three-fourths the height of the tree after the stake is driven into the ground. Drive the stake 2 to 4 inches from center of the planting hole, on the northwest side of the tree trunk. If possible, place the stake prior to planting the tree; a stake driven in after the plant is planted can strike roots and damage them, reducing the chances of a quick recovery and establishment.

Fasten the tree to the stake with a wire or plastic plant fastener that will provide adequate strength and support. Notch the stake where the wire is fastened to it so the wire will not slip down. Put a loose sheath of rubber or plastic hose around the trunk, where the wire is in contact with the trunk, to prevent injury.

Use the double-stake method for larger bare root trees and all balled and burlapped, field grown-potted, and container-grown trees. This method provides more support than a single stake in areas where the soils are light (sandy) or where there are high winds. Drive stakes at least 18 inches into the firm soil, about 1 foot beyond the planting hole. Never drive the stake through the soil ball or roots will be severely damaged. The length of the stake after being driven into the soil should be about two-thirds the height of the tree. Place the stakes opposite each other, and attach a wire to each stake, as described for the single-stake method, and encase the wires in a rubber or plastic hose.

The most commonly used support method for the larger trees is to fasten three guy wires to

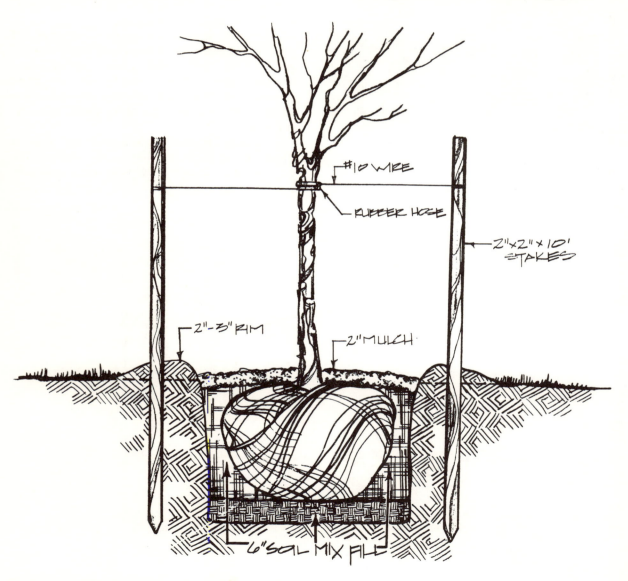

Fig. 3.8 *Two stakes provide more support than the single stake method for larger balled and burlapped and bare root trees.*

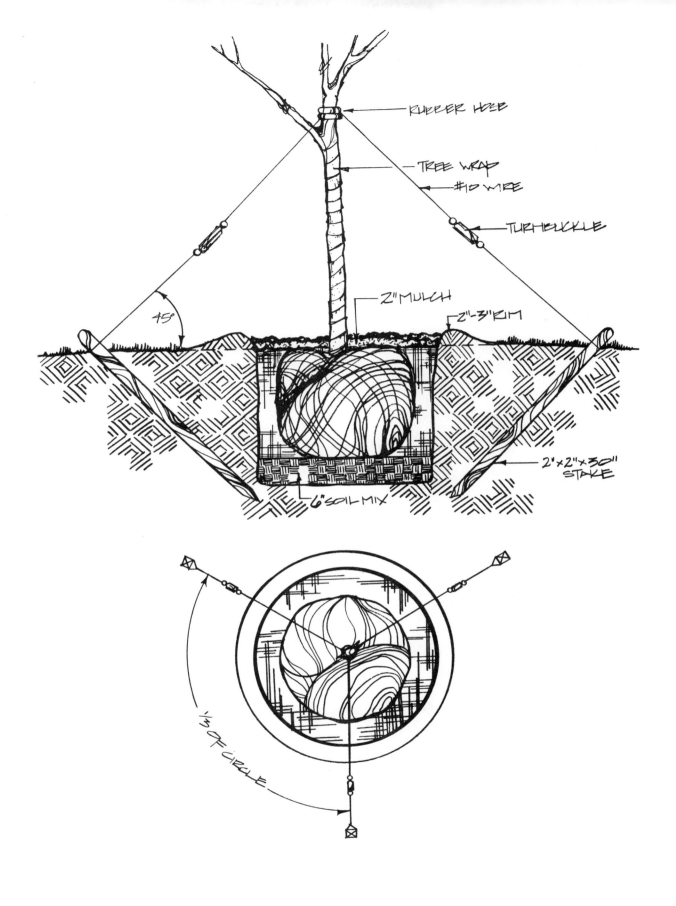

RUBBER HOSE

TREE WRAP
#10 WIRE

TURNBUCKLE

45°

2" MULCH

2"-3" RIM

2"x2"x30" STAKE

6" SOIL MIX

⅓ OF CIRCLE

Fig. 3.9   *Three guy wires are used to support larger trees up to three-inch caliper.*

stakes or "deadmen" that are positioned in firm soil outside of the planting hole. For trees that are not too large (less than 4 inches diameter), use stakes of 2 x 2-inch stock, long enough to be driven 18 to 30 inches into the ground. Approximately 10 inches of the stake should be above ground level after being driven into the ground at a 45 degree angle away from the tree trunk. One common error is to not drive the stakes deep enough into the ground. In a strong wind one or two stakes may pull out, and the tree then leans in the direction of the remaining secure stake.

Notch the top of the stakes to hold wires in place, and run wire from each stake to the tree trunk and loosely loop each wire around the trunk (always encase the wire in a rubber or plastic hose). Once all the wires are in place, tighten them so that equal support is obtained in all directions, but no excessive strain is placed on the tree trunk. Do not place the wires in the crotch of a small limb on the trunk. This is an easy way of keeping the wires from sliding down the tree trunk, but it also can be very damaging to the limb and maybe even the trunk.

Deadmen are more satisfactory than stakes for supporting very large trees (over 6 inches in trunk diameter). The forces created by a large tree in heavy winds are very great, and the stakes are not secure enough to withstand being pulled from the ground. Deadmen are made from 8-inch stock (either 8-inch logs or 4 x 8-inch lumber, approximately 4 feet long. (You can also use commercial soil anchors or 6 x 6 12-inch concrete blocks; the anchors disturb less soil when they are installed.) Bury the deadmen 3 to 4 or more feet down (the larger the trees, the deeper the deadmen should be set). Place the deadmen so they are at a 90 degree angle to the direction of maximum pull. Insert an eyebolt in

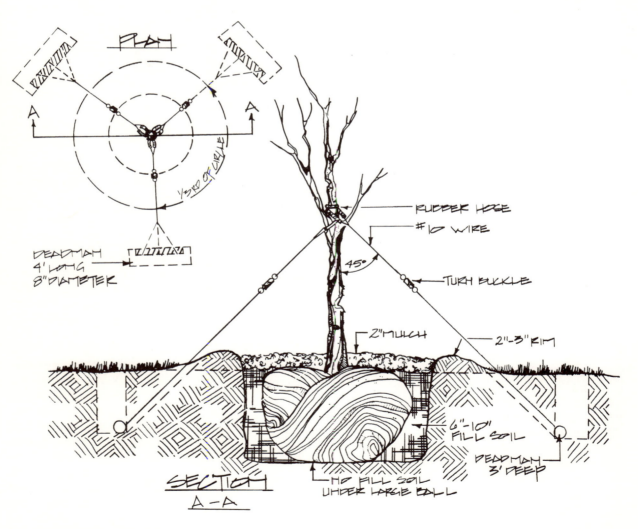

Fig. 3.10 Deadmen are used to anchor very large trees after planting. In sandy soils four deadmen may be needed rather than the three shown here.

44

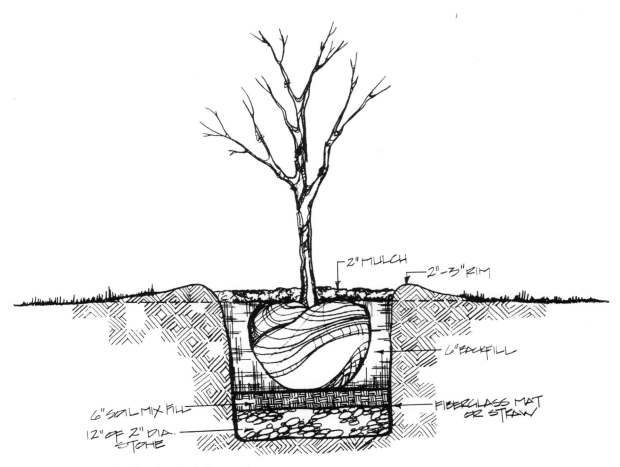

Labels on figure:
2" MULCH
2"-3" RIM
6" BACKFILL
FIBERGLASS MAT OR STRAW
6" SOIL MIX FILL
12" OF 2" DIA. STONE

Fig. 3.11 *A sump under the planting hole to collect excess water in heavy, poorly drained soils.*

the center of each deadman, and fasten a guying cable from the eyebolt to the tree trunk. Use turnbuckles on the cables to tighten the cables equally in all directions. Do not place eyebolts in the tree trunk for attaching the cable. Leave the supports up for two or more years.

PLANTING IN HEAVY, POORLY DRAINED SOIL

Unfortunately, in many sections of the country the soils drain poorly, and after construction the soil structure is often further degraded to the point that it is almost impossible for most plants to develop to their fullest potential if special planting techniques are not used. Compaction is a major problem, so insist that any temporary roadways at the site coincide as nearly as possible with the planned permanent roadways. If it can be done, restrict the movement of the general contractor's vehicles on the site to the roadways.

The special planting techniques needed depend on how severe the problem is and whether the plants selected can tolerate poorly drained soils. If the problem is only moderate—

plants in the immediate area growing satisfactory is an indication — you can slightly modify the planting methods.

Special Planting Techniques. First, do not add any peat moss, sand, or any other soil amendments to the soil used for the fill around the roots or soil balls. If the soil is amended with peat moss and/or sand, large pore spaces are left in the fill mix. During excessive rains or overwatering, the pore spaces soon fill up. The major problem of poorly drained soil is that it will not let water escape from the planting hole. In fact, the hole may act as a sump for the area surrounding the hole, collecting and holding water for long periods of time; and sometimes killing the plant roots because of the waterlogged conditions. Only certain species can survive these adverse conditions (see Chapter 1). Also, if you are planting in tight, heavy soil, make certain that the soil around plants is slightly raised, to prevent water from draining into the hole. But, again, remember to set plants at the proper depth, and do not mound the soil around the stems.

45

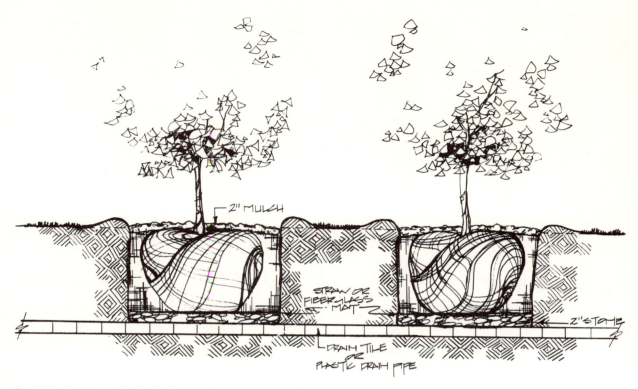

2" MULCH

STRAW OR
FIBERGLASS
MAT

2" STONE

DRAIN TILE
OR
PLASTIC DRAIN PIPE

Fig. 3.12 *Draining individual planting holes to a central collecting storm sewer.*

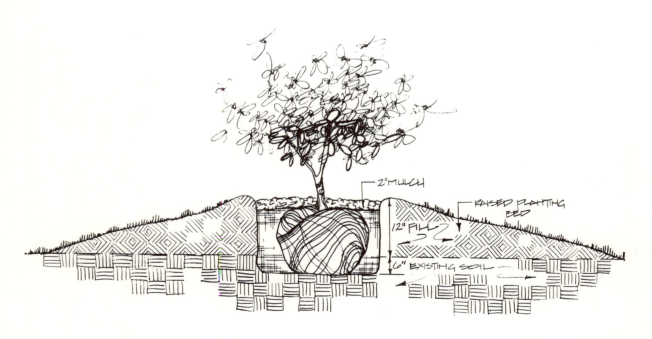

2" MULCH

RAISED PLANTING
BED

12" FILL

6" EXISTING SOIL

Fig. 3.13 *The raised bed method of planting plants that will not tolerate, heavy, poorly drained soils.*

Fig. 3.14 *Use of railroad ties to retain sides of a raised bed. The trees are flowering dogwood (Cornus florida) which will not tolerate heavy, poorly drained soils.*

depth, and do not mound the soil around the stems.

You may have to provide means for draining water from around plant roots if the soil is very tight, heavy, and poorly drained. Adding a drainage system for the entire site will help improve the chances of plants, including turf, successfully establishing themselves. However, there are alternative solutions. The simplest, if the water table is not too high, is to install a dry well at the bottom of the hole (Fig. 3.11). Dig the planting hole 12 to 18 inches deeper than normal for the plants, and fill the extra depth with coarse stone, preferably egg sized. Put straw or a fiberglass mat on top of the stone to prevent the spaces between the stones from becoming plugged or filled with the soil as it settles.

On some sites it may be practical to drain each planting pit into a storm sewer or some other water-removal system. The installation of such a system should be done by professionals or at least by someone who has experience laying tile lines. Each planting hole is tied into a drain tile or line. The dry well is installed at the bottom of the planting hole, but the stone is placed around a drain tile. The drain tile must be properly installed: the flow has to be away from the planting hole to the outlet of the drainage system. Because depressions or rises in the system prevent the flow of water through it, the tile must be laid with exactly the right slope for it to function properly.

There may be a natural gravel stratum at a reasonable depth to which the dry well at the bottom can drain but this is rare. If there is a gravel stratum at your site, dig a 6 inch diameter hole in the bottom of the planting hole to a depth that reaches the gravel. The hole is then filled with stone and covered with straw or a fiberglass mat.

A more practical way to compensate for poorly drained soils is to construct a raised bed. This technique can be used for most shrubs and small trees. Construct a soil mound that will hold most of the eventual root system of the plants. Prepare a well-drained planting medium; the specific mix depends on the plant being grown. For plants that do not have special pH requirements, use a soil mix of one part sphagnum peat moss to two parts well-drained top soil (by volume). For plants that require a soil pH of 4.5 to 5.5, such as azaleas, use a soil mix of one to two parts sphagnum peat to one part (by volume) of well-drained sandy soil. Check the pH of the mix and be sure it is within the recommended range.

Deeply till the soil surface of the planting area before applying the soil mix. Then apply 6 inches of the mix to the newly tilled surface, thoroughly working the mix into the existing soil. This helps reduce the sharp delineation between the two soil types and the possibility of a perched water table developing. Next add a second 6 inch layer, thoroughly working it into the first. Depending on the size of plants being planted, a third layer may be needed.

The height of the mound should be from 12 to 18 inches for most rhododendrons, azaleas, and smaller shrubs. For large plants, such as small trees, the mound should be up to 36 inches high. The diameter of the bed should be several feet larger than that of the normal planting hole, and the taper of the mound should gradually slope down to the surrounding soil. Use the same planting techniques described for good soils, using the mound soil as the fill soil for the hole.

In some instances, depending on the landscape design, you should retain the edge of the bed, particularly a deeper bed, with treated lumber, railroad ties, or a flagstone wall. More shallow beds can taper gradually into the surrounding area. Plant the edge with turf immediately to prevent erosion and speed the blending-in process. When plants are placed in the bed, build a rim to help retain the water. Runoff from the tapered bed could be excessive and result in plants drying out. With time the height of the bed will decrease and blend into the rest of the area.

Many plants are particularly susceptible to injury from being planted in poorly drained soils; rhododendrons and azaleas are perhaps the most well-known plants in this group. Other plants that do not do well in poorly drained soil include the flowering dogwood (Cornus florida) and Taxus. The dogwood will do well in raised beds. The Taxus sp. is a rugged plant that can survive most conditions, but poorly drained soils are its downfall. All of these plants will most likely thrive in a raised planting bed.

The initial installation costs for raised beds are higher than for normal planting procedures, but the eventual results more than make up for the added costs. If it is not possible, because of physical or financial reasons, to alter planting techniques to improve soil, select plants that are most tolerant of the soil conditions.

Poor Surface Drainage. There are four main reasons for poor surface drainage: soil is poorly graded; down spouts drain into planting beds; surface water drains from sidewalks and driveways into planting beds; and soil next to a foundation settles. All of these problem conditions direct the flow of water into plant beds instead of away from them.

The first solution is obvious: correct the cause of the poor surface drainage. If proper drainage is not possible, use the raised bed method of planting to force the flow of surface water away from the planting hole or pit and reduce the chances of the soil becoming waterlogged around the roots. If a raised bed is not practical and the water-flow problems cannot be corrected, use plants that will tolerate wet soils.

PLANTING IN SANDY SOILS

In soils that are too sandy and droughty, plant establishment is often difficult because of excessive drying of the soil. Except at pure sand sites, such as dunes and seashores, the problem can be solved easier than the problem of poor drainage. The first and most logical step is to select plants that can tolerate sandy soils, then add organic matter — sphagnum peat moss — to improve the moisture- and nutrient-holding capacities of the soil. Use a mixture of one part sphagnum peat moss to two parts sandy soil (by volume) as fill; this will greatly improve the moisture-holding quality of the soil around the soil ball or roots. If you are planting many plants, use hypnum or sedge peat moss to save money.

Construct a water basin with a 3 to 4 inch high rim 1 to 2 feet wider than the planting hole.

Fill the basin with an organic mulch, such as shredded hardwood or pine bark, that has a good moisture-holding capacity. Water plants regularly, supplying at least 1 inch of water each time. In dry periods, 2 inches of water per week may be needed. Neglecting the water needs of plants in sandy soils can, at the worst, mean the loss of the plants or, at the very least, unsatisfactory growth.

Trees planted in sandy soils need even more support than trees planted in heavier soils. Use support stakes for small trees rather than small stakes and guy wires, which tend to pull out in high winds. Support larger trees with guy wires and deadmen (as described in the section for planting in good soils). Bury the deadmen at least 3 feet deep to ensure that they will not pull out. The trees must be well established before you can remove the supports. If you leave the guy wires on for longer than 1 year, inspect them every 3 or 4 months to be sure the wires are not injuring the trunks.

PLANTING HEDGES

Since so many plants are used for a hedge, the planting of each plant in an individually prepared planting hole may not be practical either due to the time involved or the cost. One way this time requirement can be reduced is to dig with a back hoe trench the approximate size of the planting hole needed. The planting hole for each plant can be finished quickly by hand and the plants are planted in the same basic manner as described for planting individual shrubs.

CARE OF PLANTS AFTER PLANTING

Once trees and shrubs are planted, initial maintenance of the plants determines how rapidly they will become established and start to grow. In fact, poor maintenance during the first season may result in many losses. The most critical requirement is to supply an adequate and even amount of moisture. Too much water can be as detrimental as too little. It is impossible to present iron-clad watering "rules" because of the wide variation in soil types and the different moisture needs of plant species. Use common sense, and carefully observe plant conditions. If there is an extended period without rainfall or if plants begin to wilt in mid-day, check the soil to see if it is dry by digging down 3 to 6 inches. If the soil is dry, water immediately, applying at least 1 inch of water. Apply the water slowly enough so that it soaks in and does not run off. It may be practical to supply 1 inch of water per week on well-drained soils, up to 2 inches on lighter sandy soils. Do not use automatic watering systems unless the system can be turned off during periods of heavy rainfall. Make certain that during the fall there is an adequate supply of moisture in the soil for the winter months.

Plants' need for water vary. Generally, deciduous plants require more water during their growing periods (spring and summer) than do the evergreens. Larger plants require more water than smaller ones. Rapidly growing plants will require more water than slowly growing or dormant plants. Some trees and shrubs require supplemental waterings several years after transplanting until they are fully established.

Pest and disease control is discussed in Chapter 8. There is very little difference between pest control for newly planted trees and shrubs and established plants, except that newly planted trees may be attacked by rodents. In the winter months in northern states, most often when there is snow cover, the bark of young trees is a food source for mice and rabbits. The rodents will eat the bark at the base of the trees, sometimes completely girdling the trees and killing them. A mechanical barrier, such as a wire mesh screen or plastic barrier, is the best protection from this type of injury, since baiting and trapping, and the use of repellants is not satisfactory for most landscape sites. Inspect the wire mesh periodically to make sure it is not too tight. A height of 2 to 3 feet is recommended so that rabbits cannot reach over the top. You can also use solid metal sheets, such as down spouting, and then remove it from trees when

their trunks are at least 2 inches in diameter. These barriers are more useful if they fit closely to the ground. Keep grass and weeds, which are excellent hiding places for rodents, away from the bases of the trunks.

Newly planted trees are frequently damaged by lawn mowers. In fact, this injury is more common than injury from rodents or other pests. The best protection is to use mulching around the bases of trees so you are not tempted to mow close to trees.

First year fertilization programs are generally limited to a fall application if you planted the trees and shrubs in the spring. For fall-planted plants, fertilize in mid-spring. The rates and materials to use are the same as for established plants. In the warmer climates, let the plants become established (probably in 2 or 3 months) before starting a fertilization program (Chapter 9 gives a detailed description on how to fertilize trees and shrubs).

Fig. 3.15 *Rodent guard used to protect trunks of newly planted trees from rodent injury. Use may be required for several years.*

4

Planting Ground Covers, Flowers and Bulbs

Annuals, perennials, bulbs, and ground covers can add color and textural change to your planting design and provide a pleasant relief from the typical two trees, evergreen shrubs, and bluegrass lawn of many residential landscapes. The primary difference between planting herbaceous plants and planting trees and shrubs involves the size of the plants. Herbaceous plants are often planted in beds, and the entire bed is prepared at one time. Because herbaceous plants are usually small, planting holes can be dug with a trowel or even fingers and preparation of individual planting holes need not be as great as when trees and shrubs are planted. Also, planting techniques vary depending on whether annuals, perennials, bulbs, or ground covers are being planted. In some instances, certain species have specific planting requirements. Each main category of herbaceous plants is discussed in detail in this chapter.

ANNUALS

As their name implies, most annuals have to be replanted every year. These plants complete their life cycle and die in one season, or they go through several stages of a life cycle, including flowering, and then die from low temperatures. The latter type of plants may be perennials in warmer climates, but in areas where winters are cold, low temperatures kill them, and thus they become annuals. Some annuals reseed themselves every year, but because of the number of hybrids being grown,

you should not depend on this method of establishing an annual flower bed: frequently the offspring do not resemble the parent plant.

There are two ways to obtain annuals: the method depends on the species being grown. You can seed some annuals directly into the bed, but others must be planted as small plants which are usually started from seed or cuttings. Many gardeners start their own annuals from seeds, but it is easier and more reliable to buy plants that have been grown by professionals. The best-quality plants are produced in individual pots: transplanting shock is minimal and there is slight chance of loss. However, these plants cost the most. Some flowers, such as petunias, marigolds, and snapdragons, are sold in peat pots that can be planted. Larger flowers such as geraniums and begonias are sold in plastic or clay pots that must be removed prior to planting.

Another method is to buy plants in small packs that hold 4 to 12 plants. You must separate the plants at planting time, which can cause excessive root damage if you do not do it carefully. Plant loss from packs is greater than with individually potted plants, but a pack costs much less than the same number of individually potted plants. Be sure to check the number of plants being sold in each pack; the price is usually per pack, and the number of plants per pack varies with the species and the seller. Either ask the number of plants per pack, or count the plants and then compare price on a per-plant basis.

Fig. 4.1 *The petunia is the favorite annual grown in American flower gardens.*

Always buy insect- and disease-free plants. If the place from which you buy plants has wilted and dead plants in view, chances are that the plants you are considering have dried out at some time during their time at the store and are in poor condition from bad care. Buy only small, vigorously growing plants because they transplant more readily. Crowded, larger plants already in flower are not always a good buy. Also, examine plants carefully for discolored (blackened) stems and yellow, brown, or spotted leaves, which indicate plant disease. If there are insects on the plants, do not buy them unless the insect can be identified as harmless, such as a ladybug. Beware of end-of-the-season specials; often these are hard, stunted plants, and their performance in the garden may never be satisfactory.

Plant Bed Preparation. The preparation of the flower bed is just as important as buying quality plants or seed. Good plant-bed preparation helps make the annual flower bed a success. You should start with a weed-free bed, and proper soil preparation will help ensure this. Always obtain a soil test before starting, and then retest again every few years. The test results will indicate if the soil pH needs adjustment. A soil analysis will also indicate how much fertilizer is needed and what ratio (analysis of fertilizer) to use. A pH range of 6.0 to 6.8 is desirable for most annuals. If you do not obtain a soil analysis, do

not add lime or sulfur to change the pH, because you may do more damage than good if you use the wrong material. A basic fertilizer ratio of 1-2-1, or approximately 3 pounds actual nitrogen per 1,000 square feet, 6 pounds phosphorus, and 3 pounds potassium, will supply most of the new plants' nutrient needs during the first part of their growing season. If you use a 5-10-5 ratio, apply 60 pounds per 1,000 square feet, or 6 pounds per 100 square feet. However, for best results the first year, have the soil tested and apply the recommended amounts of fertilizer and lime or sulfur if the soil pH needs to be modified.

Planting Seeds. In the spring you can sow annual seeds in rows or broadcast (scatter) them. Broadcasting gives a more natural appearance; planting in rows results in a formal look. Most seed packets give explicit, easy-to-follow directions on how to space seeds. The key is to get the seeds *evenly* distributed over the area to be covered. Do not overplant. Space the seed as recommended on the package. Seeds too close together will result in crowded young plants that you will have to thin out if they are to develop into normal-sized plants.

Most packages indicate the depth seeds are to be planted. As a general rule, never cover very fine seed. Fine-seeded annuals, such as petunias, should be sown on the surface, with the soil firmed or pressed lightly to ensure good contact between the seed and the soil, otherwise germination and growth will be very erratic. Sow medium-sized seed at a depth of 1/8 or 1/4 inch and then cover them. Plant larger seeds even deeper. If you sow later in the season, increase the depth as much as 1/4 to 1/2 inch so that the roots of the young seedlings do not dry out. When planting deep, do not let the surface dry out and become crusted or many of the seedlings will be unable to push through the soil surface. The color display from seeded annuals usually occurs much later in the season than that from young started plants, which bloom earlier and longer.

After you sow the seed, water the area with a fine mist to further firm the soil and to soak the seed so that the germination process will start. To prevent the seed from washing away during heavy rainfall, use a very light mulch, or cover the area with tied-down, coarse burlap. Remove the covering when the seedlings emerge. During the first stage of growth it is important not to let the young seedlings dry out.

In 1 or 2 weeks, seed leaves will emerge, followed by a set of true leaves. This is the time to do any thinning. Keep the strongest plants;

remove the weakest. When you finish the thinning, the plants left should have the necessary space for growth to occur. Some species have to be pinched back when they are 2 to 4 inches high. Pinching is the removal of the top or growing part of the plant. This forces branching and the development of a low, stocky plant. However, not all plants require pinching, so check with an experienced gardener if you are uncertain whether or not to pinch.

Started Plants. In the spring you can plant young plants in rows or randomly place them throughout the bed; the random method gives the bed a more natural appearance. Arrange the plants for the final desired spacing, because they will not have to be thinned out. When you buy plants, ask the personnel for the recommended spacing of the species. Table 4.1 provides recommended spacing for selected annuals.

Plant started plants at the same depth they were growing. Dig the planting hole with your hands or with a trowel, and do not plant too deeply. If you use plants in peat pots, break away the top rim of the pot. If you let the rim remain above the soil surface, it could dry out and act as a wick, pulling moisture from the pot and causing harmful moisture stress during dry periods. Place the plant in the hole, and firm the soil around the plant by pressing it with your

Fig. 4.2 a, b, c *Annuals come in a variety of shapes, colors, and textures and add color to the home landscape.*

hands. As mentioned previously, carefully separate any plants grown in packs to reduce the damage to root systems.

After you firm the soil around the plant, there should be a slight depression, which will serve as a mini water basin. Water each plant with a starter fertilizer solution. Use a water-soluble, high-phosphorus fertilizer and add the recommended amount to water; water each plant with approximately 1/2 pint of the mixture.

Table 4-1 Height and correct spacing of home annuals.

Plant	Height (inches)	Spacing (inches)
Ageratum		
(Ageratum houstonianum)	8-18	10-12
Alyssum (Lobularia maritima)	3-6	6
Balsam (Impatiens balsamina)	10-18	8-12
Begonia (Begonia semperflorens)	18-24	24
Browallia (Browallia Spp.)	10-15	12
Calendula (Calendula officinalis)	14-18	8-10
Calliopsis (Coreopsis Spp.)	18-24	12
California Poppy		
(Eschscholzia Californica)	10-12	6-8
Candytuft (Iberis Sp.)	10-15	12
Carnation (Dianthus Spp.)	10-18	8-10
Celosia		
(Celosia argentea Cristata)	12-48	10-18
China Aster		
(Callistephus chinensis)	12-36	12
Christmas Cherry		
(Solanum pseudocapsicum)	12-15	10-12
Coleus (Coleus blumeii)	24-30	18-24
Dahlia (Dahlia Spp.)	18-24	18-20
Dianthus (Dianthus chinensis)	8-15	6-8
Dusty Miller (Cineraria maritima)	8-12	12
Dwarf Marigold (Tagetes patula)	8-15	6-8
Geranium		
(Pelargonium hortorum)	18-24	24
Godetia (Godetia Spp.)	18-24	12
Hollyhock (Althaea rosea)	36-72	12
Impatiens (Impatiens sultanii)	12-24	8-12
Joseph's Coat		
(Amaranthus tricolor)	10-15	6-8
Lobelia (Lobelia erinus)	8-10	4-6
Marigold (Tagetes erecta)	24-36	12-18
Nasturtium (Tropaeolum Spp.)	12	6-8
Pansy (Viola tricolor)	10-12	6-8
Periwinkle (Vinca rosea)	6-18	8-10
Petunia (Petunia hybrida)	10-18	
Phlox (Phlox drummondi)	8-18	6-12
Rose Moss (Portulaca grandiflora)	6-8	6-8
Rudbeckia (Rudbeckia hirta)	24-36	15-18
Salvia (Salvia splendens)	12-24	8-10
Snapdragon (Antirrhinum majus)	8-36	10-15
Statice (Limonium Spp.)	12-30	8-10
Stocks (Matthiola incana)	12-24	8-12
Sunflower (Helianthus annuus)	36-84	12
Sweet Pea (Lathyrus odoratus)	36-60	12-18
Tritoma (Kniphofia uvaria)	24-36	12-18
Verbena (Verbena hortensis)	6-14	6-8
Zinnia (Zinnia Spp.)	12-36	1215

Weed Control. Initial weed control in the flower bed is very important. It can be accomplished in a variety of ways, but a combination of methods is best. See Chapter 8 for details on weed-control methods. After planting use a recommended herbicide for the particular plants being grown. Carefully follow the label recommendations for rates and application techniques. However, do not expect 100 percent weed control from a herbicide; it will reduce the weed population, but not eliminate it. Remove by hand any weeds that come up. By spacing the plants at their proper distance, they will fill in solid by mid-season and markedly reduce the number of competitive weeds. Too wide spacing leaves room for weeds to grow and develop and compete with the flowers.

Rejuvenation of Annuals. Some annuals, such as petunias, need special mid-season training, cutting back, and fertilization to revitalize them and bring about new growth and flowers. Cut off from up to one-half of the top of the plant. Also, cutting flowers for use in the home will help keep the plants flowering. You should remove old flowers from plants like geraniums to prevent the formation of seed heads, which often reduce the number of future flowers because plant nutrients are used for seed production rather than flowers. Moreover, many plants look better when their old flowers are removed. Plants such as pansies will flower longer when their flowers are either picked off or removed before seeds form.

PERENNIALS

Perennials are herbaceous plants that grow in the flower garden year after year. A perennial garden is often considered too much trouble, but the subtle, quiet beauty of the pastel flowers adds variety to gardens. A well-planned perennial bed will produce color nearly all year, from early in the spring until late in the fall. The key to a good perennial garden is planning not only for the colors but also for the height and spread of the plants and the sequence of flowering.

Terms. Perennials are sold or propagated in a variety of ways: as seeds (started at the nursery), as seedlings in flats or individual pots, or as under- or above-ground mature plant parts, such as bulbs, corms, rhizomes, tubers, tuberous roots, divisions, crowns, or runners. For propagation, the parts of mature plants are usually transplanted when the plants are dormant. Each species will probably require some specific planting techniques but there are several general methods that will apply to nearly all the perennials used in the landscape.

A *bulb* is a modified shoot that consists of a shortened, disk-shaped stem surrounded by fleshy, leaflike scales. In the center a shoot or flower bud is enclosed by these scales. When people speak of a tulip bulb, they are correct in calling it a bulb. However, a gladiolus "bulb" is actually a corm, not a bulb. A *corm* is a short, fleshy, underground stem similar to a bulb, but

Fig. 4.3   *Annuals may also be grown in containers for color on a deck, patio, or home entrance, but these plants will require more attention to appearance than garden grown annuals.*

the corm has only a few rudimentary leaves rather than the many scalelike leaves of a bulb.

A *rhizome* is a fleshy, horizontal, underground stem, that occurs in such plants as iris, lily of the valley, and cannas. Many grasses are also rhizomatous, but their rhizomes are not fleshy. A *tuber* is an enlarged underground stem that is not covered by leaf scales or rudimentary leaves, nor is there a basal plate or center from which a stem or flower shoot develops. A tuber is covered with a tough skin. "Eyes," dormant buds that will grow and produce new plants, are arranged around it in a spiral. The caladium "bulb" is actually a tuber, and the potato is a tuber that we eat.

A *tuberous root* is thickened and fleshlike, and it has dormant buds only on its neck. When the buds start to grow, they produce a new shoot. At the other end, the bare end, fibrous roots develop. Dahlia and ranunculus are grown from tuberous roots.

Above-ground plant parts are

Fig. 4.4 *A perennial border garden provides season long interest to the landscape.*

Fig. 4.5 *The lily is a true bulb that provides summer flowers in the garden. Not all bulbs are spring flowering.*

modifications of the stem. A *crown* is the portion of a plant just below and just above the soil line. Some plants have a crown that is compressed, with many fleshy buds. This crown can be divided and new perennial plants obtained by planting the *division*. Some plants have modified stems called *stolens* that grow along the surface of the soil. If the internodes of the stolen are long, the stem is called a *runner*. Often new plants develop at the nodes on a runner. The strawberry is a good example of a plant that can be propagated this way.

Planting. As indicated in the previous section, the perennials category includes some bulbs and ground covers. Because of the specialized techniques required for planting bulbs, these are covered later in their own section. Take special care when preparing the bed because perennial gardens can be permanent. With annuals, you can make corrections in the planting methods each season, but making changes in the soil of a perennial planting is more difficult and most likely will disturb established plants.

When to plant depends on several factors. First, the species dictates planting times. Some perennials can be planted only at certain times of the year. Form also affects planting time. Seeds or seedlings should be planted in the spring, but bare root plant parts such as rhizomes, tuberous roots, and divisions of certain species may have other requirements. Generally, plant bare root perennials in the fall if the site is located in hardiness zone 6 or further south. (See Hardiness Zone Map — page 7 — to locate your area in relation to the climate zone.) For colder areas (zone 5 and north), plant in the spring. Peonies are usually planted in the early fall (September), and bearded irises should be planted soon after flowering. Bare root perennials are usually much cheaper than actively growing container plants and usually are easy to establish.

Bare root plants are sold dormant in individual packages, with the roots packed in sphagnum moss or some other moisture-holding material in a plastic bag. The plastic bag is often placed in a cardboard box that has a picture of the actively growing plant, the plant name, and planting instructions. Later in the spring these plants start to grow in their plastic bag containers. This is not a problem unless the plant has been at the garden center too long, in which case the plant becomes pale and stretched from lack of light. In some extreme cases the new growth will be white and very spindly, with even the tips of the shoots dying. Do not buy plants in this condition.

You can plant perennials actively growing in containers anytime in your area's normal growing season. Container perennials are the most expensive, but they allow you to establish or add to the garden at any time.

An inexpensive way to obtain perennials is to ask for divisions, roots, and so on from a friend's garden. A word of caution: the plants should be free of insects and disease, and the contributing garden should not have perennial weeds, since these weeds may be moved along with the plant.

Weed Control. The common enemy of almost all perennial gardens is perennial weeds. The best approach to weed control is to eliminate them from the site before planting the perennials. This used to be difficult because perennial weeds are very persistent and able to propagate themselves in many ways. However, a new herbicide called glyphosate (trade name "Round-up" "Kleen-up" or "Doomsday") has been developed to control those weeds. This environmentally safe herbicide has no soil activity, and can be used on the entire perennial area prior to planting to kill all existing vegetation.

Glyphosate is not selective; it will kill or injure everything green with which it comes in contact. This means that you apply it when the weeds are up and actively growing. About 10 days later the area is ready for preparing the soil. You cannot use glyphosate if the perennials are already planted or if the bed has existing plants. Check the application techniques prior to planting. If there is a serious perennial weed problem, you might want to consider applying the glyphosate a year in advance. This herbicide is expensive, but the cost is minor in relation to the work involved in removing perennial weeds year after year.

Plant Bed Preparation. Special soil preparation techniques should be used for the perennial flower bed, since this is the key to planting perennials. Do any necessary pH adjustment of the soil and add any fertilizer or organic matter at least 2 weeks prior to the initial digging and working of the soil. Mix the material thoroughly and deeply in the future root zones. Adjustment of the pH is even more effective if it is done in the previous fall, before spring planting. Separate times for adding materials means working the soil twice, but mixing fertilizer, manure, and lime could release chemicals injurious to newly planted perennials. A soil test is absolutely essential before adding any lime or sulfur to change the pH. Most perennials prefer a pH of 6.0 to 6.8.

Add substantial quantities of organic matter unless the soil already contains high percentages of organic matter. Normal rototilling does not work the soil to sufficient

Fig. 4.6 *Perennials may be purchased at the garden center in attractive packages that show the flower of the mature plant. Also, often planting instructions are included.*

depth. For small areas, spade under 3 to 4 inches of the organic matter. For larger areas, deep rototilling or, preferably, plowing has to be done. The best source of organic matter is from a compost pile, or use well-rotted manure or peat moss. Sphagnum peat moss is excellent but very expensive.

At the time you work the soil and turn under organic matter, add a high-phosphorus fertilizer such as superphosphate to provide the necessary element for good root growth. Use 4 or 5 pounds per 100 square feet as a good base for future plant growth. Since phosphorus does not move in the soil, turn it under so it is in the root zone. Nitrogen and potassium can be added later in amounts determined by soil tests.

Make the height of the bed slightly higher than the surrounding area to ensure the surface flow of water away from the landscape bed, not into it, which could waterlog the soil.

Planting Container-Grown Perennials. Use the same techniques described in Chapter 3 for container-grown trees and shrubs, but do *not* make any additions to the fill. Make the planting hole large enough, and do not under any circumstances plant the perennial too deep. The depth that the plant was growing in its container, or just slightly higher to allow for settling, is best.

Planting Seeds. Those perennials that are to be established from seed should have the planting bed prepared in the same manner as that for plants. Depth of planting depends on the seed size; spacing is determined by the species being grown. Spring is the planting time for seed of almost all annuals, but the time for planting perennial seed depends on the species. For specific information, consult your nursery. Also, most perennials are not started from seed in the garden. The planting of perennial seedlings is done in the same way as that for annual flower seedlings.

Planting Bare Root Perennials. This is somewhat complex, depending on what part is being planted. Follow two general rules: (1) always plant at the proper depth (planting too deeply will cause severe problems), and (2) dig big enough planting holes (do not fold the roots to get them in the hole). Place the soil around the roots and firm with your hands. Do not leave any air pockets. Mark each plant with a stake so the plant will not be accidently dug up when it is dormant. Obtain specific planting instructions for each species if you have any doubts.

Do not plant crowns too deeply. When planting divisions, use only the newer, most vigorous growth; remove older, dried parts and any damaged or broken roots. Inspect iris rhizomes closely for evidence of iris borer, an insect particularly destructive to perennials. Use the recommended spacings for perennial parts, and do not crowd them. Often the beauty of a

perennial garden is the presence of individual plants, not the closeness and mass found in most annual plantings.

Once you plant the perennial, water it with the same starter fertilizer described for annuals. Use a preemergence herbicide if you can find one that will not injure the wide variety of perennials you may be growing. Often there will be considerable bare soil between plants that will harbor weeds, so mulch the first-year garden with 2 inches of shredded hardwood or pine bark. The mulch will also help maintain an even moisture supply for the establishment phase of the garden. The first-year maintenance program should emphasize applying water as needed, removing weeds by hand, and staking plants that need it when they start to flower.

BULBS

Many people think of bulbs as only spring flowers, but certain bulbs will supply color in the landscape during the entire growing season. Buy only top-quality, insect- and disease-free bulbs. If you are buying bulbs from a mail-order firm, order only from a reputable company. When buying from a garden center or other type of garden supplier, check the bulbs to be sure they are healthy and firm, with no bruises, signs of mechanical injury, disease spots or insects. Soft or mushy bulbs are not satisfactory. Buy bulbs early in the season so that you have a good selection to choose from. Beware of "bargains," which are usually undersized or poor-quality bulbs.

The sizing of bulbs is difficult to understand, and each genus has its own terminology. Sizing is based on a bulb's diameter in centimeters, particularly among such spring-flowering bulbs as tulips. Terms such as "jumbo," "first size," "medium," and "flowering size," are all used by the bulb industry, but these terms do not denote any definite size. Deal with reliable firms that will supply the proper size bulbs for your needs. Most garden centers have printed information available or personnel who can advise you. The term "bulb" used in this section refers to that general group of plants started from underground plant parts. Most bulbs used in the landscape are perennials. The exceptions are tender bulbs that cannot survive the low winter temperatures in many areas of the country. These must be grown as annuals: plant them in the spring, dig them up in the fall, and store them in a place where the temperature is above freezing. The gladiolus (a corm rather than a true bulb) should be handled in this manner.

Fig. 4.7 *These perennials are in the correct stage for planting. The crown will be apparent so do not plant too deep.*

Planting Bulbs — Naturalizing Or-Bed Planting.
The site for most bulbs should be well-drained and free of standing water at any time of the year. Good surface drainage as well as internal drainage is very important. This does not mean that the site must be sandy, only that the soil should not be heavy or have a tendency toward water logging. In most situations bulbs will do quite well in the perennial garden, or even where shrubs have been planted. You should be aware of a problem that my occur. Bulbs are food sources for mice, chipmunks, and gophers, and once the bulbs are planted most control methods do not work particularly well. Install a rodent barrier at the time of soil preparation by putting a 1/2-inch hardware cloth screen around the planting area to a depth of 12 inches. For individual prized bulbs, make a wire basket at least 2 inches deeper than the planting depth of the bulb.

There are two general methods of planting bulbs: naturalizing and bed planting. Naturalizing is the planting of bulbs in rough turf or in ground cover. Bed planting means creating mass plantings in beds that feature large areas of color during the flowering period. Usually the beds are planted with annuals after the spring bulbs flower. One landscape architect has suggested that the best way to place the bulbs in a naturalized planting is to throw them in the air and plant them where they fall. This advice should not be taken too literally, since you would risk damaging the bulb, but the point is well taken that the bulbs should *not* be planted in straight rows, with equal distance between bulbs. Place the bulbs randomly about the area; daffodils, tulips, and crocuses are good bulbs for naturalized plantings. For smaller bulbs, dig individual holes up to 6 inches deep in the turf or ground cover with a trowel and a bulb-planting tool, setting aside the soil you dig out. Loosen the soil in the bottom of the hole. Add no more than 1 teaspoon of superphosphate or bone meal to the hole, and work the fertilizer into the loose soil in the bottom of the hole. Next plant the bulb at its proper depth (see Table 4-2). Finally, replace the soil removed from the hole and firm it into place.

For larger bulbs or groups of bulbs, you may have to dig the holes with a spade. In this case, lift the turf or ground cover as you would a small piece of sod from turf. Save this piece; dig

Fig. 4.8   *The tulip is the most popular of the spring flowering bulbs.*

Table 4-2 Some information on a few spring flowering bulbs.

Flowers (in order of appearance in garden)	Planting time	Flowering time	Height in inches	How to plant
Crocus	Sept.-Dec.	March	5	4" deep, 4" apart
Grape Hyacinth (Muscari)	Sept.-Dec.	April	5	3" deep, 3" apart
Tulip - Species	Sept.-Dec.	April	5-15	4" deep, 5" apart
Daffodil & Narcissi	Sept.-Dec.	April	14-18	6" deep, 6" apart
Tulip - Fosteriana	Sept.-Dec.	April	16	5-6" deep, 6" apart
Tulip - Early	Sept.-Dec.	April	14	4-5" deep, 6" apart
Hyacinth	Sept.-Dec.	April	10	6" deep, 6" apart
Tulip - Dlb. Late, Triumph Darwin Hybrid, Lily	Sept.-Dec.	April-May	18-24	5-6" deep, 6" apart
Tulip - Darwin	Sept.-Dec.	May	26-32	5-6" deep, 6" apart
Tulip - Parrot	Sept.-Dec.	May	20-24	5-6" deep, 6" apart

From: Forrest Keeling Nursery, Elsberry, MO.

Fig. 4.9 *Crocuses may be naturalized as well as bed planted but if in a lawn situation delay the first mowing for as long as possible.*

Fig. 4.10 *The hyacinth is pleasantly scented and is an interesting landscape plant though not used in the quantities that tulips are.*

the holes to the depth the bulbs are to be planted. Loosen about 4 inches of soil in the bottom of the hole, add 2 tablespoons of superphosphate to the loosened soil, work it in, and then plant the bulbs. Firm all the soil, and then replace the sod or ground cover and firm it into place. Finally, thoroughly water the sod or ground cover. A planting bed for bulbs is prepared the same way as for perennials. You can dig a hole to the proper depth with a trowel and then replace the soil and firm it by hand over the bulbs. If fertilizer was added during the perennial bed preparation, no additional fertilizer is needed. Use the recommended spacing for each species, and remember that mass plantings of the same variety are more impressive than scattered plants or many different flower colors mixed together. Sometimes clumping several bulbs in a realtively small area can also be effective. Plant larger bulbs such as tulips and daffodils in individual holes; smaller bulbs such as crocuses can be planted several to a hole. In all cases be sure you closely follow the proper planting depths.

First-Year Maintenance. The first-year maintenance program for bulbs is realtively simple. Let spring-flowering bulbs grow until their foliage begins to turn brown and die, then remove it by cutting it off at the soil line. You can cut off old flowers and flower stems as soon as they look bad. However, do not remove any of the foliage until it does turn brown because it manufactures food reserves for the bulbs which will be used for the following year's flowers and the production of new bulbs. For example, the flower stalks of many lily species have productive foliage long after the flowers have died, so this stalk should not be removed until the foliage is also dying. An exception is crocuses that have become naturalized in a lawn: delay mowing the lawn as long as possible to maintain their future vigor.

The flower stalks of some species, such as certain lilies, have to be supported. However, if staking is a problem because of time limitations, grow only those bulbs whose stalks do not require support.

If you carry out the initial elimination of perennial weeds as described for the perennial bed, the weed-control problem in a bed of bulbs is simpler. There are only a few preemergence herbicides that can be used on bulb plantings. Check the label carefully, and use the herbicide only on those plants listed. A coarse mulch will greatly reduce weeds. Also, with spring-flowering bulbs, once their tops die down, you can use a very, very shallow cultivation to remove any weed seedlings prior to planting annuals.

Some bulbs must be treated as annuals; these must be dug up in the fall for sorting and replanting. Dig most tender bulbs, corms, tubers, and rhizomes before heavy frosts. Be careful that you don't cut into the bulbs with the digging tool; a potato fork is useful for this purpose. Remove the soil from the bulbs, and store them as recommended for the particular species. Some bulbs, such as tulips and hyacinths, produce the largest flowers from the largest bulbs. If you do not dig up the bulbs each fall, they will continue to multiply and eventually become overcrowded, causing the bulbs to remain small, thus, drastically reducing the size of the flowers. By digging up the bulbs you can grade and replant them immediately by size grouping.

GROUND COVERS

Blending ground covers with the lawn, trees, shrubs, gardens, and constructed features can greatly enhance the landscape. Ground covers generally fall into two categories: (1) herbaceous perennials and (2) woody species. The planting techniques for each category are similar to the methods already discussed in this chapter or in Chapter 3 "Planting Trees and Shrubs." However, you should consider certain facts about ground covers. Too often ground covers are used where turf grasses will not grow well, the assumption being that ground covers will grow there without any special planting attention. This is far from the truth! You must analyze the site.

Site Analysis. A good site analysis will enable you to make a correct decision as to which ground cover to use and which planting methods to follow to ensure good establishment of the plants.

The following five questions must be answered:
1. What will be achieved by planting the ground cover?
2. Will a bare soil area be covered?
3. Is the planting for ecological reasons, such as for preventing erosion?
4. Is the planting to tie together areas of the landscape, such as turf with trees and shrubs?
5. Are the plantings for their own desirability and beauty, or are they just part of the landscape?

Once you decide why you want ground covers, you should make an on-site analysis to determine what factors will influence the establishment of the planting.

Consider the question: "Will a bare soil area be covered?" If your answer is "yes," then you should answer some further questions:
1. Why is the area bare?
2. If turf grasses will not grow, why?
3. Is there too much shade?

4. Is the soil poor?
5. Does heavy traffic prevent the growth of turf?

Fig. 4.11 Pachysandra terminalis *is a herbaceous ground cover that requires winter and summer shade.*

A.E. Bye and Associates

Fig. 4.12 *Some low growing forms of juniper (*Juniperus *sp.) make excellent ground covers but they require full sunlight to grow well.*

Fig. 4.13 *This bank has shade and low traffic. English ivy (Hedera helix) is an excellent ground cover for this site but it must have winter shade.*

Browning - Day Assoc.

Fig. 4.14 *The ground cover helps tie the plant material and the wall to the stone walk.*

Some plants must be grown in the shade in the winter time, so winter exposure is as important as light conditions in the summer.

Soil conditions are also important, especially texture and drainage. Such factors as pH and nutrient levels can be modified at planting time with minimum effort when compared to the problem of making major changes in soil texture and drainage patterns. If a soil is a heavy clay, sometimes the best approach, even with good bed preparation, is to use ground cover plants that will tolerate the conditions present. Likewise, if a soil is sandy, consider drought-tolerant species. If irrigation is available, your choice of species is greatly increased.

Make a *total* site analysis before starting to select a ground cover. It is always tempting to answer just a few of the questions about a site and then select the ground cover. But for best results, complete the analysis, looking at *all* the conditions described in the list.

Planting Ground Covers. Planting ground covers in containers is very similar to the planting techniques described in Chapter 3, "Planting Trees and Shrubs." For smaller plants use the planting methods described for annuals and perennials. Regardless of the planting method, prepare the bed as you would for perennials, because most ground covers are perennials. Do any soil modification, including required pH changes, at this time; most ground covers do better in a pH range of 6.0 to 6.8. Deep tillage is very important for good, rapid growth. Eliminating perennial weeds before you plant will greatly reduce future weed control problems. Also, if at all possible use fill soil free of perennial weeds, particularly perennial weed roots and rhizomes.

Once the bed is prepared, plant the ground covers according to techniques for perennials. For small peat-potted plants or crowns, dig holes with a trowel, and then firm the soil by hand. For larger plants, such as container-grown junipers, follow instructions for shrubs.

Use a preemergence herbicide to help control annual weeds. Your local county agricultural agent can recommend the proper herbicide. Follow the label recommendations carefully or you may injure sensitive plants. Use the herbicide only on those species listed on the label. After applying the herbicide, install a 2-inch deep mulch. Once the ground covers fill in, this herbicide application will not be necessary in the following years.

You can draw some obvious conclusions at this point. If the area is too shaded for turf, then use shade-tolerant species of ground covers (not all ground covers are shade-tolerant). Poor soil conditions for turf generally mean that the site must be drastically modified for ground covers unless the area is rough and plants that will establish themselves on poor soils can be used, such as the nitrogen-fixing crown vetch or Hall's honeysuckle. But remember that these plants can be invasive and can escape their designated area, so use them carefully. If the site is to be modified enough for ground covers, it will probably grow turf grasses if there is enough light. You should then base your choice on whether turf grasses or ground covers best suit the site. Finally, if traffic is the cause of the bare area, then the choice of ground covers is limited to only those that tolerate heavy traffic. There are few ground covers in this category, so your best choice is to reroute traffic to a less sensitive area. If you are planting ground covers to control erosion, select plants that will establish themselves quickly to check the erosion as rapidly as possible.

Next you must decide how to plant the ground cover. If the area is large, seeding is about the only economical way to establish a cover, but keep in mind that not all ground covers can be established by seeding. For smaller areas use young potted plants or divisions. Another factor to consider is the accessibility of the slope. Sometimes slopes are so steep that only hydroseeding can be used (discussed in Chapter 5). Regardless of the method used, the ground cover must establish quickly, spread rapidly, and, in most instances, be deep rooted.

If your reason for planting the area is to tie together portions of the landscape, then you must consider not only the selection of the ground cover but environmental conditions that affect plant growth and how the ground cover will blend into the total landscape (color, texture, height of the plant). Finally, if you are using a ground cover because you like the plant, make certain that the location and the plant's characteristics fit the total landscape.

There are certain environmental factors you must consider when choosing ground covers. Besides summer shade or sunlight, winter shade is important! Certain broadleaf evergreens such as English ivy *(Hedera helix)* and *Pachysandra* spp. cannot tolerate winter sun. On a bright, cold day, when the soil is frozen, they lose an excessive amount of water and are injured by winter burn (dessication).

For rapid fill-in and good growth, maintain an even moisture supply during the season, but do not overwater. Remove any weeds that penetrate the herbicide and mulch barriers. The following spring the plantings will probably benefit from fertilization. Apply between 2 and 3 pounds of actual nitrogen per 1,000 square feet, using an approximate ratio of 2-1-1. This is 10 to 15 pounds of fertilizer with an analysis of 20-10-10. Apply it over the top of foliage when the foliage is dry so that the fertilizer will not stick to the foliage and burn it. Use overhead irrigation immediately after application to wash the fertilizer particles from the foliage and prevent burning.

5

Establishing Lawns

The lawn is an important part of the residential landscape and often, in area covered, is the largest part. Probably more time and money is spent on maintaining the lawn than any other part of the landscape. Thus, selection of the right turf grasses, proper installation, and initial maintenance are all important factors in establishing a satisfactory lawn that will add to the total beauty of the landscape. Turf grasses can be installed by (1) sodding, (2) sprigging or plugging, and (3) seeding.

Sodding involves cutting and lifting strips of established, actively growing turf (including a thin layer of soil containing the roots) and transplanting these strips to the landscape site. Tightly fitted together, the pieces create an

Fig. 5.1 *The lawn is an important part of the total landscape.*

almost "instant" lawn. Sprigging or plugging, on the other hand, is the installation of plant parts (underground stems called stolons) or plugs of sod. This is generally limited to warm season grasses such as Bermuda and zoysia grasses. Plugging can be done with the cool season grasses, but is rarely done since it is almost impossible to establish a high quality lawn with this method. Finally, seeding is the uniform application of seed over the surface on which turf is to be established.

FACTORS INFLUENCING THE METHOD OF INSTALLATION

Factors to consider when deciding which method of turf installation to use are:
1. cost;
2. geographic location of the site;
3. rapidity of cover desired;
4. season of the year the installation is to be made;
5. availability of water (either through rainfall or irrigation;
6. the size of the area to be planted; and
7. the type of grass selected.

Cost. The cost of installing turf varies with the method selected. Sodding is the most expensive method and seeding the least. A general rule of thumb is that sodding costs five to seven times that of seeding and sprigging costs three to four times more than seeding. However, compare the costs of all three methods because prices vary greatly between geographic areas of the country and even among landscape contractors in the same area. Be sure that the prices are based on the same quality of sod, sprigs, or seed since there can be a marked difference.

Location of Site. Climate will influence greatly the selection of turf grasses. Grasses are either warm season or cool season grasses. Warm season grasses must have soil temperatures above 60° F for best growth; when temperatures reach near freezing they will go completely dormant and turn brown. Warm season grasses are zoysia, Bermuda, St. Augustine, and dichondra. Dichondra is a ground cover broadleaf type of plant rather than a grass. Using warm season grasses in northern climates is not practical because even if they survive, the lawn color will be brown for a significant part of the year.

Cool season grasses grow best if soil temperatures remain below 80° F and above 40° F. They will remain green after frosts and green up early in the spring, thus making them a more satisfactory selection for northern climates. In southern climates growth ceases when temperatures are much above the 80° F mark. Cool season grasses include bluegrass (or Kentucky bluegrass), fescue, bent, and rye grass. From this it is apparent that if you are living in the south you would not select a cool season grass and likewise if living in the north a warm season species would not be used. It is those persons living in the border or transition areas that will have a difficult decision. Observe through the seasons the different types of grasses used in your area and select the one that best meets your needs.

Rapidity of Cover Desired. If you want or need instant cover then you must use sod because it has the appearance of a finished lawn immediately upon installation. The lawn will be ready for normal use once the turf roots knit the sod down to the soil, usually within 2 or 3 weeks

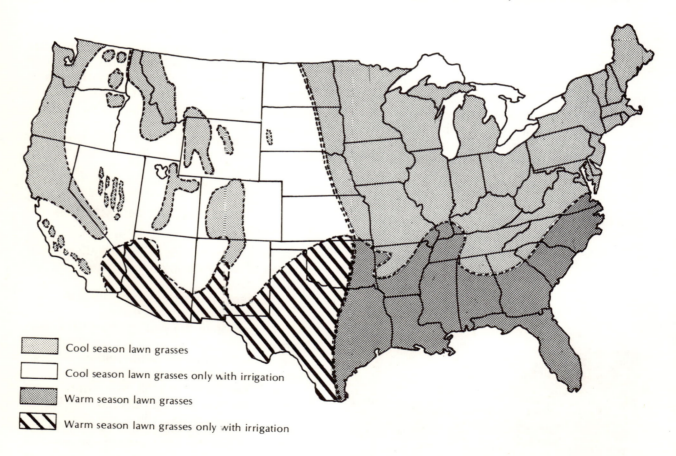

Cool season lawn grasses

Cool season lawn grasses only with irrigation

Warm season lawn grasses

Warm season lawn grasses only with irrigation

Fig. 5.2 *Specific turf grasses are suited for particular sections of the country. (Taken from Robert W. Schery, "No Frills Future May Require Closer Attention to Turf Selection." Weeds, Trees & Turf, February, 1980, p. 38).*

Fig. 5.3 a *Preparing the site for sod.*

Fig. 5.3 b *Laying the sod.*

Fig. 5.3 c *Instant lawn three days later.*

after it is laid. Sprigging or plugging will take at least 2 months to fill in; seeding takes up to 4 months to fill in and become usable. Obviously the cost factor must be weighed against the time required to obtain a usable lawn.

Season of Installation. Cool season grasses require lower soil temperatures for seed germination. This means seeding must be done in the early to mid-spring or in the fall. In many sections of the country, fall seeding is preferred over spring seeding. Summer seeding will not provide immediate germination or growth of the seedlings if the temperature is above 80° F. For rapid cover in the summer, sod must be used. Your county agricultural agent can usually provide information on the best times of the year to seed lawns.

For good germination, warm season grasses require a soil temperature of approximately 60° F. Seeding is limited in most areas from late spring to mid-summer. Seeding late in the summer does not allow sufficient time before cold weather occurs. In the deep south and in southern California, seeding can be done for much longer periods of time. Delay seeding in the border areas until continued warm weather is a certainty. Too early seeding will result in damage to newly germinated seedlings when periods of cold weather return. The restrictions for sprigging are not quite as critical as for seeding, but sprigging should be done early enough in the spring/summer so that the newly developing grass plants can become established before cold weather occurs.

The season of the year the work is to be done restricts greatly which method of installation that can be used. The greatest restrictions are placed on the time cool season grasses can be seeded. The general rule of

Fig. 5.4 *Zoysia plugs require at least 2 months to fill in.*

thumb is that when seeding of both cool and warm season grasses or sprigging of warm season grasses cannot be done then sod must be laid. The exception is in the winter months in the colder climates when the establishment of turf by any means should not be attempted.

Water Availability. If the site has irrigation, there is no influence of water availability on the method of installation. However, if irrigation is not available and the site is located in an area that characteristically has a dry season, seeding can only be done in the season when adequate rainfall is available. Young grass seedlings are very susceptible to moisture stress injury, so adequate moisture must be available to ensure their establishment. The supplemental waterings required for sod are not as great as for seeded areas.

Size of Area. For small and medium sized areas (2,000 square feet or less) sodding is probably the best means of establishing turf. The overall cost may not be any greater than for seeding, because the initial maintenance period is shorter and weed control problems are nearly eliminated during the first growing season. Also, the use of sod prevents surrounding landscape beds from being unintentionally sown with grass seed. This creates a severe weed problem in the beds.

Types of Grass Selected. If you select one of the cool season grasses, the option of either seeding or sodding is available. Some other factors must be considered when making the choice. If a pure fine fescue lawn is desired, it must be seeded, since fescue sod does not hold together. Tall fecue, on the other hand, is nearly always seeded. It is a coarse grass and is not grown for lawns by most sod producers. Bentgrass is usually seeded, although it can be established with sod.

Warm-season grasses are established primarily by sprigs or seeding. But here again the method is controlled by the species. Common Bermuda grass can be seeded, but if the better hybrids are used they must be established either by sprigging or by sodding. Bahiagrass, which is often used in high traffic areas in the south, is best established by seeding, but sod or cuttings can be used. Centipedegrass and dichondra can both be seeded, but centipedegrass can also be sprigged; use plugs when establishing dichondra vegetatively. St. Augustine and zoysiagrass are rarely, if ever, established by seeding. Both may be planted using sprigs or by sodding of St. Augustine and plugging of zoysia.

Fig. 5.5 *A fine bluegrass lawn area.*

LaPorte County Landscaping

Fig. 5.6 *It is necessary to have some full sun for a bluegrass lawn and the shade areas must be planted to other plants.*

Clearly, the type of grass selected has a great influence on the method of planting that can be used.

DESCRIPTION OF GRASS SPECIES

Cool Season Grasses. Bentgrasses are a very fine texture grass frequently used on golf greens in the northern areas of the country. There are two types of bents — Colonial and creeping. Because of the thick mat-like growth, bent lawns must be thatched regularly, and in warm weather they are subject to disease attack which requires the use of a fungicide program. Bent lawns require frequent close mowings — Colonial at 3/4 inch and creeping at 1/2 inch. The bents definitely demand high maintenance and must be grown as pure stands. If a bluegrass lawn is invaded by bentgrasses a real control problem develops because the bent is very competitive. Those considering a bent lawn should be prepared to carry out a professional type maintenance program. See Table 5.1 for other details on some cool and warm season grasses.

Bluegrasses are the most widely used of all the cool season grasses. Lawns are established with pure stands of bluegrass or with mixtures of bluegrass and some other cool season species. The bluegrass in the mixture is or will become the dominant species on sites receiving full sun. Bluegrasses generally thrive only in full sun or light shade. This is the grass used on most golf course fairways. Bluegrass lawns require relatively high maintenance, which includes fairly frequent mowings at heights of from 1 to 2 inches. For most varieties a height of at least 1-1/2 inch is considered best. Kentucky bluegrass and common Kentucky bluegrass are terms used to describe the mixture of bluegrasses often found in stands of native grasses in the midwest. The seed is far less expensive than the selected varieties of bluegrass, but the resulting lawn is much less vigorous than one established with the new selections of bluegrass.

Because of the differences in susceptibility to disease and adaptibility to a particular site, never established lawns of a pure selection or strain. Always use a mixture of several bluegrass varieties to help ensure a more permanent stand that will be less susceptible to attack by disease and other bluegrass problems. If possible, use at least four different varieties when seeding the lawn or buy sod from a source that uses a mixture of bluegrasses. If the desired mixture is not readily available, buy seed of several varieties recommended for your area and prepare your own mix. Mix varieties prior to application so that only one seeding is necessary.

To create a very fine appearance in a bluegrass lawn requires a substantial maintenance program, but due to the very large market for bluegrass lawn maintenance products, many products are readily available to make the maintenance of a bluegrass lawn fairly easy. Usually one can maintain such a lawn without too much difficulty.

Fine fescues are considered more tolerant of adverse site conditions than bluegrasses. They will also germinate more rapidly than bluegrass, and thus establish a quicker cover. The fine fescues are often used in blends of other grasses for lawns. When used with bluegrasses in full sun, they do not compete well and are soon crowded out, but the fine fescues function as a "nurse crop" for the bluegrass to protect it until it becomes established and takes over. In shaded areas, on the other hand, the fine fescues dominate most varieties of bluegrass. Creeping red fescue is probably the most shade tolerant and will do well in moderate shade. No cool season grasses thrive in areas of heavy shade, so do not be misled by advertising or claims for turf grasses that grow well in such conditions. There are selections and mixes that will do well in moderate shade, but not heavy shade such as that found under a large sugar maple (Acer saccharum).

Fine fescues can be mown at 1-1/2- to 2-inch heights and the fertility requirements are somewhat less than for bluegrass. Usually, the same pests that attack bluegrass attack the fine fescues, so the same pest control program can be used. An increasing number of pure fine fescue lawns are being installed because they

Table 5-1 Turf grass characteristics.

Species	Texture	Uniformity	Wear	Shade tolerance
Cool				
Bent	Fine	Good	Moderate	Low
Bluegrass	Fine	Good	Moderate	Low
Fine Fescue	Fine	Good	High	Medium
Tall Fescue	Coarse	Poor	High	Low
Perennial Ryegrass	Fine	Fair	Moderate	Low
Warm				
Bahiagrass	Coarse	Poor	High	Low
Bermuda	Fine	Good	High	Low
Zoysia	Fine	Good	High	Low
St. Augustine	Coarse	Fair	Low	Low

establish quickly, tolerate more adverse conditions and possibly require a little less maintenance than bluegrass.

Tall fescue is a rugged, low maintenance grass used along roadsides in many sections of the country. The texture is coarse, and this grass will withstand traffic. For this reason, it is commonly used for athletic fields, play grounds and other areas that might have more traffic than bluegrass or fine fescue would tolerate. It has a tendency to clump, so it should be sown in pure stands and not used in mixture with the fine bladed grasses such as bluegrass and fine fescue. Tall fescues are resistant to most turf grass diseases, and damage from insects is rare unless large insect populations are present.

Mow tall fescue at a height of 2 to 3 inches with a sharp blade. Dull blades shred the ends of the grass blades, which turn brown and give the turf an unsightly appearance. This grass is more drought resistant than bluegrass and will maintain a green appearance longer during the hot dry periods of summer. Though its maintenance requirements are fewer, it is not selected for most lawns due to its coarse texture and tendency to clump.

There are two types of ryegrass: annual and perennial. Annual rye is a temporary, one season grass used as a nurse crop or quick cover crop, particularly at times of the year when other cool season grasses would be slow to establish. Bermuda grass is sometimes overseeded with annual ryegrass to extend the green appearance of the Bermuda lawn later into the season. Since annual rye does not survive through the winter, it will not become a weed grass problem in the Bermuda lawn.

Perennial ryegrass is a semi-permanent grass that is often the main species used in inexpensive lawn mixtures, but it is attacked by diseases in certain areas of the country. This grass has a medium to coarse texture but can be mown at the same height as bluegrass or fine fescue (1/2 to 2-1/2 inches). It is not easy to mow in the summer if it has gone to seed because the seed stalks tend to lie prone to the ground. Pure stands do not make good lawns because in time perennial rye tends to become clumpy and does not fill in tightly. Perennial rye grasses do not require as much maintenance as bluegrasses, but do require more than tall fescue.

Redtop is a temporary or nurse type grass used in some seed mixtures. It is not used to any great extent now and so is rarely found in better seed mixes. It germinates rapidly and grows in most conditions, including shade, but provides only temporary cover until permanent grasses can become established. This clump grass does

LaPorte County Landscaping

Fig. 5.7   *A shade tolerant ground cover must be used here in place of turf grasses.*

not compete with the bluegrasses or fine fescues.

Warm Season Grasses. Bahiagrass is used to a limited degree in the subtropical areas of the southern United States. It is coarse textured and tolerates heavy use, in much the same manner as tall fescue, and is mainly used along roads and in playgrounds. It does not form a dense sod and does not provide the tight, close appearance of a fine, high quality lawn.

Bahiagrass is mown at a height of 2 to 3 inches and demands high maintenance. It will be brown in the winter months even in the warmest parts of the United States, and is often overseeded with annual ryegrass to improve the winter appearance.

Bermuda grasses are the most commonly used of the warm season grasses. They make a fine, high quality lawn if maintained. The newer varieties are fine textured and will compete vigorously with all other grasses and weeds in the lawn only when grown in full sun. They definitely cannot tolerate heavy or even medium shade.

The maintenance requirements for Bermuda grass are high even though the grass is vigorous. It should be mown at a height of 3/4 to 1 inch. In periods of rapid growth it may need up to three mowings per week. Common Bermuda grass may be mown less frequently. To maintain rapid growth will require frequent fertilization (as often as once per month). It is susceptible to some of the same diseases and all the insects that attack bluegrasses. In areas of the country where both cool and warm season grasses are grown, Bermuda grass infestation of a bluegrass lawn is considered a serious problem that is almost impossible to correct without killing everything and starting over. Because of its vigor, plant Bermuda grass in pure stands.

Centipedegrass, like bahiagrass, is used in the southeastern United States. It is medium textured and is mown at a height of 1-1/2 inch. It will tolerate moderate levels of shade or in areas that receive sun during only part of the day. It is relatively disease resistant and has only one very serious insect pest — ground pearl. Centipedegrass is considered a relatively low maintenance turf but it does require fertilization and cannot tolerate much traffic. This turf grass will not grow on alkaline soils (high pH). Also, frequent waterings are needed during dry weather.

St. Augustine grass is used in the southern parts of Florida and California, and to some extent on the southern Gulf Coast. It has a coarse texture, but in pure stands it presents a uniform and pleasing appearance. The mowing height is greater than that of lawn grasses — 1-1/2 to 3 inches. Close mowing may result in injury. Unlike centipedegrass, St. Augustine grass will thrive on alkaline soils and actually is adaptable to a wide range of soil conditions.

Fig. 5.8 *A zoysia grass lawn (on left) is invading the bluegrass lawn (on right). The zoysia is brown due to low temperature.*

This grass requires relatively high maintenance, and lacks resistance to any of the more common turf diseases. St. Augustine grass has a low wear resistance, and during unusually cold periods in areas where it is commonly grown it will freeze out. If your site has moderate to heavy shade, St. Augustine will still thrive.

Zoysiagrass has been widely advertised as the solution to all lawn problems. Unfortunately, this just is not true. A zoysiagrass lawn has a fine texture and a heavy dense sod results once it is established. However, it is slow to establish and requires care, particularly watering, during establishment. Watering is necessary even for established turf during dry periods. Zoysiagrasses are relatively shade tolerate and can be used in most home landscapes except in areas of extremely heavy shade. The mowing height is low, 3/4 to 1-1/2 inches.

Zoysiagrass requires a good maintenance program because it is neither disease nor insect resistant, but on the other hand it develops such a dense growth mat that weeds are generally not a problem. Frequent fertilization is required, as much as once per month during the growing season (up to four times per year). In the transition zone between cool and warm season grasses, zoysia spreading from nearby lawns can become a serious weed pest in bluegrass lawns. Though edgings have been suggested as a way for containing zoysiagrasses, this generally does not work because the stolons will go under the edgings and invade surrounding areas.

Dichondra is not a true grass but a low growing, broad-leaved perennial. Its use is limited to the extreme southwest and southern California, Gulf Coast, and southeast. Dichondra tolerates heavy traffic and can grow in the shade. There is some disagreement on recommended mowing heights. One recommendation is to mow it short — 3/4 to 1-1/4 inches for best plant performance. Another recommendation is to fertilize heavily and grow it to a height of 6 inches. However, at that height it has an uneven appearance.

Dichondra requires moderate maintenance because it does not have insect or disease resistance, and fertilization every 2 or 3 months is needed. It should not be grown in areas where temperatures might drop below 25°F.

LAWN INSTALLATION

Proper installation is absolutely essential if a satisfactory lawn is to be established. Poor site preparation and installation mistakes are difficult and expensive to correct later. The initial cost of good installation is higher than a haphazard, inexpensive job, but the results will be worth it in future years because the lawn will provide a more satisfactory and pleasing appearance, with less maintenance.

Too often a site is graded, the seed sown or sod laid and the project is considered complete. But there are nine steps required in a good lawn installation. If these steps are followed, except in unusual circumstances, a fine lawn will result.

1. Install all drainage and irrigation systems and all utility lines.

2. Till the subsoil and establish rough grade levels.

3. Spread the topsoil.

4. Apply lime or sulfur, basic fertilizer, and any soil modifying materials indicated by soil tests.

5. Use deep tillage and then smooth.

6. Apply a starter fertilizer.

7. Allow the soil to settle and establish final grade.

8. Firm the seed bed if soil has not settled to your satisfaction.

9. Install lawn by seeding, sprigging, or sodding.

Each of these steps is discussed in detail below.

(1) It is logical to install all underground utilities and drainage and irrigation systems prior to establishing grades. It is common to see a newly finished lawn with a trench cut across bringing in a power or telephone line. For several months or even one or more years, the ridge from the overfilling of a trench remains; or, if the filling was not complete, a small depression will be left in the lawn. The installation of the lawn irrigation and drainage system should also be completed at this time. Once the systems are in, do not use any heavy equipment over the area.

(2) Deeply till the subsoil. If heavy soil compaction has occurred use a chisel plow. After plowing or rototilling, follow with a rough disking or harrowing. Do not smooth, since a rough surface will permit a gradual transition zone between the subsoil and the topsoil that is added and reduce the chances of a perched or artificial water table developing. Establish a rough grade at this time. All surface drainage patterns are established by the rough grade and if a satisfactory job is done the topsoil may be applied at a uniform depth over the entire site.

(3) A layer of not less than 6 inches of topsoil should be spread evenly over the site. The cost of bringing in that much topsoil may be

Fig. 5.9 *Make sure all drainage systems, wires, pipes, etc. are installed before starting the lawn preparation.*

Fig. 5.10 *Establish rough grades.*

prohibitive, so it would be wise to require that the topsoil from the site be stockpiled prior to starting the construction. The cost is reduced to just the movement of the soil to the pile and then after construction is completed replacing it on the site. Before any topsoil is spread, have it analyzed for nutrient levels and pH. For most turf grasses a soil pH of 6.5 is best. A pH below 6.0 means the soil will need lime if the pH is much above 7.5, add sulfur or an organic material such

Fig. 5.11 *Work subsoil prior to replacing topsoil.*

Fig. 5.12 *Work topsoil thoroughly and smooth after applying fertilizer, lime or sulfur.*

Table 5-2 Use the following nutrients if a soil test is not run.

Element	Actual nutrient
	per 1,000 sq ft.
Nitrogen	2.5 - 4.0
Phosphorus (P_2O_5)	5.0 - 8.0
Potassium (K_2O)	2.0 - 3.0
Example: 5-10-5	50 to 80 lbs

Based on data in Vengris, J. 1969. Lawns. Thomson Publications, Fresno, CA.

as peat moss. This will be considerably more expensive than lime addition. The soil test results will, also, provide information on the basic fertility needs of the site.

Never apply the topsoil when the site or the topsoil is wet. Working the soil when it is wet can cause a breakdown of soil structure (puddling). Also, the site can be rutted by equipment used to spread the topsoil.

(4) Apply lime or sulfur in amounts determined by soil tests. General fertilizer ratios to use should be either 1:2:1 or 1:3:1. The amount used will be based on the amount of nitrogen added. If soil tests are not available use the rates given in Table 5.2. The table is based on a fertilizer ratio of 1:2:1. Spread the fertilizer uniformly over the surface. If possible apply the lime and the fertilizer at separate times with a delay of at least several days between.

(5) Once the fertilizer is applied, use deep tillage (6 to 8 inches) to incorporate the fertilizer and prepare the seed bed. Smooth the area close to final grade with a drag.

(6) Apply the starter fertilizer to the surface. The starter fertilizer should have a high nitrogen content (a ratio of 3:1:1 to 2:1:1). Apply at a rate of 40 to 60 pounds of actual nitrogen per acre or 1 to 1-1/2 pounds per 1,000 square feet. Do not use more than the recommended rates or the emerging grass seedlings will be injured by excess fertilizer. An example of a rate for a readily available fertilizer with an analysis of 20-10-10 is 200 to 300 pound per acre (5 to 7.5 pounds per 1,000 squre feet). A 10-5-5 analysis is applied at 400 to 600 pounds per acre (10 to 15 pounds per 1,000 squre feet). "Slow release" fertilizer can be used at higher rates of up to 160 to 200 pounds of actual nitrogen per acre (4 to 5 pounds per 1,000 square feet). The "slow release" fertilizer should be applied according to manufacturers' label recommendations.

(7) Let the soil settle and establish final grade. If rainfall is inadequate to properly settle the soil, the site should be watered to aid the settling process. The final grading should be done carefully on a dry surface. Final grade stakes, if present, should be rechecked for level and location. Eliminate all low places where water might stand. Hand rake and use level boards on small areas; larger areas require special leveling equipment pulled by a tractor. It will be necessary to touch up the area with hand raking and smoothing around established plantings, trees, landscape features and structures.

(8) If the soil has not settled adequately, firm the seed bed with a light rolling. Recheck the site for low spots to make sure the rolling did

not change the finished grade. For large areas use a tractor drawn roller.

(9) Install the lawn by seeding, sprigging, plugging, or sodding, according to the methods discussed in the next section.

SEEDING THE LAWN

Seed Mixture. The best bed preparation is pointless if you use poor quality seed, so buy the best. The cost of seed is a very small part of the total cost of installing a lawn, and it is false economy to buy cheap seed mixtures that contain a high percentage of temporary or less desirable grass species. Read the seed label carefully: all certified grass seed must have a label indicating what and how much of each grass is present in the mixture. The seed is also tested and certified pure, usually by a state agency, and each bag should have a label so stating.

Cool season grass mixtures, particularly bluegrass should contain several different varieties to help ensure a more disease resistant stand and a lawn that is more adaptable to the environment present at your site. A general rule is to have at least 60 percent permanent grass species in the mixture. The mixture might be dominated by bluegrass but still contain a significant percentage of other permanent grasses such as the fine fescues. Cheaper grass mixtures contain higher percentages of temporary grasses such as annual ryegrass or redtop. These temporary grasses are good in a mixture only when seeding is done during the warm season when germination and growth of the bluegrasses would be poor. Some seed companies prepare mixtures for various sites such as for full sun, shady areas, playground areas, etc. Select a mixture that is best suited to your site.

Of the warm season grasses most used, only common Bermuda is established by seed. Hybrid bermudas, zoysiagrass, St. Augustine and centipedegrass are all established either by sprigging or by sod.

Seeding Methods. Sowing of the seed can be done using a variety of equipment, but the most important factor is that the seed be spread uniformly. Professional firms use both seed drills and hydroseeders, tools normally not available to homeowners installing their own lawn. Usually most people use either a gravity-feed or an impeller type spreader. For small areas the seed may be spread by hand.

Seed drills place the seed in rows, cover it and firm the soil. This method provides good

Fig. 5.13   *Smooth, well prepared area is ready for seeding, sprigging, or sodding.*

Fig. 5.14   *Two types of seeders that can be used by the homeowner to apply seed. On each end are impeller type spreaders and a gravity-feed is located in the center.*

Fig. 5.15   *A hydromulcher applying grass seed to a bank.*

conditions for seed germination, but the seed is planted in narrow bands with wide bands of bare soil in between the rows. This bare soil can become a weed control problem until the grass fills in the space. Also, drilled seed requires more time to establish a filled in turf with a good appearance than seed sown by other equipment.

Hydroseeding or hydromulching is being used more frequently for seeding residential areas. In the past it has been restricted to commercial sites, roadsides, and hard-to-reach slopes. Grass seed, a cellulose mulch and fertilizer are mixed in a water slurry which is pumped under high pressure onto the site. The advantages of this method are that the seed is watered, fertilized and covered with a mulch in the same operation. The disadvantage is that the distribution of the seed is not nearly as uniform as when seed is sown by other types of equipment. Consequently, a uniform, fine quality lawn develops slowly.

Gravity-feed and impeller type seed sowers are available in small models that can be purchased or rented. The gravity-feed spreaders are hoppers on wheels that drop the seed onto the soil surface. The rate is controlled by adjusting the size of the opening on the bottom of the hopper. Spreaders that can be pushed by hand are generally from 2 to 3 feet wide. If you use a gravity-feed spreader, divide your seed supply in half and make two applications, spread half the seed in one direction then, in a direction 90 degrees from the first, make a second pass (see Fig. 5.11). This will not take much more time, and the result will be more uniform distribution of the seed with less chance of bare spots.

The impeller spreader applies seed in an 8-foot band. The time required to cover an area is considerably less than when using a smaller, gravity-feed spreader. Use the same two direction method of application. This spreader will give the most uniform application if the mixture contains seed of approximately the same size. If the mixture contains both large and small seeds, the impeller spreader will throw the larger seeds further than the smaller, resulting in uneven distribution.

For small areas the seed is best spread by hand. Again, use the two direction method. Regardless of the sowing method used, care should be taken that the seed is not thrown into nearby shrub and plant beds. This can create a serious weed problem.

Once the seed is sown, cover it. The depth of covering varies with the seed size. The bluegrasses are covered not more than 1/4 inch, while the larger seed of the fine fescues and rye grasses can be covered up to 1/2 inch. Cover small lawns by light raking. Do not redistribute the seed into uneven patterns by raking too long or hard in an area. On large areas cover the seed using a spiked tooth harrow or drag.

After covering the seed the soil should be firmed with a small hand-pushed roller. (Do not do this if the soil is excessively moist.) Next, apply a mulch to help ensure an even moisture supply during the germination and early growth of the seedlings. Small grass seedlings will die if the soil surface dries out for even a short period of time. However, if the soil is kept too wet the seedlings are susceptible to a disease called "damping off" which attacks at the soil line. To be active, the "damping off" organisms must have extra moist soil conditions.

A variety of materials are used as mulches for newly seeded lawn areas. Wheat straw is considered by many to be the best, but it is not always available. Straw is usually applied at a rate of 1-1/2 to 3 tons per acre (75 to 150 pounds per 1,000 square feet). For most city lot size areas and smaller, spread the straw by hand. Tie down the straw with binder's twine or other string run between stakes on each side of the newly seeded area. This reduces the amount of straw that will blow away and helps maintain a uniform cover. On larger areas hire a professional with a straw blower; the straw is bound together with a non-injurious asphalt.

Wood chips, sawdust, shredded bark, peat moss, hay and commercially prepared cellulose fiber mats are also used as mulches. Sawdust or peat moss are used in the western United States. Sawdust should be aged to reduce its nitrogen demand from the soil as it decomposes. Apply a very shallow layer — 1/8 to 1/4 inch. Wood chips or shredded bark are spread to depths of 1/4 inch. These products must be of a much smaller particle size than the bark mulches used in landscape beds. Do not use hay in most areas of the country, since it introduces a large number of weed seeds. Salt marsh hay can be used in the east if it is weed free.

Cellulose fiber mats are satisfactory for slopes or small areas. They are too expensive to use on larger areas, but on slopes where erosion may occur their use may be necessary. On very small areas the old method of tacking down coarse burlap is still satisfactory.

Once the area is mulched, the site is ready for the initial maintenance program. Water is the most crucial item, but all phases of the initial maintenance program will be discussed in a later section of this chapter.

Sprigging. Sprigging is the planting of plant parts, such as cut up stolons (runners) of the grass species desired. Several warm season grasses are established this way, particularly the hybrid bermudas, centipedegrasses, St. Augustine and zoysia. One cool season variety, bentgrass, is planted in some areas by sprigging. Use of sprigs may be necessary if the grass is a poor seed producer. In some cases it may be the only way (except sodding) that a true variety can be established. Plants produced from sprigs are identical to the parent plant.

Prepare the site as for seeding. For small areas plant the rows 3 inches deep and 12 inches apart for Bermuda and St. Augusine grasses and 6 inches apart for zoysia, since zoysia is much slower to fill in and cover. Plant the sprigs vertically every 8 to 12 inches. Cover the trenches with soil, smooth, and firm by rolling, and mulch as for seeding.

On larger areas broadcast sprigs over the surface at a rate of 3 to 5 bushels per 1,000 square feet depending on the species. Follow recommendations on the rate for your area of the country. Cover the sprigs with 1/4 to 1/2 inch screen topsoil — do not allow the sprigs to dry out. Peat moss, shredded bark, or aged sawdust may be used in place of screened soil if it is not available. After applying the covering, firm the area with a light to medium weight roller. For best results use a mulch as described for seeding.

Purchase good quality sprigs from a reputable source. The sprigs should be kept moist and not be wilted or limp. There should be no evidence of dark brown or black tissue which indicates that the stolons have been damaged in storage. Do not store sprigs more than 24 hours

before planting and keep them in a cool dark place until planted. If you are making sprigs from existing sod or purchased sod, cut them 6 to 9 inches in length. It is best to prepare the pieces immediately before planting.

Initial maintenance is much the same as for a newly seeded lawn except that the times between watering can be longer. It will take 3 to 4 months for the lawn to fill in solidly and be ready for normal use. Zoysia lawns may take longer.

Plugging. Do not use plugs if you desire a uniform, fine lawn because they fill in slowly, it takes 1 to 3 years or longer to achieve a smooth lawn. However, zoysia grass can be plugged into an existing lawn, and it will take over in 3 to 5 years and establish a solid zoysia lawn. Plugs of the hybrid bermuda grasses and zoysia grasses are planted in holes made by the plugging tool used to cut the plugs from the existing sod. Plant plugs at the same depth as they were grown in the original sod. Bermuda plugs are usually planted on 8 to 12 inch centers, and zoysia is planted on 6 inch centers. Dune grass, used to control sand dunes, is generally established by plugging.

Sodding. Sodding provides an instant lawn, at least from the point of view of appearance. It takes 2 or 3 weeds for sod to "knit" down to the soil surface and be ready for use. To obtain excellent results, install sod by preparing the soil as for seeding. Many will consider the added costs of sodding well worth the expense.

Buy high quality sod. Even proper preparation of the site will not make a good lawn if cheap, poor quality sod is used. Avoid using sod from pastures, meadows or old lawns because it will not contain the best, new varieties of turf grasses and serious weed pests could be introduced. When buying sod, ask what seed mixture was used to produce it. Remember that bluegrass sod should contain a mix of several varieties to help ensure a long-lasting vigorous lawn. Warm season grass sods may be pure strains without as great a danger to the longevity of the lawn. Sod should be freshly cut, or, if cut previously, spread out so that it can be kept watered until ready for laying. Do not buy or accept dry sod, since it has gone dormant and may take several weeks to return to active growth. Dry sod may even be dead if it remains dry for an extended period.

Bluegrass sod has a soil depth of 1/2 to 3/4 inch and is well grown so that when the pieces are picked up they do not break apart. The strips are 1 to 2 feet wide and 4 to 6 feet long. Sod is

Fig. 5.16 *Watering of newly seeded lawns is a must until the new lawn is well established.*

sold flat or rolled. There is no difference in quality, but do not allow it to remain stacked or rolled for more than 24 hours before laying.

Before you lay the first row of sod, mark a straight line perpendicular to the sidewalk or driveway or parallel to the property line by stretching a string or laying boards precisely between two stakes. Some lay the sod diagonally to the street, but nevertheless lay out the straight line first. The first row of sod is laid precisely along this line. The next row is laid tight to the first but the joints between pieces should be staggered. Care should be taken in fitting the joints so that they are very tight. The pieces of sod should be laid perfectly flat without bulges or humps. Never overlap the joints. Cut pieces from a whole strip of sod to fill in where needed. Once you lay the sod, lightly roll it and check to make certain all pieces are laid flat and smooth.

INITIAL LAWN MAINTENANCE

Watering is the single most important aspect of maintenance during the establishment phase of the lawn. For newly seeded areas apply frequent light waterings so that the upper surface does not dry out. Sometimes several waterings per day may be necessary, particularly on hot, dry, windy days, and the frequent waterings may be necessary for up to 30 days with a gradual tapering off toward the end of the period. When the seedlings begin to be well established, more normal watering practices will be sufficient: apply 1 inch per watering so that soil penetration is at least 6 inches deep. Usually a common lawn sprinkler is satisfactory. If a turf irrigation system is installed, it will be ideal for providing the necessary water.

A watering program for sprigs will be less vigorous than that for seeded areas, but be certain that the soil surface does not dry out for more than a few hours. The frequently of waterings is determined by the soil type and the weather conditions: heavier soils take less water and lighter soils take more. On dry, windy days more waterings are necessary. Again, water penetration should be at least 6 inches.

Sod requires more frequent waterings than established turf; the frequently depends on the weather. Do not let the sod dry out until it goes dormant, because the recovery period may be as much as several weeks. Irrigation systems for turf areas are ideal for watering both sod and sprig planted lawns.

The first mowing is done when the grass is 1 to 2 inches higher than its normal mowing height. Check the earlier sections in this chapter for the normal mowing heights of the individual species. The surface for the first mowing should be dry and firm (withhold water until after the mowing) so that the mower will not leave ruts on the surface.

Weed control is not a problem if you use good quality sod. Usually a herbicide for broad-leaved weeds is not needed until the following growing season. However, in seeded and sprigged lawns the situation is different; weeds are usually a serious problem, but control means have to be limited the first year because the new seedlings or plants from sprigs are more sensitive to herbicide damage during the first year. The best thing to do is to follow current recommendations for newly planted lawns. Recommendations are available from the county agricultural extension agent, the seed company that supplied the seed, or the garden center where the seed was purchased.

Regardless of any other maintenance practices that might be carried out the first year, proper watering is the most important consideration for ensuring the establishing of a high quality lawn.

6

The Vegetable and Fruit Gardens

More and more people are using a portion of their landscape site for the production of food. As food costs continue to rise the financial reasons for gardening are becoming very real. However, people garden for many other reasons, and these reasons are just as important. Most gardeners believe the quality of home produced vegetables or fruits is superior to what can be purchased at a store. There is no question that produce picked at its prime in ripeness and not shipped is of superior quality. Also, if you choose to have vegetables and fruits that are produced without chemical fertilizers and pesticides, you can do so in your garden. Some people garden for recreational reasons. Caring for a garden provides exercise, and, as the produce is harvested, there is satisfaction in seeing the results of one's hard work. Regardless of the reasons for gardening, there is an orderly process that should be used prior to starting a new garden venture.

GARDEN SITE SELECTION

The vegetable garden should be located in a sunny spot — at least 6 hours of sunshine or more is preferred. Vegetables just do not grow well in the shade and the results of a garden in shade will be most disappointing. However, there are some vegetables that will do better in less sun. Table 6.1 provides a list of vegetables and their light requirements.

The site should be level and the soil well drained, since good water drainage is a requirement for vegetable production. Avoid low areas and pockets of poor drainage in your garden. If only a slope is available, a south facing slope is best. To prevent erosion it will be necessary to build terraces in the garden (see Fig. 6.1).

If the site has heavy clay or subsoil (often found at many home sites after construction) the use of several inches of peat moss, leaves, compost, or strawy manure is recommended to improve soil structure. Work the organic matter thoroughly into the soil by spading or rototilling.

Finally, the garden should be located so that it is part of your total landscape plan. It should be conveniently located for work and for harvesting of vegetables. But at the same time it

Table 6-1 Light needs of some vegetables.

Partial sun (4 to 6 hours a day)	Full sun (over 6 hours a day)
Beets	Beans
Carrots	Broccoli
Cauliflower	Cabbage
Swiss chard	Corn
Cucumber	Eggplant
Lettuce	Muskmelons
Onions	Summer squash
Parsley	Tomatoes
Peas	
Radishes	
Spinach	
Winter squash	

From: Square Foot Gardening by Mel Bartholomew. Rodale Press, Emmaus, Pennsylvania.

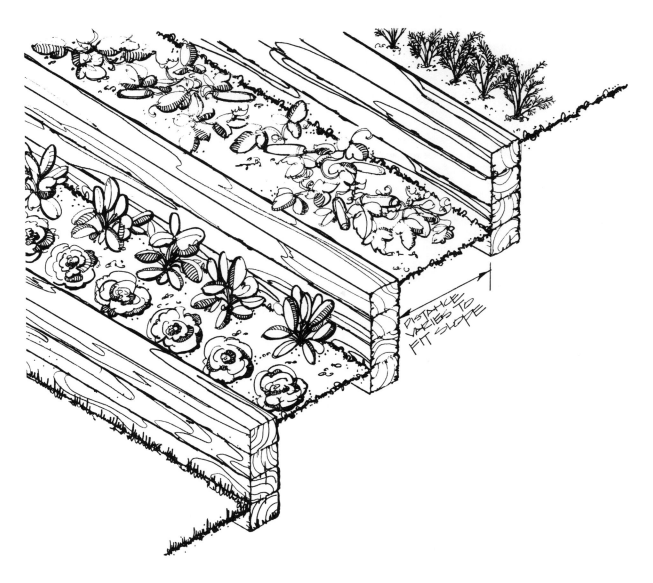

Fig. 6.1 *A terrace system should be used when gardening on a slope.*

should not interfere with the use of the rest of the landscape site. Also, remember that the garden may not be very attractive late in the season or if you let the weeds get ahead of you.

SIZE OF GARDEN

There are two main factors that will control the size of your garden — physical restrictions and needs of the family. It is obvious that you cannot have a garden larger than the space available in your landscape or larger than the area that is suitable for a vegetable or fruit garden. The amount of space you utilize from your site for the garden will depend not only on the lot size, but also on the other needs of your family such as play areas for children, recreational space for the entire family, or the aesthetic use of some of the area for ornamental plantings, etc.

Once the available space for the garden has been determined, another physical factor that must be considered is the person or persons doing the gardening. Are you prepared to take care of the garden throughout the growing season? Gardening is more than just planting seeds in the spring. It is a continual program of care for 6 or 7 months of the year, longer if you live in a warm climate. The garden should be no larger than you can care for or have the equipment to assist you in managing the garden. Gardening is a time consuming project, so if you are a first time gardener make certain that your schedule will permit you to spend the time it takes. It has been suggested that a small 20 x 50 foot garden may take 2 or more hours of care per week, and in the spring during planting time even more time will be required.

Next you should determine the food requirements of the family and how a vegetable or fruit garden might supplement these needs. If the primary reason for having a garden is financial, then the size should be sufficient to provide substantial quantities of produce for immediate use as well as for items to process for use in the winter. Usually, gardens to supplement the family food budget are much larger than the garden that is for recreational or hobby reasons. The produce from a hobby garden is generally for eating fresh and for show.

Regardless of the reason for gardening, the selection of vegetables and quantities to be grown will depend on the likes and dislikes of the family. It is pointless to grow a large number of eggplants if no one or only one person eats eggplant. A computer program has been developed by Dr. John Wott and others at Purdue University for the design of a vegetable garden. This program designs the garden based on the size of space available, the vegetable needs of the family, and compares the two factors so that the most efficient use of the available space is achieved. Tables 6.2 and 6.3 are

from this computer program, and they show the approximate yearly vegetable needs of an adult (both fresh and processed) and also the expected yields from a specific length of row of a particular vegetable. This information can be used in planning the size of your garden and how much to plant of each vegetable.

GARDEN DESIGN

The size of the garden in part determines the distance between the rows of vegetables. In large gardens the distance will be wider so that mechanical equipment such as rototillers can be used for cultivation between rows. For smaller gardens where space is limited the distance between rows will be much closer, and planting beds and hand cultivation will be necessary. Table 6.4 is a planting guide that provides row spacings (minimum) and distances between plants as well as the depth to plant seeds. Also given are the average days after planting until harvest.

You may want to lay your garden out in small plots if space is limited. Cultivation must be done by hand, but this technique will make maximum use of the space you have available. A

Table 6-2 Vegetable needs per person.

Vegetable	Amount grown for one average adult's fresh use	No. of adults-fresh use	Amount grown for one average adult's processed use	No. of adults-processed use
Bush Green Beans	9 lbs.	1	18 lbs.	1
Lima Beans	2 lbs.	1	2.6 lbs.	1
Broccoli	4.5 lbs.	1	6.3 lbs.	1
Cabbage	15 lbs. (5 head)	1	15 lbs. (5 head)	1
Cauliflower	4 heads	1	6 heads	1
Cucumber	6 lbs.	2	12 heads	2
Cantaloupe	10 fruit	2	2 fruit	1
Summer Squash	19 lbs.	2	6 lbs.	1
Winter Squash	48 lbs.	1	48 lbs.	0
Pumpkin	36 lbs. (6-12 fruit)	1	36 lbs.	1
Watermelon	4.5 lbs.	1	not processed	--
Tomato, cased	35 lbs.	2	70 lbs.	2
Tomato, nonstaked	35 lbs.	0	70 lbs.	0
Tomato, staked	35 lbs.	0	70 lbs.	0
Onion (Green/Bulb)	10 lbs. (60 green)	2	not processed	--
Turnips	3.5 lbs.	1	7 lbs.	1
Irish Potatoes	56.25 lbs.	1	not processed	--
Beets	3.6 lbs.	1	7.2 lbs.	1
Carrots	7.5 lbs.	2	7.5 lbs.	1
Radishes	5 bunches (10/bunch)	2	not processed	--
Pepper	3 lbs.	1	7 lbs.	1
Eggplant	2.4 lbs.	1	4.8 lbs.	1
Okra	3.25 lbs.	1	3.9 lbs.	1
Sweet Corn	25 ears	2	50 ears	1
Peas	4.5 lbs.	1	7.5 lbs.	1
Leaf Lettuce	5 lbs.	2	not processed	--
Spinach	3 lbs.	1	5 lbs.	1
New Zealand Spinach	4.5 lbs.	1	4.5 lbs.	1
Swiss Chard	3 lbs.	1	5 lbs.	1

Table 6-3 Yields given row length.

Vegetable	Amount to plant	Expected yield	No. of average adults supplied by yield: fresh use	processed use
Bush Green Beans	12 feet	7.2 lbs.	.3	.3
Lima Beans	6 feet	1.2 lbs.	.3	.3
Broccoli	5 plants*	4.5 lbs.	.4	.4
Cabbage	2 plant	12 lbs.	.4	.4
Cauliflower	3 plants	2.97 heads	.3	.3
Cucumber	18 feet	18 lbs.	1	1
Cantaloupe	5 hills	10 fruit	.9	.5
Summer Squash	3 hills	19.2 lbs.	.9	.4
Winter Squash	1 hill	24 lbs.	.5	0
Pumpkin	2 hills	36 lbs.	.5	.5
Watermelon	2 hills	3 fruit	.7	0
Tomatoes, Cased	4 plants	52 lbs.	.9	.9
Tomatoes, Nonstaked	--	--	--	--
Tomatoes, Staked	--	--	--	--
Onion (Green/Bulb)	20 feet	20 lbs.	2	0
Turnips	11 feet*	7.7 lbs.	.7	.7
Irish Potatoes	24 feet	18 lbs.	.3	0
Beets	14 feet*	100.8 lbs.	.8	.8
Carrots	11 feet*	16.5 lbs.	1.5	.7
Radishes	4 feet	8 bunches	1.6	0
Pepper	3 plants	2.7 lbs.	.3	.3
Eggplant	2 plants	2.4 lbs.	.4	.4
Okra	3 feet	1.95 lbs.	.3	.3
Sweet Corn	48 feet	48 ears	1	.5
Peas	15 feet*	4.5 lbs.	.4	.4
Leaf Lettuce	8 feet*	8 lbs.	1.6	0
Spinach	12 feet	6 lbs.	.8	.8
New Zealand Spinach	3 feet	2.25 lbs.	.3	.3
Swiss Chard	4 feet	2 lbs.	.3	.3

*This amount must be planted twice to obtain the expected yield. The expected yield is the total from both spring and fall plantings.

A 30 by 30 foot garden design.

Table 6-4 Vegetable planting guide.

Vegetable	Space between rows	Space between plants	Amount seed or no. plant per 50 ft.	Depth to plant
	feet	inches		inches
Beets	1	3	1 ounce	1/2-1
Broccoli (plants)	3	18	36 plants	--
Cabbage (plants)	3	18	36 plants	--
Cantaloupe	4	48	1 packet	1
Carrots	1	2	1/2 ounce	1/2
Cauliflower	3	18	36 plants	--
Cucumber	4	18	1 packet	1
Eggplant (plants)	2	24	24 plants	--
Irish potato (pieces)	3	10	60 pieces	4
Sweet Potato (plants)	3	12	50 plants	--
Leaf Lettuce	1	4	2 packets	1/2
Lima Beans (bush)	2	6	1/2 pound	1--2
Onions (sets)	1	2	1 pound sets	1--4
Peas	1	1 (no thin)	1/2 pound	2
Peppers (plants)	2	18	36 plants	--
Radishes	1	1	1/2 ounce	1/2
Snap beans (bush)	2	2	1/2 pound	1--2
Spinach	1	3	1 ounce	1--2

Table 6-4 Continued.

Vegetable	Space between rows	Space between plants	Amount seed or no. plant per 50 ft.	Depth to plant
	feet	inches		inches
Summer squash	4	48	1 packet	1/2
Winter squash & pumpkins	6	72	1 packet	1
Sweet Corn	3	12	1 packet	1--2
Tomato (plants)	4	24	25 plants	--
Turnips	1	4	1 packet	1/2
Watermelons	6	48	1 packet	1

*In large gardens, distance should be adjusted for cultivating equipment.

Fig. 6.2 a&b *Some suggested garden designs. You probably will vary the design to meet your individual needs and site requirements. (pp. 80-81)*

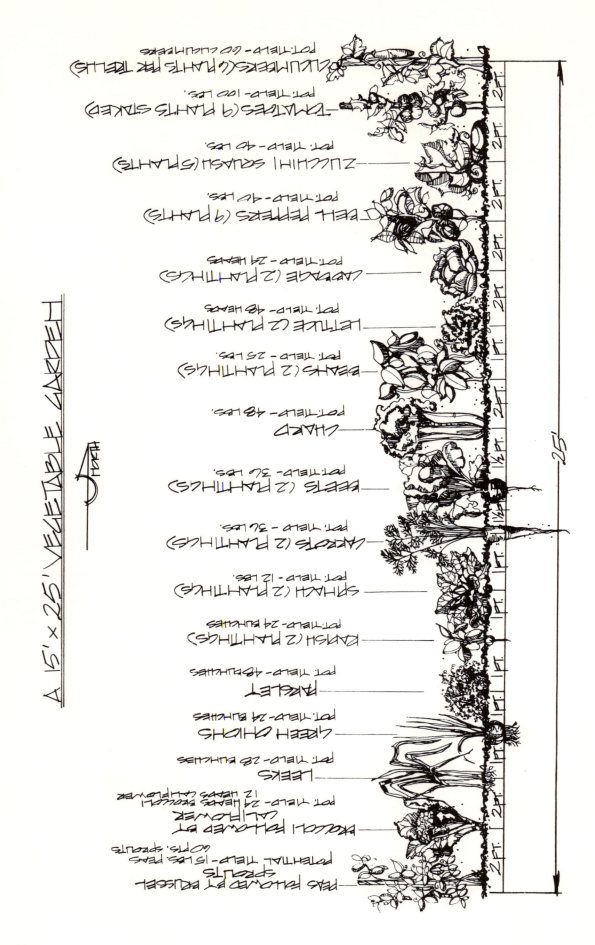

A 15' × 25' VEGETABLE GARDEN

80

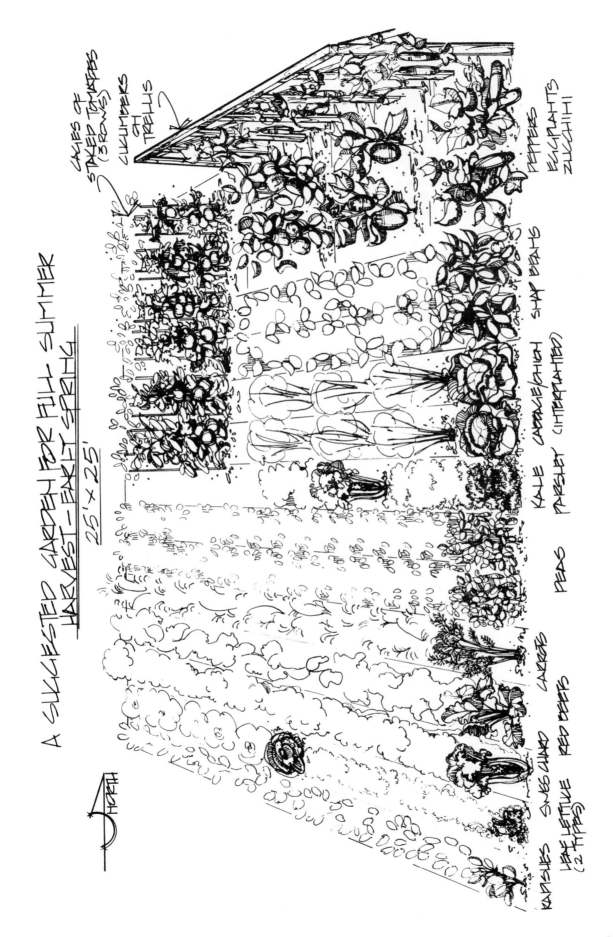

A SUGGESTED GARDEN FOR FULL SUMMER
HARVEST—EARLY SPRING
25' × 25'

CAGES OF
STAKED TOMATOES
(3 ROWS)

CUCUMBERS
ON
TRELLIS

PEPPERS

EGGPLANTS

ZUCCHINI

SNAP BEANS

KALE

CABBAGE/CHARD

PARSLEY (INTERPLANTED)

PEAS

CARROTS

SWISS CHARD

RED BEETS

RADISHES

LEAF LETTUCE
(2 TYPES)

81

book by Mel Bartholomew entitled *Square Foot Gardening* describes a method for laying out a garden in squares (plots) rather than rows to make maximum use of space and reduce labor required. He also describes how to use trellises and stakes to make "vertical" gardens that take less garden area for plants such as cucumbers, tomatoes, etc. Of course the disadvantage to plot gardening vs. row gardening is that, if the space is available, rows permit the use of mechanical means of cultivation and weed removal.

Some general pointers in garden design will be helpful in having a successful project. Always put the tall vegetables such as sweet corn on the north side of the garden so they will not shade the shorter vegetables. Plan the rows so that they run across the slope if there might be an erosion problem. For at least the first year, it will be worthwhile to prepare a sketch of the garden to help you determine the space requirements of each vegetable and also the best location for each. Plan on a fall or second season garden to make maximum use of the space available, and, if the space permits, rotate the individual vegetable species to different locations to reduce the chances of disease problems.

PREPARING THE GARDEN SITE

Initial preparation of the soil should include a deep plowing if the garden spot has not been a garden before. This is particularly important if there is heavy sod since the sod must be turned completely under to kill the grass. Otherwise you will have a very tough grass problem to control the first year of your garden. Once the garden is plowed, it should be left to dry out 3 days and then disked to prepare the surface for planting. If you are adding organic matter such as manure or peat moss, it should be plowed down the first year. Also, any lime or sulphur addition should be plowed down. But do not add lime or sulphur without having a soil test run. Contact your local Agricultural Extension agent for information on how to have a soil sample analyzed.

Taking a soil sample is a fairly simple process and should be done prior to starting a lawn or planting a flower garden as well as before starting a new vegetable garden. After the initial test, retesting is needed only every 3 or 4 years. The best time to take the sample is in the fall so that there is ample time to have it tested before spring planting. The recommended amounts of fertilizer and lime or sulphur may be applied in the spring when the garden is plowed

or tilled. Samples may be taken with a trowel at a depth of 6 inches. Place the sample in a clean bucket and take approximately 10 samples from a 20 x 50 foot garden area. The samples should be distributed evenly throughout the area. Thoroughly mix the samples together and follow these directions:

1. Dry samples at room temperature.
2. Break up lumps and remove stones.
3. Mix dry samples again and shred or crush soil to size of wheat grain.
4. Remove the required amount for the soil test (the amount will be specified in the directions from the soil test laboratory).

If you are taking samples from more than one area make certain that you label each sample and record information such as crops, previous fertility programs, etc., for each area. A sketch of where the samples came from is helpful. The soil test laboratory will run the tests and usually make recommendations on how to improve the pH and fertility levels of your garden site. See Chapter 1 for more information on the importance of adjusting the soil pH prior to planting.

1. To take the sample you will need a trowel and a pail. Get ample bags from your county agent.

Fig. 6.3 *How to take a soil sample and prepare it for testing.*

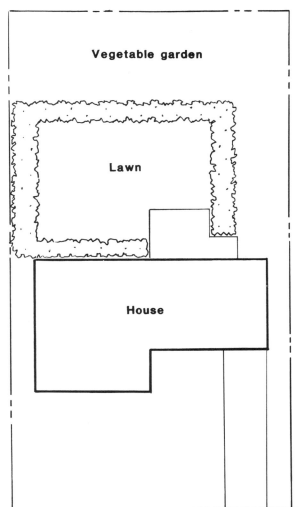

2. Sketch the areas of the home yard. Sample the areas of the yard separately.

4. Place samples in a clean pail. Mix them together thoroughly, breaking up the samples. If soil is muddy, dry it before mixing. If soil crumbles easily, dry after mixing.

Spread mixture out on clean paper to dry. Do not heat in oven or on stove. Do not dry in places where fertilizer or manure may get in sample.

3. Sample to proper depth of 6 inches.

5. Identify the sample and record the area, plants used and any previous cultural treatments on the information sheet.

Fill sample box with the air-dried mixture of soil. Discard the rest. Label and number the sample box. Be sure the numbers correspond to your sample numbers on your sketch.

A basic fertilizer addition can be made at the time the garden is plowed or when it is disked or tilled after plowing if soil testing was not done. A general recommendation is to add 40 to 50 pounds 5-10-5 per 1,000 (50 x 20 foot) square feet to improve the general fertility levels of poor soils or 20 to 25 pounds 12-12-12 if it is easier to obtain. But, again, obtain a soil test if at all possible. This will enable you to apply the right amount of fertilizer and/or lime and sulphur to help ensure success in the garden.

PLANTING THE VEGETABLE GARDEN

There are two general ways of establishing a garden—by seed or by plants. You will do both in your garden. Almost all vegetables are annuals, at least in the garden, with the major exceptions of asparagus and rhubarb, so you will be planting every year both seeds and plants.

Work the soil in the area to be planted just prior to planting. Do this when the soil crumbles in your hand after you squeeze it. Soil that is too wet should not be tilled or worked as this will destroy the structure and seed emergence will be difficult. Once the soil is tilled it should be raked to help make a good seed bed. Break up any large clumps of soil that might be left.

Seeding. Lay out the rows in straight lines using a string stretched between stakes at the end of the row. Make sure the space between the rows will allow you to use your cultivation equipment between the rows. If you are using a small plot gardening method you would not leave space for tilling equipment, but the short rows still should be straight and spaced properly for good development of the individual plants. Make a furrow for small seed using a hoe handle (Fig. 6.5) and for larger seed use the hoe blade (Fig. 6.6). Do not plant the seed too deep or they may not come up. Plant the seed with the proper space between the seed. Usually instructions will be given on the packet on how far apart the seed should be planted. Also, the depth of planting is usually given. If this information is not given, consult Table 6.4 for information that will help you space the seed in the rows. Cover the rows with soil and firm gently with your hands or tap lightly with the bottom of the hoe blade. Mark each end of the row with a stake so that you know where the seeds have been sown and to guide you so that the rows are not walked on, since this could damage newly germinating seeds.

Some vegetables such as carrots and beets require thinning after seeding. When the first

Fig. 6.4 a   *Soil that is too wet to work (plow or till) will stick together when a handful is squeezed.*

Fig. 6.4 b   *Soil that can be worked (plowed or tilled) crumbles easily when squeezed.*

Fig. 6.5   *Use the hoe handle to make a furrow for small vegetable seeds.*

Fig. 6.6 *The blade of the hoe is used to make the furrow for larger vegetable seeds.*

Fig. 6.7 a *Unthinned carrots are often deformed due to crowding.*

Fig. 6.7 b *When properly thinned carrots are well shaped.*

true leaves are fully formed, thin to the spacing suggested on the package (see Figures 6.7 and 6.8).

A word of caution: plant at the recommended time for your area of the country. Planting too early may result in poor germination due to cold temperatures or frost damage to newly emerged seedlings. Also, some vegetables such as peas, radishes, and lettuce are cool season crops, and planting too late may result in poor yields due to too warm a temperature.

Plants. You will be able to purchase vegetable plants in packs, usually 6 to 9 plants per pack. Plants such as cabbage, peppers eggplants, etc., are sold this way. Or, you may buy individually potted plants such as the more expensive tomato varieties. When removing plants from the packs cut the soil in cubes around each plant and carefully remove the plant, doing as little root damage as possible. The soil in the pack should be moist (not wet) when you are removing the plants. When planting peat potted plants, always break off the top rim of the pot so that it will not act as a wick to remove water from the pot and soil after planting. Finally, buy top quality, disease and insect free plants. If the plants are wilted or have black or darkened stems, do not buy them.

The soil is prepared in the same manner as for seeding and rows are marked the same way. Usually you can dig a hole with a trowel in the freshly worked soil, and you should make the hole slightly larger than the soil ball of the plant to be transplanted. Set the plant in the hole a little deeper than it was growing and firm the soil around the roots. Each plant should have a small basin around it to hold water. Water each plant with a starter fertilizer solution that is high in phosphorus. Usually 1/2 pint per plant is enough. The fertilizer analyses should be approximately 10-52-17 or 11-48-0. Follow directions on the label for the amounts to add to the water.

During the next few days after transplanting, carefully watch the moisture supply for the newly transplanted plants. Do not allow them to dry out, and, if the days are to be excessively hot and sunny, you may need to shade the plants with newspaper tents. Leave the north side open so that the heat will not build up during the day.

In northern areas the urge to start gardening is often great in the early spring. Temperatures warm up, the countryside starts to turn green, and everyone is anxious to get into their garden. But exercise caution and make certain that it is past the average frost free date for the area before you set out tender plants such as tomatoes, peppers, and eggplants. It may save you the expense of buying more plants to start over again after a frost. Sometimes a late frost may occur, but if there is adequate warning you may cover the plants with cardboard boxes, hot caps, tents made of blankets, or newspaper tents. Do not use metal containers. Do not allow the plant foliage to touch the protective cover and always remove the protection in the morning as soon as the temperatures have started to warm up. Remember, it is best not to plant tender plants too early.

STARTING YOUR OWN VEGETABLE PLANTS

Some gardeners start their own vegetable and flower plants from seed. This practice will save money and can be rewarding, but it must be done using correct methods. First, buy good quality seed from a reputable seed company, and read on the package any special instructions for germinating the seeds. You probably should avoid saving seed from the previous year, since germination percentages may decline greatly. Also, saving seed from the vegetables in your garden should be avoided. Seed from hybrids will not come true to variety and other plants are easily cross pollinated and their seed would not be true. Also, seed can carry viruses and other diseases. The expense of purchasing new seed is low in comparison to the risks taken when trying to save seed from your garden.

A variety of things may be used as containers for starting seed, but they all should have certain characteristics. First, they should be very clean and have absolutely no soil residues from previous use. Wash all containers, even new ones, in a solution of one part chlorine bleach and ten parts water, and allow to dry before planting. Dirty containers may introduce diseases to which newly germinated seedlings are very susceptible. The container should have sufficient drainage holes in the bottom so that water will not stand in the container, and the container should be sufficiently deep (2 inches or more) so that the soil does not dry out too rapidly.

You may start your plants in trays, flats, or large pots and then transplant the young seedlings to individual pots or space them in other flats. Or, if time is limited, you may sow two or three seeds in small, individual pots. When the seeds germinate you should remove the weaker plants so that only one plant per pot remains. Do this when the first true leaf develops.

Fig. 6.8 *Use a trowel to dig the hole for transplanting vegetable plants to the garden. At planting break off the top rim of the peat pots.*

Fig. 6.9 *Use shade to protect newly transplanted plants from excess sun and wind or if low temperatures threaten from frost.*

A variety of soil mixes can be used for germinating seed. If you are just starting a garden, you should purchase a commercially prepared mix for germinating seed. Most garden centers will have a mix available. Do not buy "potting soil" since it varies widely in quality and often is not sterilized. You may also use mixes that you prepare yourself. Table 6.5 gives an example of such a mixture with the proper additives of fertilizer and limestone.

Some of the materials that are used for starting seed are:

Vermiculite — A fine grade of this material works well as a germination medium. Be careful not to contaminate it when handling and place in very clean germination flats or pots. A 1/2 strength feeding of fertilizer will be needed after germination. Use water soluble fertilizer and dissolve 1/2 the amount in the full amount of water that is recommended on the package. Water the new seedlings with this solution.

Table 6-5 Suggested soil mixtures.

Ingredients	1 gallon	1 bushel	2 bushels
Shredded sphagnum peat moss	2 qts.	1/2 bu.	1 bu.
Vermiculite #2, 3 or 4	2 qts.	1/2 bu.	1 bu.
Limestone, dolomitic preferred	1 Tblsp.	5 Tblsp.	10 Tblsp.
20% superphosphate (powdered)	1/2 Tblsp.	2-1/2 Tblsp.	5 Tblsp.
5-10-5	--	7-1/2 Tblsp.	15 Tblsp.
Iron (chelated such as NaFe, 138 or 330)	--	1/2 tsp.	1 tsp.
Nonionic surfactant*	--	1/2 tsp.	1 tsp.

*Mixed at rate of 1/2 gal. per bushel of mixture. **Note:** Bushels are level full, not packed. Tablespoons and teaspoons are level amounts.

From: Starting Seeds Indoors *by John A. Wott and Allen E. Bozer. Cooperative Extension Service, Purdue University, West Lafayette, Indiana.*

Table 6-6 Guide to sowing vegetable seeds in the home.

Vegetables	Time to seed before last frost	Comments
Cool season crops		
Broccoli	10 weeks	Grow cool. Will tolerate
Cabbage	10 weeks	light frost outdoors after
Cauliflower	10 weeks	hardening and may be
Head lettuce	10 weeks	transplanted to garden early.
Warm season crops		
Tomato	7 weeks	Keep warm; do not
Eggplant	7 weeks	subject to frost.
Pepper	7 weeks	
Vine crops		
Cucumber	4 weeks	Sow directly in peat pots.
Cantaloupe	4 weeks	Keep warm at all times.
Squash	4 weeks	
Watermelon	4 weeks	

From: Starting Seeds Indoors *by John A. Wott and Allen E. Bozer. Cooperative Extension Service, Purdue University, West Lafayette, Indiana.*

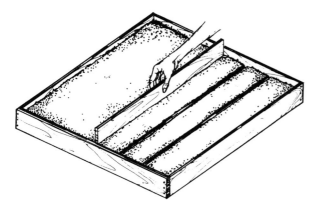

Fig. 6.10   *Make seed rows 1 to 2 inches apart with a wooden board.*

Soil: Vermiculite Mix — Mix about 1/3 garden soil by volume by 2/3 of vermiculite. The garden soil must be sterilized prior to using. This may be accomplished by baking in the oven at 180°F for 30 minutes. Make certain the center of the container of soil has reached 180°F before starting the time. You do not need to fertilize the newly germinated seedlings after they emerge.

Soil:Peat:Sand — For large seeded plants such as cabbage, you may use two parts garden soil, one part shredded peat moss, and two parts perlite, sharp sand, or vermiculite. This *mixture* should be sterilized as described above for the garden.

Milled Sphagnum Moss — This material is sold for starting seeds and it works well for those seedlings that are suspectible to damping-off disease. (This is not peat moss but new sphagnum moss — see Chapter 3.) Seedlings need to be fertilized after emergence as described above for seeds started in vermiculite.

Seeding. The time to plant the seed will depend on what is being started. Table 6.6 provides approximate times to start seed prior to planting the new plants in the garden. Do not start plants too early since they will often get leggy or too hard and not develop satisfactorily once they are planted in the garden.

These steps in sowing seed will help you be successful in starting your own vegetable plants.

1. Fill the seed flat or pot to 1 inch from the top with the medium you are using for germinating the seed, and moisten the medium thoroughly before placing in the container. If the holes in the bottom of other container are large, cover with sphagnum moss so that the mix will not wash out.

2. Level the mix in the container and firm.

3. Make rows approximately 1 to 2 inches apart by pressing a narrow board or wooden label into the mix (Figure 6.10). If just one variety is being planted in the container, the seeds may be broadcast on the surface of the mix.

4. Sow the seeds uniformly and thinly. If planting in rows, label each row.

5. Large seeded plants, such as melons and cucumbers, should be planted directly into 2-1/2 to 3 inch pots. Peat pots work well for these plants. Use 2 seeds per pot and thin to 1 plant after germination.

6. Cover the seeds with dry vermiculite or the milled sphagnum moss. The depth of covering depends on the size of seed, but usually 1/8 to 1/4 inch covering is sufficient. Moisten the surface with a fine mist or water by placing the container in a pan of water so that

water is absorbed through the holes in the bottom of the container. Do not allow the water to cover the top of the container.

7. Some prefer to cover the container with a piece of clean plastic or a sheet of glass. This is not necessary if the surface is not allowed to dry out during the germination process. At the same time do not overwater. Keep the container moist, but not waterlogged.

8. Most seeds germinate better if kept in a warm room (65 to 75°F). Some do better at cooler temperatures of about 55°F. Members of the cabbage family are in this latter group.

9. Check containers daily for germination and when it starts move to an area with bright light. If plastic or glass was used to cover the container, remove at this time.

GROWING THE SEEDLINGS

Once the seedlings have emerged, they should be given as much light as possible. Insufficient light will result in spindly, poor quality plants. If a south window that has full sun during the day is not available, place the plants under fluorescent lights (two tube fixture). One tube should be cool white and the other either daylight or warm white. The tubes should be 6 inches above the seedlings and the fixture should be raised as the plants grow.

Keep the seedling containers well watered but not overwatered. Allow them to dry out between waterings but not to the point that the plants wilt. The seedlings may be fertilized with a water soluble fertilizer. Follow the label directions on the amount to use and the frequency. Most vegetables will grow well if the day temperatures are between 70 to 75°F; if possible, the night temperature should be 10 degrees lower. Members of the cabbage family and lettuce should be grown at lower temperatures of 55 to 60°F.

Watch for damping-off. This is a disease that attacks the seedlings at the soil line. The stem is girdled and the seedlings die. Remove any infected seedlings and treat the flat with a fungicide. Keep the seed containers in full light, at the proper temperature, and do not overwater. This will help reduce the chances of plant loss due to damping-off. Also, remember that clean containers and sterilized soil will help prevent damping-off attacks.

Transplanting and spacing. When the first set of true leaves have good development (not necessarily full grown), the seedlings should be spaced out in flats or placed in individual pots so that they may develop into sturdy, healthy plants. Place the seedlings in 1-3/4 to 2-1/2 inch pots or 2 inches apart in flats or packs. Carefully remove the seedlings from the seedling container. Lift several out at one time using a label or small spatula, do not pull them up. Carefully separate the seedlings, doing as little root damage as possible. Place the individual seedling in a hole poked in the soil in the pot or flat. Firm the soil around the roots being careful not to damage the tender stem of the seedling. Water carefully after transplanting. Be sure to water after a flat or several pots have been planted. Do not allow to dry out. Table 6.7 shows which vegetables can be transplanted and which must have seed sown directly in a pot.

Table 6-7 Ease in transplanting from seed container to pots.

Vegetable	Easily transplanted	More difficult	Must be seeded
Broccoli	X		
Cabbage	X		
Brussels sprouts	X		
Lettuce	X		
Tomatoes	X		
Cauliflower		X	
Celery		X	
Eggplant		X	
Onions		X	
Pepper		X	
Cucumber			X
Muskmelon			X
Squash			X
Watermelon			X

Preparing for planting in garden. Plants started indoors should be hardened before planting in the garden. The tender plants cannot take the shock of being planted directly into the wind and temperature variables found in the spring in the garden. Start the hardening process approximately two weeks before you anticipate planting the garden.

Gradually reduce the temperatures by placing the plants out of doors during the days. Protect them from the bright sun and wind. A cold frame works well for this purpose. They should be protected at night from low temperature injury (frost). Reduce the waterings so that the plants harden but do not allow the plants to wilt. Gradually increase the exposure of the plants to the elements, particularly full sunlight. High winds may cause severe wind burn.

CARE OF THE GARDEN

Weeds are the number one enemy of the garden. Nothing is more discouraging than to have the weeds take over the garden, but there are several ways that the weed population in the garden may be reduced. One is to use an organic mulch 2 inches deep. Some people catch the clippings from the lawn mowing to use for the mulch, and this works fine. *But you should not use the clippings for several weeks after the lawn has been treated with a weed killer.* Some use newspaper mulch and others plant vegetables such as tomatoes and melons through black plastic (available in garden and hardware stores).

Weeds can be removed by hoeing and hand pulling. Use a sharp hoe and cut the weeds off 1/4 to 1/2 inch below the soil surface. You can use a herbicide, but you must follow label directions very carefully. Also, no one herbicide can be used on all vegetables in the entire garden.

Water is essential during dry periods. Apply water in the early morning so that the foliage dries before evening. This reduces chances of foliage disease. Be sure to apply

Fig. 6.11 *Measure the amount of water being applied at several locations in the garden.*

enough water to soak the soil 6 to 8 inches deep by apply 1 to 1-1/2 inch of water in one watering. Use a straight sided can to check the amount of water being applied. Use several cans in several locations to check water distribution patterns. Apply water slow enough to soak in and avoid run off. Avoid frequent, light waterings as this only wets the soil surface and does not encourage deep rooting.

You may have some vegetables attacked by insects and diseases. If you spot trouble, check with your county extension agricultural agent for ways of controlling the pest. Do not just routinely apply pesticides; determine what the problem is and apply the correct control measure.

Harvest your vegetables when they are in the proper stage of maturity. As an example, a tomato should be red ripe, while a zuchini squash should be picked when it is only 5 to 6 inches long. Beets for pickling should be approximately 2 inches in diameter, but some people like larger beets. Check specific garden references for the best time for harvesting fresh produce.

FALL GARDENING

To make maximum use of space, some gardeners like to plant a fall garden in which some of the "cool season" crops are planted again. The fall garden is planted in sections of the garden where the spring-summer vegetables have been harvested.

The soil is prepared in the same manner as planting in spring, including fertilizing and deep tilling. Add 1 to 2 pounds of 12-12-12 per 100 square feet and thoroughly mix in the soil by deep rototilling or spading. Smooth and plant in the same manner as described for the spring garden. In some areas of the country the fall is dry, so water requirements of the vegetables must be watched. Add sufficient water to soak the soil 6 to 8 inches deep. Weed control will be a problem, so use the same procedures as described previously. Table 6.8 gives a list of vegetables suitable for fall gardening and days to harvest from the planting date. Information in this table is for the midwest and you should adjust the dates for your section of the country. Further information can be obtained from local county extension agricultural agents offices.

THE FRUIT GARDEN

The fruit garden can be divided into two major categories — small fruits and tree fruits. There is some controversy concerning tree fruits

Table 6-8 Vegetables suitable for late summer planting.

Vegetable	Date[1]	Days to harvest
Seeds		
Beets	August 1	40-50
Carrots	August 1	50-60
Collards	August 15	65
Endive	August 1	65-80
Leaf Lettuce	August 1	30-45
Kale	August 1	50-70
Kohlrabi	August 1	55-70
Onions (green)[2]	Sept. 1	30-45
Radish	August 1	25-35
Snap beans	August 1	50-60
Spinach	Sept. 1	40-50
Swiss Chard	August 1	40-50
Turnip	August 15	(roots) 50-60
		(tops) 20-40
Trasplants		
Broccoli	August 1	45-60
Brussels Sprouts	August 1	45-60
Cabbage	August 1	45-60
Cauliflower	July 15	-
Chinese Cabbage	August 1	45-60

[1]Dates are for the midwest, adjust to your area.
[2]Onion sets are for the midwest, adjust to your area.

in the home garden. Certainly from a cost point of view the production of apples, pears, and peaches is not a money saving venture. The care of tree fruits is a very time consuming project and the cost of pesticide materials is quite high. To produce blemish free, insect free fruit requires frequent (every 7 to 10 days) pesticide applications from early spring until near time the fruit matures. And this requires the purchase of at least a small, power sprayer so that the pesticides may be applied efficiently and evenly to control the various pests that attack fruit trees. For this reason the production of tree fruit in the home landscape should be done only as a hobby and not to save money in the family food budget.

Since tree fruit production is somewhat specialized in nature, it is recommended that before starting you consult references on this subject to determine if you have the time to give to the project. Also, these references will provide the technical information needed to grow fruit trees and to produce high quality fruit.

Small fruit production is another matter. The techniques used are similar to vegetable gardening and the time requirement is considerably less than for tree fruits. Also, the costs of production and space requirements are less. Besides the pleasures of producing fresh fruit, there could be savings in the family food budget. There are three small fruits commonly grown by home gardeners: strawberries, raspberries, and grapes.

Strawberries. Strawberries work well in your vegetable garden, but they must be assigned a permanent location (at least 3 years). Their production is approximately 25 to 35 quarts of berries over the spring season for a 50 foot row (25 plants). Of course to obtain this production you must take good care of the plants.

Location of the strawberry patch is very similar to the vegetable garden. It should be on well-drained soil in a sunny spot. Avoid low areas that might be frost pockets. Because of disease problems, do not establish a new strawberry planting where strawberries, tomatoes, peppers, potatoes, eggplant or raspberries have been grown during the last 3 years.

If the soil is low in organic matter due to the top soil being removed or heavy cropping, add organic matter as described for the vegetable garden. Add 2 pounds of 6-24-24 or equivalent to 100 square feet and plow down or deeply rototill. This should be done as soon as possible in the spring so that planting may be done early. But do not work the soil if it is too wet. The plants need to be well established before the warm weather of late spring and summer starts.

Select varieties suitable for your area. Check with the county extension agricultural agent for recommended varieties. Buy plants from a reliable nursery or garden center, and make sure that the plants have not dried out.

Rows should be at least 4 feet apart and the plant 2 feet apart in the row. If a small bed is desired, the rows may be 2 feet apart and the plants closer in the rows. The correct planting depth is cruicial. Plants set too deep die due to the crown being covered, and those set too shallow may dry out. The crown (junction of the top with the roots) should be level with soil surface. Firm the soil around the roots and water with 1/2 pint of starter fertilizer solution (see Plants in the Vegetable section).

During the first year all the flowers should be removed to encourage runner production. Next year's fruits are produced on this year's runners. It may be necessary to sidedress the plants with 1 pound of 12-12-12 per 50 feet of row in June and then repeat in mid- to late July if the plants do not seem to be growing rapidly enough. Keep the fertilizer off the foliage and work it lightly into the soil.

Keep the patch weed free by removing the weeds by hoeing or pulling as they develop. Weeds compete with the strawberries, and their

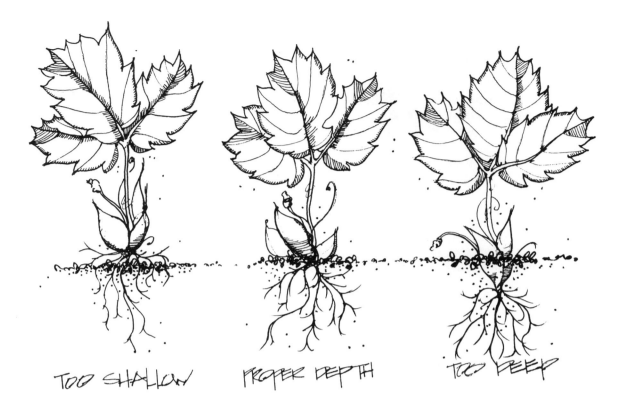

TOO SHALLOW   PROPER DEPTH   TOO DEEP

Fig. 6.12   *Set strawberry plants so the crowns are at the soil surface.*

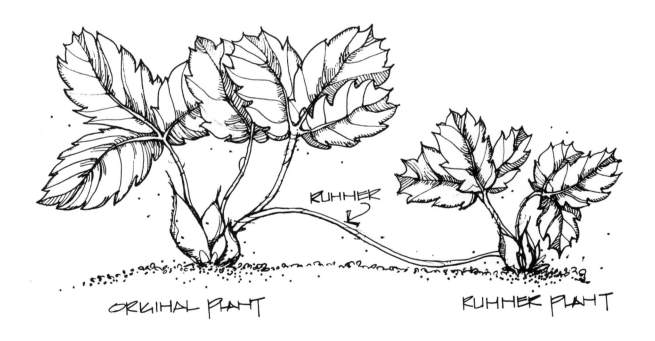

ORIGINAL PLANT   RUNNER   RUNNER PLANT

Fig. 6.13   *Pinch off all flower blossoms the first year to obtain early "runner plant" formation.*

appearance will hurt production of next year's crop.

Set the runner plants approximately 6 inches apart and firm the soil around their base to encourage rooting. The rows of berries will be about 15 to 18 inches apart as the runners fill in. Water as needed during the summer using the same methods described for the vegetable garden.

In the winter the strawberries will benefit from a 2-inch mulch of straw. The straw keeps the soil frozen in the spring and reduces the amount of frost heaving of the plants, which means the plants are pushed out of the soil so that they dry out and die. Other materials may be used as a mulch, but straw is considered by most to be the best. When growth starts in the spring, pull the straw off the plants but leave it between the rows. If there is danger of frost while the plants are in bloom, the straw may be pulled back over the plants to provide some protection from the frost.

Strawberries bear fruit well for the second spring after planting. Once the crop is planted the bed should be renovated. This is done by mowing off the old leaves immediately after harvest with a rotary mower that is set high enough so as not to damage the plant crowns. Rake off the old leaves and burn. Narrow the rows down to 8 inches wide with a rototiller and then thin the plants in the row to 8 to 20 inches apart. Fertilize with 2 pounds of 12-12-12 per 100 square feet of bed and care for the bed as a newly planted bed, as described previously. By renovating every year immediately after planting, the bed will bear satisfactory amounts of fruit for several years.

Raspberries. There are several colors and varieties of raspberries to choose from and the selection will in part depend on your personal likes and also on the part of the country in which you live. Again, check locally to determine what varieties you should be growing and then buy healthy, vigorous plants from a reliable nursery. Getting plants from a friend's patch may result in your obtaining diseased plants.

The planting site should have similar characteristics as the vegetable garden. A sunny location is best though the raspberry will bear fruit in some light shade. The soil should be well drained but not sandy. Avoid low areas that might be frost pockets, and avoid planting where tomatoes, potatoes, eggplant, peppers, or strawberries have been grown. If you are planning on growing red raspberries, they must be separated from the black or purple

BEFORE PRUNING

AFTER PRUNING

Fig. 6.14   *Red raspberries should be pruned by thinning as shown and at the proper times for good fruiting (check text).*

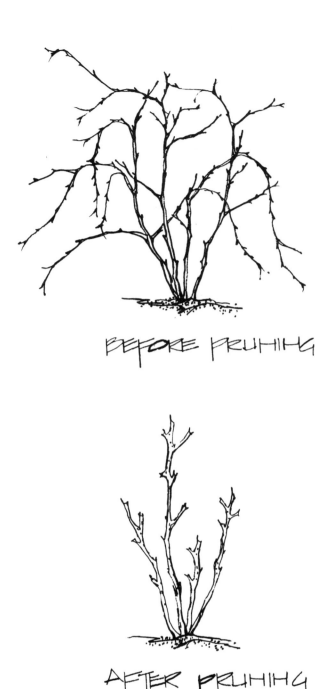

BEFORE PRUNING

AFTER PRUNING

Fig. 6.15 *Black and purple raspberries before and after pruning. Check text for correct methods and timing.*

raspberries by at least 300 feet to prevent the spread of disease.

Weeds are always a problem in raspberry plantings, so start clean. Eliminate any perennial weeds prior to planting, and add organic matter if needed. Before the final spading or plowing, add 1 to 2 pounds of 12-12-12 per 100 square feet.

Plant the plants as soon as the soil is prepared in the early spring. Plant in the same manner as described for planting bare root nursery stock in Chapter 3, but set the plants slightly (1 to 2 inches) lower than they were growing in the nursery. The cane or canes of black or purple raspberries should be cut back to the soil level and cut back red raspberries to 6 to 8 inches above the ground. Remember, the crown should not be above the soil surface.

The plants should be spaced 2-1/2 to 3 feet apart in the rows for red raspberries and 3 to 4 feet for the purple and black. The row widths, by pruning and cultivation, should be kept to 12 to 15 inches wide. Standard distance between the rows is 6 to 8 feet. This forms a narrow hedge row and plants may be trained to a system of wires (2 or 3) stretched between posts.

They also can be planted in hills with each plant developing 6 to 8 canes and the hills are 5 to 6 feet apart. The berries are harder to pick in this type of planting.

Once the plants are established, they should be fertilized every year with 4 to 6 pounds of 12-12-12 per 100 feet of row. Apply as a sidedressing by each row early in the spring before growth starts.

Cultivate between the rows 2 to 3 inches deep in the spring as soon as it is possible to work the soil. Cultivate as needed until harvest begins and start again after harvest is completed. Do not cultivate in late summer. A cover crop of annual rye or oats may be sown between the rows after the last cultivation. Turn the crop under in the spring with a cultivation.

To reduce the number of cultivations, you may want to mulch the area or at least mulch the raspberry rows to reduce the weed population. A 3-inch layer of straw is a good mulch, and this will reduce the amount of irrigation that might be needed. Use the same watering principals as for the vegetable garden.

All raspberries must be pruned every year. The canes are biennial, growing the first year and fruiting the second. Thin in the spring and remove fruiting wood after fruiting. The techniques vary depending on the type of raspberry.

Red raspberries — remove the old fruit canes at ground level after fruiting. In the spring before growth begins, remove any weak, diseased or damaged canes by thinning so that strong canes are left every 6 to 8 inches apart and cut back to 4 feet. Keep the row 12 to 15 inches wide. In the hill system, thin to 6 to 8 canes per hill and shorten them to 5 to 6 feet.

Everbearing raspberries — these bear the summer crop on the old canes and the fall crop on the tips of the new canes. Remove the tips of the new canes after fruiting, and next year's summer crop will be borne on the remainder of the cane. During the next summer remove the old cane at ground level after fruiting. Thin in the spring as described for red raspberries.

Black and purple raspberries — on new plants pinch off the top 3 to 4 inches of the shoots in the summer. Keep the height at 2 to 2-1/2 feet by frequent pinching of the new growth during the summer. After fruiting is complete remove the old canes. In the spring remove all canes less than 1/2 inch in diameter and, of course, remove any damaged canes. Shorten lateral branches to about 8 to 10 inches for black varieties and 12 to 14 inches for the purple ones. Cut any unbranched canes back to 2-1/2 to 3 feet.

As you can see, pruning raspberries can be time consuming and some skill is required. You may want to observe someone's planting to see how they pruned their plants, but make sure they are doing it correctly.

Grapes. Two or three plants of most varieties of grapes will provide adequate fruit for fresh use, but more will be required if you desire to make juice or wine. So you must first decide the reason for growing grapes, since this will control the number of plants and the variety selection. Different varieties have different uses, so it is important to check on the variety recommendations for the areas, since there is a great difference in the cold hardiness of grape varieties. Also, some varieties are better adapted to the soils found in different sections of the country.

Grapes should be planted in a well-drained garden soil. Prepare the soil in the same manner as for strawberries or raspberries including the elimination of serious perennial weeds.

Buy 1 year old plants from a reputable nursery and plant in the early spring just as soon as your site is prepared. Before planting, remove all but the one, strongest cane and cut back any damaged or extra long roots. Plant in the same manner as bare root shrubs as described in Chapter 3.

Space the vines 8 feet apart and if more than one row is used, 9 to 10 feet between the rows. The grapes will be trained to a wire trellis or grape arbor. After planting, cut back the cane to two strong buds just above the soil line.

During the first season, sidedress each plant with 1/3 cup of ammonium nitrate spread in a ring around the plant and repeat twice at 3 week intervals. This nitrogen will encourage rapid growth.

As usual, weeds are a problem, so keep the planting free of weeds by either mulching or cultivation. Use a shallow cultivation so as not to injure the root system, and stop cultivating by late summer. If you mulch with grass clippings, do not use clippings after the lawn has been treated with an herbicide. Also, since grapes are susceptible to 2,4-D damage (common lawn herbicide) be very cautious about drift from this herbicide.

The pruning and training of grapes is an art. First, unlike raspberries, the grape bears on this season's wood. A vine that is trained properly will have a trunk that reaches the top of the trellis. There are arms that arise from the trunk from which the fruit bearing arms arise. These trunks and arms are the permanent part of the grape plant.

During the first year at planting, cut back the cane to two large buds. During the first winter tie the new shoots to a stake and then in the second spring start to train the plant to the trellis. The trellis is constructed by placing two 10-foot end posts in the ground 2-1/2 to 3 feet. The posts are as far apart as the row length and there are line posts every 16 to 24 feet. These posts are set 2 to 2-1/2 feet in the ground. Make certain the end posts are braced well. Use two No. 9 or 10 galvanized wires placed at 3 and 6 feet above the ground. Fasten the wires to the windward side of the posts.

Use the four-cane Kniffin system of training. After the frost danger has passed in the second spring, tie the strongest shoot to lowest wire and cut back to the first strong bud above the wire. Cut off all other shoots and growth, since this shoot will become the trunk. After frost in the third spring, tie the strongest shoot to the top wire and cut back to a strong bud above that wire. Also tie two shoots to the lower wire, and cut back to 6 or 7 buds. Tie these shoots to the wire with cloth strips, and trim out all other growth. Every spring after that select four pencil sized branches and tie to the wires. Cut each back to 8 to 10 buds. Always use new shoots, they will be thinner and lighter in color. Also, cut

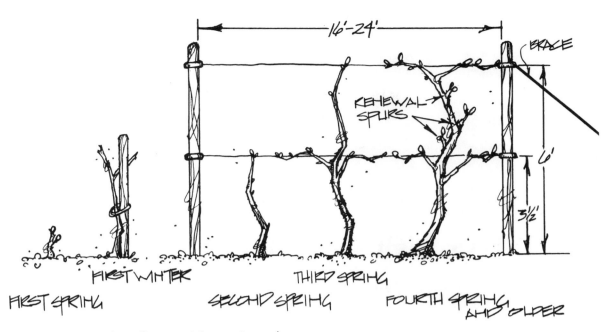

Fig. 6.16   *Best method (Kniffin system) for pruning and supporting vines.*

back 4 additional canes to 2 buds to serve as renewal spurs. This guarantees canes in the best locations for next year.

Fertilize every spring with 1 pound of 12-12-12 spread in a 2-foot wide circle around each plant keeping 1 foot away from the trunk. Work the fertilizer in by shallow cultivation (2 inches) and then water. It will be necessary to apply a general purpose fruit spray to grapes when the shoots are 4 inches long, 8 inches long, just before bloom, just after bloom, and at mid-summer. These five sprayings will help ensure quality fruit. Follow label directions carefully. Of course some will prefer to grow the grapes without pesticides.

Harvest your grapes when they are fully ripe. Color is not always a good indicator. Grapes that ripen in full sun in the autumn have the best quality. Until you know when the grapes are ripe, you might sample one or two and when they are sweet they are ready.

A fruit garden can be as enjoyable as a vegetable garden. If space permits and you are interested, be sure to include small fruits in your gardening projects.

7

What is Needed to Maintain the Residential Landscape

Once a landscape planting is installed it must be properly maintained to achieve the desired effect. The key to proper maintenance is completing each task correctly at the proper time. Timing of the operation is often just as important as the actual performance of the task. This chapter shows how to build a maintenance schedule that will help you plan each operation during the year ensuring that each needed task is completed. Also, the length of time needed for each job can be computed.

DEVELOPING THE SCHEDULE

A well prepared schedule tells you what should be done at a particular time. By following the schedule you can keep your landscape maintained. The first step is to classify the level of maintenance desired: high, medium, and low. A residential site might require all three levels or if in a modern suburban setting possibly only high maintenance. For example, a high maintenance site contains some or all of the following: well maintained turf areas, annual and perennial flower beds, shrubs and trees, and ground cover plantings. There will probably be landscape features such as walks, patios, decks, fences, etc., that will require maintenance and the turf next to them will need trimming and edging. A well-manicured lawn requires frequent fertilization, waterings when necessary and regularly scheduled mowings. Flower beds, ground covers, and shrub plantings require weeding, watering, fertilizing and manicuring (pruning and faded flower removal). A

residential site that has a high level of maintenance has well-ordered and well-cared for plantings.

Medium levels of landscape maintenance are found at many residential sites. The total area may be maintained at a medium level or just part of the site while the rest may have high or low maintenance. Typically, a medium maintained site involves less lawn care, perhaps fewer flower beds, and more maintenance free woody plants and ground covers. The lawn receives one or two fertilizations per season and maybe only one weed control application. Supplemental waterings needed in the summer may not be carried out with any degree of frequency. Old flowers and seed heads will probably not be removed from flowers and shrubs. A medium maintenance site has a nice appearance, but it does not have the finely manicured appearance of one that is maintained at a high level.

The low maintenance area is left in its native state and needs only minimal care. As an example, irradication of obnoxious weeds such as poison ivy or heavy pollen producers might be done. Any trails or paths will be maintained and dead or dying trees might be cut down to avoid the hazards of them falling in an unwanted place. Generally, the purpose behind a low level maintenance program at a residential site is to leave the area as near as possible in its natural state.

Determining the type of maintenance will depend on three factors. The cost of the program both in monetary terms and in time

Fig. 7.1 *A highly maintained courtyard that is part of a site that has both high and low levels of landscape maintenance depending on the area.*

Theodore Brickman Co.

needed to perform the work, if the work is carried out by the owner, must be considered. The high level program will be expensive if the work is hired out and time-consuming if the homeowner carries out the program. Do not attempt such a program unless you are financially able to do so or if you have a great interest in landscape gardening. A more modest approach to maintaining the site is more practical.

How the site is designed and used determines how much maintenance is needed. Larger wooded residential lots can be left natural, with only a small portion of the lot maintained at high or medium level. The basic landscape design should be based on your interests and abilities to maintain the site. Intensively planted areas generally demand more maintenance than areas left native. If you want a manicured appearance but do not want to spend the money or time to achieve this appearance, design the site using plants with lower maintenance requirements.

Fig. 7.2 *Flower beds are high maintenance features of the landscape.*

Fig. 7.3   *A natural low and medium maintenance level site.*

Fig. 7.4   *Only a small portion of this wooded site has been developed into a high maintenance level site.*

Plant Categories. Once you decide the level of maintenance, inventory the landscape plants you are growing and put them into one of three groups that relate to their needed maintenance: trees, shrubs, and herbaceous plants. The plant categories are based on their size and their growth habits. The sub-categories or groups for trees and shrubs are based on their timing requirements for pruning or in some instances, their use in the landscape (see Table 7.1). At most residential landscape sites all the plants will fall into one of these groups. If you have trouble deciding in which group a plant might belong, the person that designed the site should be able to provide assistance. Identification of some of the plants may require some assistance from the

Table 7-1a Plant classifications based on maintenance.

Group	Plants
	Shrubs
I	Deciduous - Non-flowering or Inconspicuous Flowers
II	Flowering Before June 30th (Early Flowering)
III	Flowering After June 30th or Prized for Fruit (Summer Flowering)
IV	Broad-leaved Evergreens
V	Narrow-leaved Evergreens
	Trees
I	Deciduous
II	Small Trees Flowering Before June 30th (Early Flowering)
III	Small Trees Flowering After June 30th (Late Flowering)
IV	Broad-leaved Evergreens
V	Narrow-leaved Evergreens
	Ground Covers and Vines
	Flowers

You may not have plants in all groups so adjust classifications accordingly.

Table 7-1b Plant lists.

Botanical name	Common name
SHRUB-GROUP I	
Deciduous-Non-flowering or Inconspicious	
Cornus Baileyi	Bailey dogwood
Cornus stolonifera 'flaviramea'	Yellow twig dogwood
Viburnum tribolum compacta	Dwarf cranberry bush
Euonymus alatus compacta	Dwarf burning bush
Cornus stolonifera 'Kelseyi'	Dwarf redosier dogwood
Elaegnus umbellata	Autumn olive
Cotoneaster apiculata	Cranberry cotoneaster
SHRUBS-GROUP II	
Flowering Before June 30th	
Viburnum carlesii	Mayflower viburnum
Forsythia intermedia spectabilis	Showy forsythia
Rhododendron catawbiense	Catawba rhododendron
SHRUBS-GROUP III	
Flowering after June 30th or Prized for Fruit	
Pyracantha coccinea "Lelandi"	Lelandi firethorn
Weigla florida cv. Eva Rathke	Eva Rathke Weigla
Viburnum opulus	European cranberry bush
SHRUBS-GROUP IV	
Broad-leaved Evergreens	
Euonymus fortunei vegetus	Bigleaf wintercreeper
Viburnum rhytidophyloides	Lantanaphyllum viburnum
Ilex glabra	Inkberry

Table 7-1b continued.

Botanical name	Common name
SHRUBS-GROUP V	
Narrow-leaved Evergreens	
Taxus cuspidata	Spreading yew
Taxus media nigra	Nigra yew
Juniperus horizontalis 'Bar Harbor'	Bar Harbor juniper
TREES-GROUP I	
Deciduous	
Acer rubrum	Red maple
Acer saccharum	Sugar maple
Betula nigra	River birch
Fagus sylvatica	European beech
Fraxinus americana	White ash
Fraxinus pennsylvanica	Green ash
Quercus alba	White oak
Quercus rubra	Red oak
Quercus imbricaria	Shingle oak
Quercus palustris	Pin oak
TREES-GROUP II	
Small Flowering Trees Before June 30th	
Cercis canadensis	Red bud
Cornus florida	Flowering dogwood
Cornus florida rubra	Red flowering dogwood
TREES-GROUP III	
Narrow-leaved Evergreen	
Pinus strobus	White pine
Tsuga canadensis	Hemlock
GROUND COVER AND VINES	
Vinca minor	Myrtle or periwinkle
Hedera Helix	English Ivy
Pachysandra terminalis	Japanese spurge
Euonymus fortunei 'coloratus'	Purple leaf wintercreeper

local county agricultural agent or he/she will be able to tell you how to get the plants identified.

Once you place the plants in their proper categories, prepare a schedule of the specific maintenance activities required. The time in the year the activities will be done depends on your geographic location. The example schedule for a midwest residence would have to be modified to meet the needs of the landscape site based on its climatic location in the country. The best approach is to base the schedule on the calendar months, planning the activities for each week of the month. The sample site has both low and high maintenance requirements, and the lot covers approximately 1-1/3 acres. This is somewhat larger than most residential lots but it does permit the use of examples of both low and high level maintenance practices. More importantly this is an actual site and the maintenance practices have been tested, and deficiencies are noted.

About 1/2 acre is devoted to a high maintenance area of bluegrass turf, brick sidewalk and drive, wooden decks, ground cover plantings on slopes from a walk-out basement and brick patio, large and medium-sized trees, deciduous and evergreen shrubs, a small vegetable garden, and annual and perennial flowers. The rest of the land is left in its natural state of large trees and some shrub underplantings. The area has been developed for approximately 5 years. Here is the schedule prepared for this site:

SCHEDULE

January - February

Comments

Equipment repair can be done much more quickly during the winter rather than the growing season. Check pruning guide list in Chapter 9.

Weeks 1 through 4
■ Check equipment and have any needed repairs made. Change engine oil and lubricate as needed. Prune shrubs in Groups I, III, IV, and V (see lists at end of schedule). Prune trees in Group I. All pruning should be done when temperatures are above 40° F.

March

As soon as the weather starts to warm up, maintenance of the landscape should also start. Do not change grass seed mixture or the lawn will have a spotted appearance. Dormant oil is an environmentally safe insecticide that helps reduce insect problems in the summer. Use on plants listed on the label.

Weeks 1 and 2
■ Turf – If there are thin or bare areas, overseed these areas with the same seed mixture as used originally. Use approximately 1 pound of seed per 1,000 square feet.
■ Trees and Shrubs – Inspect the *Euonymus fortunei coloratus* (purple leaf wintercreeper) for scale; and if this pest is present use a dormant oil spray, following directions on the label carefully.

Fertilize the shrubs and perennial plantings with 2 to 3 pounds actual nitrogen per 1,000 square feet. Use an approximate ratio of 2-1-1. If the analysis is 20-10-10 apply 10 to 15 pounds per 1,000 square feet.

Finish pruning any trees listed for January–February. If preemergence herbicides are to be used in the shrub and perennial beds, they should be applied according to label directions at this time.

If your area is relatively free of crabgrass, do not apply a crabgrass herbicide.

A slow release fertilizer is sometimes used, in which case the rate is higher since frequent applications are not necessary.

Weeks 3 and 4
■ Turf – If crabgrass is a problem in a few areas of the turf, apply crabgrass herbicide only to those areas and do not apply to areas that have been overseeded.

Fertilize the turf area with high nitrogen fertilizer, at approximate ratio of 3-1-2, at the rate of 1 pound nitrogen per 1,000 square feet. An analysis of 15-5-10 would be applied at the rate of 6 to 7 pounds per 1,000 square feet. A first mowing may be necessary if the season is advanced.
■ Trees and Shrubs – Continue work outlined for weeks 1 and 2.
■ Annuals and Perennials – Remove winter debris from perennial plantings and any winter annual weeds.
■ Landscape Features – Inspect walks, patio, and driveway for bricks that might have heaved up in the winter. Place bricks at their original level. Lower wooden edging along bricked areas in places that have frost heaved.

Do not be in a hurry to remove rodent barriers.

If crabgrass has been a problem, apply the crabgrass herbicide used for the lawn area.

Apply preemergence herbicide to brick area to control weeds that will grow between cracks.

Check railroad tie steps to ensure that frost heaving has not displaced or loosened them. Maintain as needed.

April

Weeks 1 through 4

■ Turf – If broad-leaved weeds are a problem apply an herbicide such as 2,4-D for control.

Follow label directions carefully and do not allow the herbicide to drift onto shrub beds, perennial flowers or other landscape plantings.

Mow turf as required and mow frequently enough so that not more than 1 to 1-1/2 inches are removed per mowing. Mow at heights of 2 inches.

Inspect turf for insect and disease. If problems are present, contact a turf expert to determine what is needed to correct the problem.

■ Trees and Shrubs – Inspect trees and shrubs for winter damage and remove any damaged limbs and branches.

■ Annuals and Perennials– If new perennial plants are to be set out this spring, prepare the area as described in Chapter 4.

■ Landscape Features – Inspect decks to determine if any lumber replacement is necessary. Do any resealing with wood preservatives when the deck is completely dry. Do not use preservatives during rainy periods.

May

Weeks 1 and 2

■ Turf – Mow as needed. This may be every 4 to 5 days if the weather is ideal for turf growth. If turf insects such as grubs are a problem apply the recommended insecticide for their control by the end of the first week.

■ Trees and Shrubs – Prune the shrubs that have already flowered. These will include some of the plants listed in Shrubs – Group II and Trees – Group II.

■ Annuals and Perennials – At the end of the second week prepare the annual beds for planting as described in Chapter 4. Plant at the end of the second week if the danger of frost is past.

Weeks 3 and 4

■ Turf – Continue mowing as needed. If a dry period occurs (no rainfall in 2 weeks), consider the use of irrigation. Apply water regularly and as a supplement to rainfall. Make second fertilizer application. Use same material and rate as recommended during March, Weeks 3 and 4.

■ Trees and Shrubs – Prune as needed any trees and shrubs in Trees – Group II and Shrubs – Group II. Remember to prune immediately after flowering.

■ Annuals and Perennials – Fertilize ground cover plantings at the rate of 3 pounds nitrogen per 1,000 square feet. Use a fertilizer with a ratio of 2-1-1. Apply an analysis of 20-10-10 at the rate of 15 pounds per 1,000 square feet. Remove any weeds in perennial and ground cover plantings. If annual weeds appear to be a potential problem, consider using a preemergence herbicide. Apply preemergence herbicide to annual plantings; follow the directions carefully.

There is a fertilizer-herbicide combination available for turf. This is more expensive but has the advantage of completing two operations in one. Follow directions and never use combinations in flower and shrub beds.

Casual observation or inspection of landscape plants should be done on a weekly basis. Look for changes in plants. Catching problems early can reduce the chance of serious damage.

A major task during this period will be to keep ahead of the mowing if the spring is warm and there is an excess of rainfall.

Not needed if a slow release fertilizer was used.

Pruning requirements may be only minor.

If ground covers are filled in, an herbicide will be of little benefit. In perennial plantings, adding mulch to bare soil areas may be a better choice than an herbicide.

Continued on next page...

The turf needs only nitrogen now, and the use of urea may be more economical than the complete fertilizer recommended for the first two applications.

It is important to correctly identify the insect pests before applying the pesticide.

Do not remove green foliage that will be necessary for producing food reserve for plants for next season's flowering.

An annual grass herbicide is best for most sites. Follow the directions carefully.

Use an herbicide that will control poison ivy but do not use a soil sterilant as it will damage nearby trees and shrubs.

Casual inspection trips through your landscape are rewarding in that not only will you observe problems before they become serious, but also you will enjoy the constant change occurring in your landscape.

By applying the broad-leaved herbicide in the early spring and early fall, you greatly reduce the chances of severe injury to woody ornamentals.

June

Weeks 1 through 4
- Turf – Mow as required, and irrigate if dry periods occur. Apply a third application of fertilizer during the fourth week. Use the same analysis as for the first two applications.
- Trees and Shrubs – Complete the pruning of early flowering trees and shrubs. Remove faded flower heads from the rhododendrons by the end of the first week. Inspect trees and shrubs carefully for insects. If insects are present, apply an insecticide to control them. Carefully follow label recommendations.
- Annuals and Perennials – Keep annual beds weed-free. Water as needed if the weather is dry. Cut off the seed stalks of bulbs and any other plants that have finished flowering.

July

Weeks 1 through 4
- Turf – Mow and irrigate as necessary.
- Trees and Shrubs – Continue inspections for insects and diseases, treat any problems with the appropriate pesticides.
- Annuals and Perennials – Some annuals need rejuvenation during mid-July. Cut back and fertilize with the same material used on the ground covers and at the same rate.
  Weed flower beds. If annual weeds start to become a problem, apply a second application of a preemergence herbicide.
- Landscape Features – A second application of the herbicide used in the spring may be necessary. Remove any weeds that have come up through the bricks.
- Natural Areas – Selectively kill poison ivy vines.

August

Weeks 1 through 4
- Turf – Continue mowing and irrigating as required.
  Fertilize turf during weeks 3 and 4. Use the same rate and material recommended for the end of June.
- Trees and Shrubs – Continue to make observations on health of your plants and apply insecticides or fungicides only if problems exist.
- Annuals and Perennials – Weed beds as needed and groom plants so that the appearance of the garden is one of attractiveness.

September

Weeks 1 through 4
- Turf – Apply a broad-leaved weed killer to turf areas only if broad-leaved weeds have become a problem
  Overseed any thin areas; do not apply broad-leaved weed killer to areas where overseeding has been done.
  Maintain watering and mowing programs as required.
  During weeks 3 and 4 make the final fertilizer application using the same material and rate listed for March, Weeks 3 and 4.
- Trees and Shrubs – Watch water requirements during this period. Late summer and fall droughts can injure trees and shrubs as they go into the winter.
  Begin leaf removal in plantings during late September.
  If chickweed is a problem, apply herbicide in landscape beds.

Check current recommendations for chickweed control in landscape plantings. Read the label carefully. A chickweed herbicide for lawns will injure many annuals, perennials, and woody landscape plants.

Roses fall into the category of plants that require winterizing.

September continued

■ Annuals and Perennials – Remove any weeds and continue to groom the plants as needed to keep up their good appearance. Use a fall applied herbicide on the ground cover plantings if chickweed has been a problem in the past.

October

Weeks 1 through 4
■ Turf – Mow as needed and water only if autumn is excessively dry.
■ Trees and Shrubs – Fertilize any trees that might not be benefiting from other fertilizer programs (turf and landscape plantings).

Continue leaf removal.

Replenish mulch as needed in shrub beds to reduce next spring's weed growth and help the plants overwinter.
■ Annuals and Perennials – After the first heavy frost, remove dead annual plants and plant a cover crop to improve the soil and stop erosion.

Mulch perennials (add an amount to bring the level to 2 inches) and winterize any plants that require special attention. Dig spring flowering tulip bulbs and grade and replant them according to size category.
■ Landscape Features – Make any needed repairs to the decks, railroad tie steps, and brick areas prior to the onset of winter.

November

Weeks 1 through 4
■ Prepare equipment for winter storage. Drain all gas tanks and run the engines until the carburetors are drained of gas.
■ Complete leaf removal and mulching of landsacpe beds.

December

Weeks 1 through 4
■ Complete any fall work as weather permits.
■ Remove undesirable underbush from natural areas.

PLANT INVENTORY

Plant Lists. This maintenance schedule may seem formidable but a careful examination reveals that many of the maintenance practices are common on most residential landscape sites. Mowing lawns is the big time consumer. By adding a few practices that need to be done at a precise time, the total site will be well maintained. Once your schedule is complete, you may want to prepare a calendar of events that lists each activity and permits you to maintain a running record of the maintenance programs. We have provided an example of a calendar designed for the sample schedule.

Fig. 7.5 *A sample maintenance calendar that can be adapted to your site. (see next page)*

LANDSCAPE MAINTENANCE SCHEDULE

TREES

GROUP I – DECIDUOUS – SHADE TREES
- BETULA NIGRA — RIVER BIRCH
- GLEDITSIA TRIACANTHUS — HONEY LOCUST

GROUP II – DECIDUOUS – SMALL EARLY FLOWERING
- ELAEAGNUS ANGUSTIFOLIUS — RUSSIAN OLIVE
- CERCIS CANADENSIS — EASTERN REDBUD
- CORNUS FLORIDA — FLOWERING DOGWOOD
- AMELANCHIER LAEVIS — ALLEGHANY SERVICEBERRY
- MALUS SARGENTII — SARGENT CRABAPPLE
- MALUS VARIETY

SHRUBS

GROUP I – DECIDUOUS – NON FLOWERING
- EUONYMUS ALATUS — WINGED SPINDLETREE

GROUP II – DECIDUOUS – EARLY FLOWERING
- AZALEA KAEMPFERI
- AZALEA BOUDOIR

GROUP III – DECIDUOUS – FLOWERING SUMMER, FRUITING LATE
- PYRACANTHA COCCINEA 'LALANDI' — SCARLET FIRETHORN

GROUP IV – EVERGREENS – NARROWLEAF
- JUNIPERUS CHINENSIS 'MINT JULEP' — CHINESE JUNIPER
- TAXUS MEDIA 'HICKSI' — HICKS YEW
- TAXUS MEDIA HILLII

GROUP V – EVERGREENS – BROADLEAF
- PICRIS JAPONICA — JAPANESE ANDROMEDA

HERBACEOUS PLANTS

GROUP I
- EUONYMUS FORTUNEI 'COLORATUS' — WINTER CREEPER
- HEDERA HELIX 'THORNDALE' — ENGLISH IVY

JOB BREAKDOWN

TREES, SHRUBS, AND WOODY GROUNDCOVERS

PRUNING: LIGHT PRUNING OF T1 WHEN ABOVE 40°F
ANNUAL PRUNING OF SL53 & S4 IF ABOVE 40°F
COMPLETE PRUNING OF T1,S1,S3,S4
ANNUAL PRUNING OF T2,S2 AS THEY COMPLETE BLOOM
MAINTAIN GROWTH AS NEEDED, TRIM BACK FROM WINDOWS, WALLS

FERTILIZER: RATIO 2:1:1 AT 2-3 LBS ACTUAL N/1000 SQ FT
DO NOT ALLOW FERTILIZER TO FALL OFF TURF AREA

PESTICIDES: DORMANT OIL APPLIED BEFORE LEAF &
FLOWER BUDS START TO EXPAND WHEN ABOVE 45°F
ALL PURPOSE PREVENTIVE PESTICIDE, INSPECT FOR
DISEASES, INSECTS, MINES, SCALE, APHIDS, FUNGI, SPRAY AS NEEDED

HERBICIDES: APPLY PRE-EMERGENCE GENERAL KILLER TO BEDS
INSPECT FOR LATE EMERGENCE, TREAT IF NEEDED
KEEP AS NEEDED TO KEEP BEDS WELL GROOMED

WATER: AS NEEDED TO PROVIDE 1" PER WEEK WHEN RAIN
IS INSUFFICIENT, OR TO AN 8" DEPTH FOR ESTABLISHED
PLANTS

OTHER: REMOVE SHREDDED BARK MULCH TO 2" DEPTH
REPAIR & CLEAN UP WINTER DAMAGE
LEAF REMOVAL FROM BEDS & TURF AREAS

MISCELLANEOUS TASKS

EQUIPMENT OVERHAUL FOR THE SEASONS USE
CLEAN & PREPARE FOR STORAGE

SNOW REMOVAL: USE ONLY ENOUGH SALT TO MELT ICE, AVOID
EXCESS

ADMINISTRATIVE: EVALUATE & REVISE THIS YEAR'S MAINTEN-
ANCE SCHEDULE FOR UPCOMING YEAR
ORDER SUPPLIES
VACATION

TURF

RENEWAL PROCEDURES: OVERSEED THIN SPOTS
ROLL HEAVED GROUND
LOW MOWING TO REMOVE BROWN LEAF TIPS
THATCH–VERTICAL THINNING IF NEEDED

FERTILIZER: RATIO 3:1:2 AT 1 LB N/1000 SQ FT

PESTICIDES: INSPECT AND APPLY AS NEEDED FOR
DISEASES–MAINLY FUNGAL RUST, MILDEW, LEAFSPOT,
INSECTS–GRUBS, SOD WEBWORMS, CHINCHBUGS, & MOLES

HERBICIDES: GENERAL BROADLEAVED WEEDKILLER, PRE-
EMERGENCE, SPECIFIC HERBICIDES, SPRAYED AS
NEEDED FOR:
CRABGRASS
ANNUAL GRASSES
WILD ONIONS
CHICKWEED

WATER: TO PROVIDE 1" PER WEEK WHEN RAIN IS IN-
SUFFICIENT OR TO A 6" DEPTH (MOW WHEN VERY
WET), DO NOT ALLOW TURF TO BECOME DORMANT BE-
CAUSE OF LACK OF WATER

MOW: TO MAINTAIN A 2" HEIGHT (COLLECT CLIPPINGS)
EXPECT TO MOW TWO TIMES A WEEK

MAINTAIN: AS NEEDED SIDEWALKS & SHRUB BED EDGES
RAKE AS NEEDED

BY JIM MEAL, CAROL MICHEL, ANGELA LOTTES, ED CURTIN, TRACY CHILDRESS

LENGTH OF TIME REQUIRED FOR ROUTINE LANDSCAPE MAINTENANCE

It is important to know approximately how long a task should take not only if you are doing it yourself but also if you are hiring the work done. Of course everyone works at a different speed and there is also the avid gardener who may pay more attention to detail and take longer to complete the task. But when it is done it will be done completely right and with skill.

Table 7.2 provides information on how long various routine maintenance operations take. Note that mowing the turf area and the maintenance of this area, including fertilizing, weed killing, and edging will require more time than the other maintenance practices required for the site. Little can be done to reduce the time required for turf maintenance except to install a smaller turf area. This can be done if your site is in a semiwooded area that can be left in its natural state. In a suburban development the chances of having such a wooded or semiwooded lot is not very great, so, the easiest way to reduce the time involved in lawn maintenance is to have the proper equipment. A

second is to have a landscape design that will require less maintenance, such as large open areas of turf that can be mowed with larger mowers. Curves on beds should be sweeping so that they can be edged with the mower and trimming can be reduced. Line trimmers reduce the time needed to trim around trees, fences, patios, and so forth. All can be helpful in reducing the time needed to maintain the lawn areas of the residential landscape.

A second time consuming maintenance operation is weed control. Removing weeds by hand from the landscape plantings, annual and perennial flower beds and ground covers is tiring work that is rarely enjoyed by anyone. Note that weeding is not listed in Table 7.2 because there are so many variables that it is impossible to estimate the time needed. The number of weeds, the closeness of the plants, the size of the weeds, the soil type and the amount of moisture present all influence how rapidly weeds can be removed. By providing ideal growing conditions so that landscape plants are competitive with the weeds and by using mulches and herbicides, you will reduce the amount of weeding necessary.

Study the maintenance schedule and the maintenance calendar so you can estimate accurately the time needed to maintain your landscape site. You may, after studying the schedule and all the factors involved, elect to hire out some or all of the work. The information will also help you estimate the cost of hiring out the work. The schedule and time estimates give information about the types of equipment that will be needed.

Table 7-2 Time required to complete some landscape maintenance jobs.

Turf

Mowing			Hours
Small-	1,000 sq. ft. (catching clippings) Hand 20 inch		1/4
Large-	1 acre Riding rotary		1/2
Edging			
Hand-	100 feet		3/4
Fertilizing			
Small-	(rotary spreader) 1,000 sq. ft.		5 min.
Spraying			
Small-	(back pack) 1,000 sq. ft.		10 min.

Trees

Spraying			Minutes
small	(3 inch cal.)		10
large	(8 inch cal.)		25
Pruning (heavy)			
small	(3 inch)		15
large	(8 inch)		60
Watering			
variable			

Shrubs

Spraying			
small	(3 to 4 foot)		1
large	(7 to 8 foot)		2
Pruning			
small	(3 to 4 foot)		5
large	(7 to 8 feet) rejuvenate		30
Watering			
variable			

Ground Cover

Spraying			
	1,000 sq. ft.		10

Source: Wayne Doede.

EQUIPMENT AND TOOLS

The equipment needed to maintain your landscape site will depend on several factors. The size of the site, the level of maintenance desired or required, the tasks you will do vs. those hired, your interest in maintaining the site for recreational activities, and of course, your maintenance budget enter into the decision. You will need turf, pruning, gardening, and general tools and equipment.

Turf Equipment.*Mowers.* A major expense is the lawn mower. There are dozens or even hundreds of models to choose from so consider these factors before purchasing a mower: the size of the area to be mowed; the time available for mowing; whether the person doing the mowing is physically able to mow the area with a push type mower; and whether it would be more practical to hire out the mowing to someone who owns their own mower.

The size of the area to be mowed controls, to a great extent, the size of the mower. Small areas can be mowed by hand with a push-type rotary mower. The blade of a rotary mower runs parallel to the ground and is powered by a gasoline engine or an electric motor. For small areas of 1/8 acre (5,000 sq. ft.) or less the electric rotary mower is ideal. It is usually less expensive than the gasoline powered mower, starts immediately, is noiseless, and does not pollute the atmosphere. The disadvantage is that the electric cord can be very bothersome if it must be pulled over large areas. Another mower to consider for small areas is the push type reel mower: the grass is cut by a reel that pulls the grass over a stationary blade. Such a mower is relatively difficult to keep adjusted, but it does mow evenly for small areas. A good quality reel mower gives a lawn the best appearance.

If you are collecting the grass clippings a grass bag collection system must be included with the mower. Collecting clippings can be very time consuming, but does reduce the thatch build-up and improve the appearance of the lawn after mowing.

For large areas, a powered rotary mower is enough. Some versions are self-propelled: even though the operator must walk, the mower pulls itself making the mowing task easier. The general mowing width is from 18 to 23 inches. On large areas of 1/2 acre or more, consider using a riding mower. These mowers generally cut swaths of 32 to 60 inches wide, with 40 inches being the most common width. Some of the more elaborate mowers double as small tractors for garden tilling, snow removal, and hauling small loads. The cost can be high, so make sure to buy a quality product suited for the site.

The rest of the equipment and tools discussed here are optional, but all will certainly assist in maintaining the lawn area. In some instances renting, borrowing or joint ownership are options worth considering when obtaining equipment for landscape maintenance.

Edgers. Another piece of useful equipment is an edger to help maintain sharp lines of demarcation between turf areas. Edgers are available in three forms: hand pushed, electric, and gasoline. Professional maintenance firms will probably use gasoline powered edgers since they have more power and flexibility. For your residential landscape an electrical edger is much more economical to purchase and maintain. If you have only a limited amount of edging to do a hand edger works perfectly well.

Fig. 7.6 a, b *It may be more desirable to hire a part of all of your landscape maintenance work done by professionals who have the equipment for the job.*

Fertilizer Spreaders. Fertilizer spreaders are either of the gravity-feed or of the impeller type. The gravity-feed spreader drops the fertilizer straight down from a hopper on wheels. The rate is controlled by adjusting the size of the opening. The width spread is generally from 24 to 36 inches for hand pushed spreaders. These spreaders are easy to push and give an even distribution of fertilizer if careful attention is given to the proper overlap. However, the time required to cover an area is much longer than with the impeller type. Overlapping problems can occur causing "streaking" of the lawn. Failure to shut off the spreader quickly enough at the end of a strip can cause fertilizer burn due to a build-up of fertilizer at the end of the strip as the spreader is turned.

Impeller spreaders operate by throwing the fertilizer from an impeller that is fed from a hopper. The rate is controlled by the opening that feeds the hopper. Impeller spreaders are mounted on wheels and pushed or carried on a strap around the neck. Impeller spreaders will cover a much wider area per strip – 6 to 8 feet. The area can be covered very rapidly, up to 2 acres per hour. By going both directions, a very uniform coverage can be obtained. Note that the fertilizer should have reasonably uniform size granules because large granules are thrown farther than smaller ones, which could affect the distribution patterns. Some fertilizer suppliers will loan a spreader. The cost of a spreader is rather low, but the corrosive nature of the fertilizer will cause rapid wear. Be sure to wash the spreader with large volumes of water after each use.

Sprinklers. Lawn sprinklers come in a variety of forms, including permanent irrigation systems, which are the most satisfactory and by far the most expensive. The system should be installed by experts, but if you do it yourself, be sure you understand the directions and techniques involved before starting.

There are five general types of lawn sprinklers. A soaker hose is a length of plastic hose with a series of small holes that emit a spray when under pressure. These hoses can be used to water narrow strips of turf or long and narrow landscape beds. Turn the holes down to soak a very narrow area without any water shooting into the air. This technique can be used along a walk without dampening passersby. A canvas version of the soaker hose oozes water and soaks a narrow band along the hose.

The oscillating sprinkler covers relatively large rectangular shaped areas. The cost of this spinkler is relatively low. An oscillating sprinkler must be moved from location to location to cover a large area; the water source is a garden hose. A 3/4-inch hose is the best and the water pressure should be strong and steady for good operation.

A third type of lawn sprinkler is the pulsating sprinkler head, which throws water in an arc pattern. By adjusting the sprinkler head the coverage can be extended from a small wedge area to a full circle. The head can be mounted on a spike pushed into the ground at each location it is to be used, or it can be on a stand that rests on the surface. This type of sprinkler is fed by a garden hose; again, a 3/4-inch size is best. The pulsating sprinkler head generally delivers more water in a given period over a specific area than does the oscillating sprinkler. Pulsating sprinklers are available in very inexpensive plastic forms or relatively expensive brass and stainless steel models which will last longer than the plastic ones and can be adjusted to more patterns.

A traveling sprinkler sprays water circularly and travels to cover a large rectangular area. The traveling sprinkler moves along a hose or a cord that is staked in the desired pattern. These sprinklers are much more expensive than the other types described and have more moving parts that can malfunction. However, they cover much larger areas without needing to be reset.

The final type is the turrent sprinkler which is a series of stationary nozzles mounted on a small platform. The water is delivered in a rectangular pattern. The shape and size of the rectangle can be varied by adjusting the pattern of distribution of the individual nozzles. It will deliver good volumes of water when supplied with a 3/4-inch hose. This sprinkler costs about the same as the oscillating and pulsating sprinklers.

Trimmers. The invention of the "fish line" trimmer revolutionized the method of trimming a residential landscape because it can be used around trees and woody stems of shrubs without injuring plants. The "fish line" spins at high speeds and cuts the soft grass and weed stems but not the woody stems. It can be used to trim along walks, fences, and other landscape features with a minimum of effort and time. These trimmers are electric or gasoline powered; professionals use the more expensive and powerful gasoline models. Some electric models have either a cord or are cordless. The cordless models are more flexible because they do not need an electrical outlet, but they are not as powerful. The cord models deliver more power for as long as it is needed. The cordless models operate for only about 2 hours; after that a 24 to 48 hour recharging period is necessary. Generally the electric cord models cost 50 percent less than the cordless models but this savings can be used up on a long extension cord.

Sprayers. Sprayers for applying pesticides come in many sizes and shapes; the size of the area and the purpose dictate the type of equipment needed. For most residential landscapes the hand carried pump-up sprayer is fine. It has a two to three gallon tank capacity and the tank will usually be of galvanized metal, plastic, or stainless steel. The best material is stainless steel, but it is the most expensive. A stainless steel sprayer last indefinitely, and so is a better buy in the long run.

The pressure in the sprayer is supplied by an air pump that pressurizes the tank and forces the spray out through a nozzle mounted on the end of a hand held boom. Because the pressurized air volume is small, these sprayers do not deliver a uniform pressure consequently the rate of spray delivered is not uniform.

A better type of sprayer is a backpack continuous pumping sprayer. This sprayer delivers a nearly constant pressure, and the volume is uniform. This sprayer costs three to four times more than the pump-up type. Also, the pump must be carefully maintained or it will not last.

There is also a small inexpensive sprayer that attaches to a garden hose. This sprayer holds a spray concentrate in a small tank from which the spray is sucked up. The distribution pattern is poor for applying weed killers, although it does a good job of delivering insecticides and fungicides. It is very wasteful of pesticides and is not as sound environmentally for that reason.

One additional type to be considered is the trombone or slide sprayer. This sprayer can be adjusted to send a stream fairly high into the air to reach small trees or down to a fine mist for shrubs and garden spraying. It is a small unit that uses a common bucket as the tank, and it can be easily carried from place to place. It is awkward to use if covering large areas because the bucket must be picked up and moved, and it takes two hands to operate the sprayer. *Important:* have separate sprayers for herbicides and for other pesticides. Never use the lawn herbicide sprayer for any other purpose than for applying herbicides to the turf area. If you are applying herbicides to ground covers, annuals and perennials, keep a separate sprayer for that purpose. The sprayer for insecticides and fungicides can be used on both lawns and landscape plants.

Lawn Sweepers. Some form of leaf pick up may be desirable depending upon the number of large trees. Various types of lawn sweepers are available, from the very small hand-pushed types to the self-propelled vacuum models. The hand pushed types have met with only moderate success and have several faults, not the least of which is that they are generally hard to push. They also have limited capacity.

The most useful lawn sweepers for residential sites are the units that can be pulled by a riding mower or small garden tractor. In some instances the mower itself picks up the leaves; the action of the blades throws the leaves into the leaf trailer pulled by the mower. The self-propelled and larger vacuum equipment is very expensive and is needed only for large estates. You can buy a lawn mower with a leaf mulching attachment. As the mower is being run through the leaves, it grinds them up and deposits them as fine mulch material onto the lawn surface. This mulch soon disappears into the grass.

Rakes. You will need two types of hand rakes: a leaf rake and a level-headed rake. The leaf rake can be used to rake grass clippings if mowing has produced heavy amounts that might smother the turf or give it an unkempt appearance. Use the level-headed rake for garden and flower bed preparation. It can be used to lightly rake a turf area but be careful that you do not dig in and pull up pieces of turf.

Pruning Tools. If you have much pruning to do the proper tools are very important. It is hard to imagine a site that does not have enough trees and shrubs to warrant the purchase of at least a pair of hand shearers and a small pruning saw. Buy good quality tools and keep them sharp.

Shearers. There are two basic types of small hand shearers. One has a steel blade that cuts against a brass anvil, and the other cuts with a hook and a sharp blade. The selection depends on individual preference. The hand shearers range in lengths from 6 to 9 inches and are used to cut branches up to 1/2 inch in diameter. It is always a temptation to try to cut larger branches, but this may damage the shearers or result in a poorly cut branch. Loppers are a type of hand shearer that cuts limbs up to 1 inch in diameter. The blades are mounted on long handles 20 to 36 inches long. Loppers are invaluable for use on shrubs as they grow. To reach higher places, try a pole pruner. The cutting blades are mounted on a pole and operated by a rope attached to the blade and pole. However, pole pruners are hard to use.

Hedge shearers are designed for trimming and clipping shrubs in a formal style and should not be used for most pruning operations. The 6- to 12-inch blades fit tightly together, and using shearers for pruning will loosen and damage the blades. Hedge shearers are available in manual and electric powered models. Electric shearers are now reasonably priced; using them to prune long hedges will save time and leave a better job.

Saws. There are many types of pruning saws available, but they all have one thing in common: coarse and very sharp teeth that help prevent them from becoming gummed up or jammed in the green wood. The small curved saw is used to remove small limbs and to reach the internal parts of older shrubs. This saw can be mounted on a pole (10 to 15 feet in length) for reaching high limbs, but this tool is physically hard to use.

The inexpensive, small band saw is popular for cutting larger limbs as well as small trees and brush. The larger band saws are often quite expensive and are usually unnecessary. A small electric or gasoline chain saw is useful only if a site has a substantial wooded area.

Gardening Tools. The major piece of equipment for gardening is the rototiller, but this item is necessary only if the owner has an active gardening program. There are several types of rototillers available; the size and type depend on the size of the area that needs to be cultivated. Regardless of the type selected, the rototiller, whether bought or rented, should till deeply enough to be effective, at least 3 to 4 inches. Renting or joint ownership may be an acceptable alternative to outright purchase.

The types of sprayers described for lawn care can be used for the rest of the landscape, but not the same sprayer. Buy separate sprayers for herbicides and insecticides. The rest of the tools and equipment needed are all hand tools or special items. A brief description of the most useful garden tools will be given. The person involved at a particular site will need to decide whether he/she needs a certain tool or not. There are several types of shovels or spades available and most people will want to consider at least two of the types. The round-pointed or garden shovel, and the spade are useful. The shovel is good for any general digging; use the spade to prepare planting beds and garden plots. The spading fork is handy for digging tuberous bulbs, or preparing small beds. Scoop shovels, available in several styles, are ideal for moving quantities of sand or mulch.

The level-head rake and a garden hoe are useful for planting and maintaining landscape beds. Hand tools, such as a trowel for planting small plants and a hand cultivator, are good for weed removal and cultivation of small areas.

A cart or wheelbarrow is very handy for moving quantities of materials from one place to another. Be sure to buy a wheelbarrow that is sturdy enough to do the job. One with a pneumatic tire and a minimum capacity of 4 cubic feet is useful on large sites: the small, solid tire wheelbarrow or the light weight garden cart is fine for small sites.

The garden hose should have 3/4 inch diameter and be made of heavy duty vinyl or rubber. A good quality hose will last for years. Smaller hoses do not deliver the necessary volume of water that might be needed to water lawn areas and gardens. Also, smaller hoses have a greater tendency to kink and stop the flow of water.

Finally, if you must contend with snow, a snow shovel is a necessity. Recently gasoline powered snow blowers have been developed that remove large volumes of snow with much less effort than shoveling. However, their cost is usually relatively high and one should consider the alternative of hiring out snow removal.

8

Pest Control

You must control pests if your plants are to develop to their fullest potential. Providing optimum growing conditions means that the plants will be vigorous and actively growing and less suceptible to attack by pests. But sometimes good growing conditions are only an aid in the fight against pests; the use of pesticides may be necessary. During the past several years pesticides have been considered by many people as dangerous and harmful to the environment, but nothing could be further from the truth. When properly used, pesticides — insecticides, fungicides, and herbicides — help protect desirable plants, and this in turn enhances the environment. You should not be afraid to use pesticides, but you should learn *how* to use pesticides with confidence. Pesticides do not cause accidents, misuse does.

PESTICIDES

While controlling weeds in the residential landscape is the most frustrating and probably the most time-consuming maintenance operation other than mowing the lawn, there are actually two other major pest problem areas in addition to weeds: insects and diseases. A fourth problem, animals, may be a concern in certain sections of the country during the winter. Pesticides, materials that control pests, are divided into three groups: insecticides, which control insects; fungicides, which control fungus disease; and herbicides, which control weeds. A fungicide will not control insects, and

an insecticide will not control fungus disease. Thus it is important to know the specific pesticide and the specific purpose for which it was designed. It is impossible to describe all the insect and disease problems that could occur on all the different species of landscape plants in different sections of the country, but the proper approaches to controlling these problems are discussed in this chapter.

Diagnosis. With all pest control problems the correct diagnosis is absolutely essential. Just as medical doctors know that before they can treat illnesses they must first determine the causes of them, so homeowners must determine what the problem is before they can apply a pesticide or other control measure. But the correct diagnosis of a problem is not always easy; sometimes insect and disease symptoms are nearly identical; air pollution, nutrient deficiencies, salt injury, and herbicide injury can all look, under certain conditions, like insect or disease symptoms. If you are the least bit uncertain about what might be causing the injury symptoms present on a plant, obtain help from a horticulturist or the county agricultural extension agent. Just do not start applying pesticides haphazardly.

By providing as much information as possible, you can help the expert to make the right diagnosis and determine the proper corrective measures. Follow these guidelines for obtaining a sample for diagnosis. First, take a

Fig. 8.1 *The light areas in the lawn are due to insect damage. Correct diagnosis is essential before applying any pesticide to control the pest.*

large enough sample so that the specialist may be able to see the entire cause of the problem. A single leaf is often useless or nearly so. If possible, take a sample that has both healthy and injured tissue. If insects are present try to obtain some and place them in a sealed bottle. If the sample is to be mailed, it should be placed in a plastic bag with holes so that the sample does not decay rapidly. Mail it first class to ensure its arriving as soon as possible and in good condition.

Identify the plant, if possible, and provide information on the care it has received. Tell what pesticides were used on the plant, and do not neglect to mention any, such as herbicides, that were used nearby, for example, in a neighbor's yard. If possible, give the names of all products used, including fertilizers. Often it is helpful to describe anything unusual at the site that might have affected the plant, such as wet soils, road de-icing salt injury, the construction of a driveway, or installation of an underground pipe. Mention any major events that occurred as much as a year or two ago. Certain large trees will not show a response to a change in their environment for several months to several years.

Safety Precautions. Once the problem has been identified and a pesticide has been recommended, the next step is application. But before applying pesticides, become familiar with the safety procedures involved.

The rules apply to two main areas: storage and application. Here are seven storage procedures which will lessen any change of a pesticide accident.

1. Store all pesticides in their original containers, with their labels intact. Do not borrow or obtain a pesticide from a friend and then place a portion of it in another container. Borrow the original container, use the pesticide, then return it.

2. Read the label carefully concerning proper storage conditions. Do not let liquid pesticides freeze.

3. Store pesticides out of the reach of children and in a *locked* cabinet. Remember that small children cannot read and will be unaware of the dangers of pesticides.

4. Do not store food, pet food, or seed in the same cabinet as pesticides.

5. Do not store 2,4-D type weed killers in the same area as fertilizers and other types of pesticides. Remember that some lawn fertilizers contain 2,4-D weed killer.

6. Properly dispose of outdated pesticides. The best way is to use them. If this is not possible, contact your county agricultural agent for information on correct disposal procedures.

7. Post a warning sign on your storage cabinet stating the contents. This may help fire fighters in case of a fire.

It cannot be emphasized enough that you must read the label prior to applying any pesticide. The label tells how to use the pesticide and what precautions to take when applying the pesticide. Do not allow yourself to become overfamiliar with a pesticide: *always* read the label, and make certain that you are following *all* the label precautions; it may prevent injury to you, your family, and the plants being treated. Here are thirteen application rules. These safety precautions may seem excessive, but common sense dictates extreme care in following directions. There is *never* a valid reason for a pesticide accident.

1. *Always read the label prior to using.* Read all the warnings and cautions on the label.
2. *Never smoke while applying* pesticides, and do not eat or drink when applying or mixing pesticides.
3. Avoid inhaling sprays or dusts both during the mixing and application processes.
4. Avoid spilling the concentrated sprays or dusts on your skin or clothing. If they do spill, remove the contaminated clothing, wash your skin immediately, and change your clothing. Wash the contaminated clothing.
5. Wash your hands and face and change to clean clothes immediately after applying pesticides. Wash the clothes before wearing them again.
6. Use separate sprayers for herbicides and other pesticides.

7. Always dispose of the empty pesticide containers as recommended on the label, or contact the county agricultural extension service.

8. When applying pesticides around the home, make certain that food and water supplies for pets are not contaminated. Cover them or remove them to safe places until application is completed.

9. When spraying or dusting, never stand downwind in the drift of the spray or dust.

10. Never apply any pesticide in high winds.

11. Never apply pesticides when children or pets are present, and make certain no one is hit by the spray or dust during application.

12. Know where the local poison control center is located. The hospital will know, and there may be a listing in the telephone directory.

13. If symptoms of illness occur shortly after applying a pesticide, call a physician or the poison control center, or take the person to the hospital emergency room. Take a label from the pesticide container so that persons treating the victim will know exactly what pesticides were used.

Equipment. The minimum equipment was described in Chapter 7. All types of equipment are available, ranging from inexpensive to expensive. Small gasoline-engine sprayers do a nice job of applying insecticides and fungicides to almost all landscape plants except large trees, but do not use these sprayers to apply herbicides. Their method of distributing the herbicide spray is not satisfactory. As with other types of landscape maintenance equipment, always use equipment suited to the task involved. Do not attempt to carry out pesticide spraying projects for which you are not adequately equipped. For example, if you have a large tree that must be sprayed for insects or disease, you must use a very expensive, high-pressure sprayer that will reach the top of the tree. Using inadequate equipment will not control the pest and will just waste the pesticide. Hire pesicide applicators if you do not have the adequate equipment or know how. Do not use faulty or leaky equipment because both the area being sprayed and the person applying the pesticide can be contaminated. Herbicides can drip and damage desirable plants, and the user could inhale fumes from the sprayer. Use high-quality pesticide-application equipment in good shape; and be sure the equipment delivers the proper amount of pesticide, not too much or too little.

Fig. 8.2 *A profesional wears protective clothing when applying a pesticide. Always wear the protective clothing recommended on the pesticide label.*

Fig. 8.3 *Make sure that you do not contaminate ponds and water supplies when applying a pesticide.*

Fig. 8.4 *High pressure sprayers are required to reach the top of large trees. This is a job for professionals.*

Read labels carefully to ascertain if there are any special equipment requirements for the pesticides being used. Some pesticides can be used only in glass, plastic, or stainless steel equipment. This information will be on the label under the *Caution* section.

After each use, clean all pesticide equipment thoroughly. Run clean water through the tanks, the hoses, spray boom, and nozzles. Then drain the tanks and *all* other parts thoroughly and store them dry until the next use. Never store unused spray in the tank until the next use; always use the spray in the tank completely. Some pesticides, when left in the tank overnight, form substances harmful to plants.

Applying Insecticides and Fungicides. Once the problem has been identified and the pesticide recommended for its control, apply the pesticide. Again read the label before making any applications. Check for any plants that might be injured by a particular pesticide. The term for this type of injury is *phytotoxicity*, which means that the pesticide is toxic to specific plants and

might well injure them under certain conditions. Any problems of this type are given in the *Caution* part of the label. For instance, there is a particular insecticide that will injure only one cultivar of *Juniperus virginiana*, and then only when high temperature occurs. The cultivar is 'Canaertii'. Read the label and follow it and the recommendations made by the agricultural extension service.

Try to apply pesticides when the pests are most susceptible to it. Often this period of maximum susceptibility lasts for only a few days, so applying the pesticide at any other time is a waste of both time and money. As an example, the scale insects are most susceptible to control with insecticides during a particular phase of their life cycle. At this time the insects have not yet covered themselves with a hard, waxy coat, so the insecticide can penetrate the scales. Once the scale forms the waxy coat, control by common insecticides is difficult, if not impossible, so timing of application is very important. The correct application timing of fungicides is also important for controlling diseases because the organisms that cause disease also have life cycles, and during certain stages of their life cycles they will be more susceptible to fungicides than at other times.

The amount of pesticide to use is also critical. Apply *precisely* the recommended amount. Too little will not do the job, and too much is not only wasteful but can injure both plants and the environment. The amount to mix in a given volume of water is given on the insecticide or fungicide label. Do not vary from the recommended rates

Spray or dust the plants thoroughly. When spraying, apply enough so that the spray just starts to drip from the foliage. Any additional amounts will not improve the control. Cover the entire plant, and use as fine (small droplet size) a spray as possible. You may have to spray in the early morning to accomplish this.

The preceding guidelines should not frighten you into not using pesticides. They are merely common sense pactices that will make pesticide usage safe and provide an effective means of pest control. Preventive sprays at sites where plants are healthy and growing well are generally not needed. An exception is for fruit trees, which must have preventive sprays. If insects and diseases have been a problem in the past at a particular site, then preventive sprays may help clean the area. But in time they will not be needed if the plants are growing well. Pesticides should be used only when a particular problem appears.

WEED CONTROL

Weed control involves not only the use of herbicides but good cultural practices, biological control, and the removal of some weeds by hand. No one should depend entirely on herbicides or not use them because of a lack of knowledge. You need to develop a total weed-control system for your site, for both landscape beds and plantings and turf.

Mechanical Methods. Mechanical methods, effective if used on combination with biological and chemical controls, involve both cultivation and mulching. Cultivation is done with a hoe or hand cultivator. Although it is not precisely cultivation, weeds can also be removed by pulling. Cultivation usually cuts the tops of the weeds or, in the case of weed seedlings, exposes their roots to the air so they dry up and die. These means are effective, particularly if done after a rain. The soil works up easily, and the weeds — roots and all — can be pulled more easily. Most people feel that hoeing weeds or cultivation with a small hand cultivator will not cause any plant injury, but injury from hoes is very common and can be severe if a trunk has a substantial piece of its bark removed. In some instances, hand removal of a few weeds in a dense planting of shrubs, annuals, ground covers, or perennials is the only safe way. Mechanical removal of weeds by cultivation or pulling is not a permanent solution to the problem.

Mulches are also considered a mechanical means of weed control because they smother the weeds. The ideal mulch smothers the existing weeds, prevents the germination of weed seed by covering them deeply, and has a dry surface that prevents blow-in weed seed from germinating. Some mulch materials are better than others. A course-textured organic mulch such as shredded hard wood bark or pine bark is considered the best all-around material. The key to good weed control with a mulch is to apply the mulch deep enough so that all bare soil is covered 2 inches. This will smother most existing weeds and reduce the number of weed seeds that germinate.

Using a plastic barrier or mulch will also reduce the number of weeds that will grow in a landscape bed. Cover the plastic (except in the vegetable garden) with a stone or organic mulch for aesthetic reasons. Install the plantings carefully so that water does not drain into the planting holes. If you use plastic, it is absolutely essential that surface drainage is away from the

Fig. 8.5   *The mulch used around these junipers will help reduce weed growth until the junipers fill in.*

Fig. 8.6   *The ivy has filled in solid and very few weeds will be able to penetrate this barrier.*

plants. Do this by planting the plants slightly higher than the surrounding bed.

Biological Methods. Biological control of pests usually means that one insect species is encouraged to eat another species, or that a disease is introduced to attack only the problem insect. Weeder geese, used to remove weeds from a strawberry planting, is another (not very practical) biological control for weeds in the residential landscape. But there is one biological weed control that is far more important. When ideal growing conditions are provided, the landscape plants grow so well that they crowd weeds out completely or permit so few to survive that they can easily be pulled by hand. This is particularly true with good ground cover plantings and, in some instances, annual flower beds. This is the ideal means of controlling

a

weeds because herbicides are not needed once the ground cover plants have filled in.

Unfortunately, in most perennial plantings and some shrub beds the plants do not fill in solidly, so there is some bare soil that permits the weed seeds to germinate. Thus the use of herbicides may be necessary. But first you should know some herbicide terms. *Preemergence* is the term used to describe those herbicides that will control weeds only if the herbicides are applied prior to the weeds' emergence from the soil. Most herbicides used in annual, perennial, and ground cover plantings are preemergence. These herbicides will not kill weeds that are already growing and generally do not injure landscape plants. *Postemergence* herbicides are applied after the weeds are up and actively growing. Generally these herbicides will not prevent weed seeds from germinating or growing. The broad-leaved weed killer 2,4-D used in lawns is an example of a postemergence herbicide.

A *soil sterilant* kills all existing vegetation and prevents its regrowth. These herbicides are so hazardous in the hands of nonprofessionals that they should not be used around the residential landscape. Never use any "magical" weed killer that promise to kill all weeds because it will probably also kill all vegetation. Do not use soil sterilants to control weeds in driveways or along fences or walks because there may be roots of a desirable tree near these areas. If some soil sterilants come in contact with only one tree root, the whole tree will be killed. Also, if a soil sterilant is applied accidentally to an area, the return of any vegetation may not occur for ten or more years, depending on the material and the rate at which it was used. If the term soil sterilant is used to describe a particular herbicide, do not use it.

Drift refers to the movement of fumes or fine spray particles from the target area to the surrounding areas. In some instances, drift of an herbicide can injure nearby desirable plants. Before the development of improved formulations, drift injury could occur several lots away when 2,4-D was used for broad-leaved weeds. Tomatoes, grapes, and redbud are particularly sensitive to injury from the drift of 2,4-D. To reduce the chance of drift causing injury, never spray on windy days, use low pressure when spraying, and closely follow the application directions on the label.

The *formulation* of the herbicide is important. Formulation refers to the form in which the herbicide is sold: granules, wettable

A.E. Bye and Associates

Fig. 8.7 a, b *Do not use a soil sterilant along this roadway if tree roots are nearby or to keep weeds out of the cracks in this stone walk.*

115

powder, or liquid. A granular herbicide, the most expensive form, must be applied in its dry form. The active chemical is impregnated on an inert granule and is ready for use. The granular formulations are generally the easiest to use since they do not have to be mixed with water. They may be more difficult to apply uniformly over a small area, such as a perennial planting, because there are no granular spreaders designed for applying herbicides to small landscape beds.

A wettable powder is a dry powder that must be mixed with water and then sprayed on the soil surface. It costs much less than a granular formulation, and it is easier (if done properly) to apply a spray to small, irregularly shaped landscape beds. However, you must be able to weigh relatively small amounts (1/2 ounce or less) with accuracy and have a sprayer for herbicide use only.

The liquid herbicides are basically the same as the wettable powders in that they must be mixed with water. It is easier to measure small quantities of a liquid than wettable powder. You generally will not have a choice as to which formulations you can purchase. That is, many herbicides are available in only one formulation, but for those few that can be purchased as granulars, wettable powders, or liquids, you have the option of selecting the one that best suits your ability and means of application. The granulars are the easiest and most foolproof to use but the most expensive.

Applying Herbicides. As with insect and disease control, the first thing to do is to correctly identify the weed problem. Applying an ineffective herbicide to control a particular weed species is pointless. For example, generally the preemergence herbicides are not effective against perennial weeds, so if you have a perennial weed problem, it is useless to apply a preemergence herbicide. Often it is enough to determine if the weeds present are annual or perennial, but not always. Most preemergence herbicides will control just certain weed species, so here again, reading the label is important to determine if a particular herbicide will control those weeds. Sometimes the best approach is to use an herbicide recommended as safe for the particular landscape plants, and if any weeds are present after its use, then identify those weeds and find out how to control them.

Once the weed problems are identified, you then must read the herbicide label *completely*. The label provides information about the active ingredients, the concentration, the weeds that the herbicide will be particularly effective in controlling, the formulation, and the kinds of ornamental plants that will tolerate the herbicide. If the plants in your landscape are not listed, do not use the herbicide without checking with your county agricultural extension agent to see whether your plants will tolerate the treatment.

Also on the label is information about how much to use over a given area and any special application instructions, such as incorporation requirements. Some herbicides must be incorporated (mixed) into the soil to be effective. In addition, if the formulation dictates that the herbicide must be sprayed on, the volume of water per given area is listed, and sometimes recommended pressure for spraying is also given.

Finally, safety cautions are on the label. Read these cautions and heed their advise. A precaution section may also appear on some herbicide labels. This section concerns the plants that the herbicide is to be used on. Such things as the stage of growth and age of the ornamental plants, sensitive ornamental plants, and so on are described in this section. Study the label and become familiar with its various sections.

Using herbicides in landscape plantings presents some special problems. The landscape bed is small and often irregularly shaped, frequently bordered by sensitive plants such as turf grasses, and often includes many different species. Thus it is difficult to find a herbicide that will effectively control weeds but not injure any of the plant species. However, even with these difficulties, herbicides can be used effectively in the residential landscape to reduce weeds.

In existing plantings the herbicides are generally limited to preemergence materials. You must use these weed killers prior to the appearance of weeds in the spring or immediately after you have cleaned the area of weeds by mechanical means. Then apply preemergence granules, measure the area and then calculate the amount of herbicide needed and weigh it out. Apply this amount uniformly over the entire area. If necessary, incorporate it into the soil by raking or with irrigation (information regarding any needed incorporation is on the label).

You must calibrate the herbicide sprayer in much the same manner as the fertilizer spreader. Convert the sprayer nozzle top to a flat fan shape if this has not been done. A garden center or a farm supply store can show you how to do this and will carry the parts necessary for the conversion. The amount of an insecticide or fungicide to be applied is controlled by the amount of pesticide added to a given volume of water. But herbicides are different, a specific amount of the chemical must be applied to a given area; this is controlled by the amount of water the sprayer is putting out. Determining the amount of water being delivered is called calibration. The following is a step-by-step procedure for calibrating a hand sprayer.

1. Add a measured quantity (1 to 2 quarts) of water to the sprayer.

2. Spray an area with the measured quantity of water until the sprayer is empty.

(a) Walk at the speed you will be moving when you apply the herbicide (when sprayer is full).

(b) Hold the nozzle at the height it will be held when you are applying the herbicide.

3. Determine the area covered — width of spray on ground times the length of the sprayed area.

4. Determine how much area would be covered by 1 gallon, and add the appropriate amount of chemical per gallon. *Example:* The spray band width is 30 inches, and the distance covered with 2 quarts is 400 feet. Area covered = 2-1/2 feet X 400 feet = 1,000 square feet for 2 quarts of water, or 2,000 square feet per gallon.

5. If the recommended rates are given for an acre, you must convert the information obtained for an acre:

$$\frac{43{,}560 \text{ (sq ft acre)}}{2{,}000 \text{ sq ft covered by 1 gal.}} = 21\text{-}3/4 \text{ gal/acre}$$

6. Determine the amount of herbicide needed per acre from the label. *For example:* the amount of wettable powder might be 10 pounds per acre of X brand herbicide.

7. Convert the amount per acre of wettable powder to amount needed per 1 gallon. For example,

$$\frac{10 \text{ lbs}}{21\text{-}3/4 \text{ gal}} = 0.46 \text{ lb/gal.}$$

or

0.46 X 16 (oz/lb) = 7-1/3 oz/gal.

8. To every gallon of water add 7-1/3 ounces of herbicide to ensure the proper delivery rate of herbicide to the area. Calculate liquids in the same manner, except use volume measurement in place of pounds per acre. As an example, the rate recommended might be 2 quarts of weed killer per acre. *Example:*

$$\frac{2 \text{ qt or 64 oz/acre)}}{21\text{-}3/4 \text{ gal/acre}} = 2.9 \text{ or 3 oz/gal.}$$

Calibration is absolutely necessary and should be done fairly frequently (perhaps two to three times per season). If you need help calibrating the sprayer, carry out the steps just described and have your calculation checked by someone experienced with sprayers, such as the county agricultural extension agent. Remember that the example given is just an example; you must do your own calibration of your equipment. Someone else's calibration for their equipment will not work for you.

Once you have calibrated the sprayer and added the correct amount of herbicide to the water, start spraying. Apply the herbicide only on very calm days. Walk at the same speed as you did when you calibrated the sprayer. Most people tend to slow down to make certain complete coverage is achieved. Do not do this or too much herbicide will be applied, possibly injuring desirable plants. Do not cover an area more than once. Clean the sprayer thoroughly after use, and do not leave mixed spray in the tank for future use.

Some preemergence herbicides useful for residential weed control are Treflan (Preen), Dacthal, Eptam, and Amiben (Ornamental Weeder). Treflan (Preen) is an excellent annual grass herbicide that controls some broad-leaved annual weeds. It can be used on many annuals and perennials as well as landscape plantings. It is volatile and must be incorporated mechanically or with irrigation, so follow the label directions carefully in regards to application procedures. You can expect 8 to 10 weeks of control, after which a repeat application might be needed. Remember that this is a preemergence herbicide, so the area must be weed-free at the time of application.

Dacthal is another annual grass herbicide that also controls a few annual broad-leaved weeds. Dacthal is safe for use on many ornamental plants (check the label) and will not injure any turf adjacent to the landscape bed. In fact, it is used to control crabgrass in lawns. It is not volatile, so it does not need to be incorporated. Dacthal is available in both granular form and as a wettable powder. It is difficult to keep from settling out in the spray tank, so frequently shake the tank hard when applying Dacthal. Good control will last from 6 to 8 weeks; if the plants have not filled in, a second application may be desirable. Remember that the plantings must be weed-free.

Eptam is used only to control certain difficult weed species, and it can be used safely on only a limited number of ornamental species. It is very volatile and must be incorporated deeply to be effective, but it can be effective against some perennial grasses, which is very unusual for a preemergence herbicide. Use this herbicide only if it is recommended for a problem at your site, and follow directions carefully.

Amiben (Ornamental Weeder) is used in the same manner as Dacthal. It is not labeled for use on nearly as many ornamental plants as Dacthal, but it will control more broad-leaved annuals than Dacthal. Check the label carefully, and use it only on those ornamentals listed on the label.

The use of postemergence herbicides in the landscape is generally limited to preplant treatments with a material such as glyphosate (Roundup or Kleen-up). The application of a postemergence herbicide directly on the target perennial weed is an effective means of getting rid of that weed. This herbicide is particularly effective against poison ivy and is available in small packages, which makes it practical for the residential landscape owner. Do not get this herbicide on any desirable plants or it will injure them. Follow the label directions carefully.

LAWN WEED CONTROL

The use of preemergence herbicides in lawns is primarily limited to crabgrass and other annual grasses. These materials are applied in granular form, or sometimes mixed with fertilizer or sprayed on using the same techniques of calibration and application as described in the previous section. Apply the crabgrass herbicides recommended for your area at the time they should be applied. Crabgrass seeds germinate when the soil warms up in the spring, and the herbicide must be applied prior to their germination. Correct time of application is very important, as is following label directions.

Broad-leaved weed killers may be applied in the granular form, mixed in a fertilizer, or sprayed on the lawn. Also, there is now a 2,4-D wax bar that you pull over the lawn. The wax has been impregnated with 2,4-D, and as the bar is pulled over the foilage of broad-leaved weeds, some herbicide is absorbed by the weeds, killing them. The bar as a weed control measure is only moderately effective, but it can be used in mid-summer without much chance of injuring nearby sensitive plants because there is no drift.

Many recommendations for broad-leaved weed control in the turf call for several applications per season. We feel that this is excessive and the risk of injury to landscape plants too great. You can make the first application of a broad-leaved herbicide early in

Fig. 8.8 *A well maintained lawn will be weed-free and the use of herbicides if done properly will not injure the existing woody ornamental plants.*

the spring, when the perennial weeds are active but before the woody plants have leafed out or the annual and vegetable gardens have been planted. Make the second application in the early fall, after most landscape plants are starting to go dormant, so no injury will occur. If you fertilize the turf well, it will become dense and very competitive with weeds. Soon you can reduce this twice-per-year treatment to once a year (in the spring), perhaps even not at all. Remove by hand the few weeds that appear, or spot threat them. The special herbicide applicators for spot treating weeds in lawns are very effective and use only a limited amount of herbicides.

RODENT PROTECTION

The use of poisons and baits as a means of rodent control in the landscape is not very desirable. These poisons are not highly selective, and pets or harmless animals may be killed. Repellents are available that are somewhat effective and yet do not injure the animal. Usually the repellents need to be used more than once during a winter season.

For most residential landscape situations, rodent barriers are the best way to prevent injury to plants in the winter. Fit a wire mesh screen (1/4-inch opening) loosely around tree trunks but tight to the ground to prevent mice from going through the barrier. The height should be at least 2 feet, higher in areas of high snow fall. You can also make barriers from solid sheet metal such as downspouting, crimping them after installation. You must remove these barriers with tin cutters as the tree increases in size. There is a flexible plastic trunk guard that provides rabbit protection, but you must install it carefully at ground level so that mice will not squeeze under it and damage the trunk.

9

Watering, Fertilizing, and Pruning Landscape Plants

Well-cared for, actively growing plants are healthier and much less susceptible to attack by insects and diseases. The three basic factors that influence landscape plant growth and the health of the plant are water, fertility levels, and pruning. Each condition is important in itself, but a good maintenance program includes a balance of all three factors. The result will be a well-maintained site that will require a minimum use of pesticides.

WATER

An adequate supply of water is absolutely essential for plants' growth and survival. During the establishment phase, watering is the most critical of all maintenance practices, and water should be available to plants in optimum amounts. However, in some instances too much water can be even more detrimental than a limited supply. As plants develop and become established, water is less critical, but an even, satisfactory moisture supply is essential for healthy plantings. Because there are so many variables that influence the amount of water needed, an all-purpose watering method is difficult, if not impossible, to define. Factors such as soil type, type of planting, age of the plantings, climate, and rainfall distribution all influence the watering practices needed for a particular site. However, there are several basic principles that should be followed when watering the landscape.

How Much? Whether watering lawn or landscape plants, apply enough water to penetrate the soil to a depth of 6 to 8 inches. In most areas and soil types this will be approximately 1 inch of water, but if the soil is light and sandy, more frequent waterings are necessary to maintain an adequate moisture supply to a depth of 8 inches or more. Except for establishing newly seeded turf areas, avoid frequent, light waterings because they are a waste of water and can actually damage plants since the water does not penetrate the soil deeply enough to encourage deep rooting. Shallow-rooted plants will have less root area to survive drought periods or, hard winters. Apply water slowly enough to keep the runoff to a minimum. Runoff is a waste of water, in some areas of the country it is unforgivable.

When to Water. Watering should be done to supplement rainfall. If a rainfall is only 1/2 inch, watering should be done immediately after with another 1/2 inch to bring the total to 1 inch. Do not be fooled by the amount of measurable rainfall in a brief summer shower; supplemental watering is often needed. Water early in the morning to reduce the amount of water lost by evaporation and to lessen the chance of foliage diseases. Mid-morning is a second choice. Avoid late afternoon and evening watering, which can cause disease problems. Weekly 1-inch waterings are adequate in most areas of the

Fig. 9.1 a & b *Healthy, vigorously growing landscape plants will provide a most satisfactory setting for the home.*

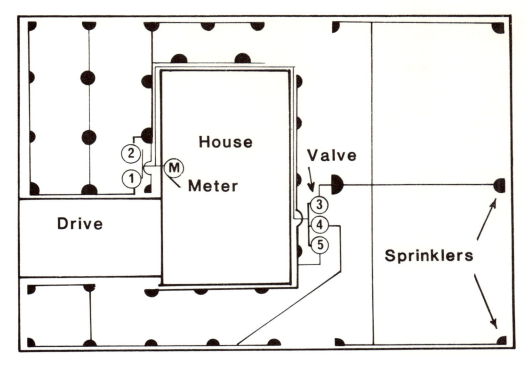

Fig. 9.2 *A permanent irrigation system is often the only way to apply water to a large landscape site in arid regions.*

country for most ornamental plantings and turf, but for light soils and in arid regions, more frequent waterings may be necessary, depending on the plants being grown.

For established trees and shrubs, the length of time between waterings or periods of rainfall can be extended. But do not neglect these plants during drought conditions when they need supplemental waterings. If there is no rainfall for longer than 2 weeks, periodically check the soil moisture supply in the root zone of trees and shrubs. Trees located in turf that is being watered properly will not be in danger of moisture stress during drought periods. To check moisture in landscape beds, dig down 6 to 9 inches and obtain a handful of soil from a place close to the plants but where it will not disturb the plant bed or root system of a tree. Squeeze the soil: if it sticks together in a ball, it has adequate moisture. If it crumbles and falls apart, water is needed; start supplemental waterings. It may take up to 2 inches of water to obtain the depth of penetration needed. Add water slowly enough so that the water soaks in rather than runs off.

When checked, sandy soils may not stick together in a soil ball even if some moisture is present. You need good judgment and instinct to determine if moisture is present at the 6- to 9-inch depth. If in doubt, remember that it is nearly impossible to overwater plants growing in a sandy soil.

Applying Water. How should the water be applied? Automatic permanent irrigation systems are popular in some sections of the country. These systems must be adjusted to deliver the right amount of water at the right rate; frequently they deliver the water too fast, resulting in excessive runoff. Also, because many of these systems are activated automatically by time clocks, water may come on even in a rain storm or after many inches of rain have fallen. The result is often waterlogged soil and plant injury or even death. If you have a permanent irrigation system, use manual activation so you can water when you judge best. This helps reduce the chance of waterlogging soils after heavy rainfall and saves water and needless expense.

You can water with the portable sprinklers described in Chapter 7. Regardless of the type of sprinkler you use, measure the rate of delivery. Do this by setting out several straight-sided cans in different locations within the distribution pattern of the sprinkler. Measure the amount of water in the cans at different times. This measuring will determine how long the spinklers must be set in one location to deliver 1 inch of water, and it will show whether the sprinkler's water-distribution pattern is uniform. Most sprinklers require from 4 to 8 hours per setting to deliver 1 inch of water. Once you determine the rate, you can control the amount of water being applied by merely timing each setting of the sprinkler.

Maintaining a lush, green lawn during the summer months in many areas of the country requires frequent irrigations. But then the nearby landscape beds may be overwatered by inefficient surface drainage patterns on the site. Too often the turf areas are sightly higher than the adjacent landscape beds, so excess water from the turf drains into the landscape beds. If the application method is improper, or the rate too rapid, the amount of water accumulating in the landscape bed from runoff can be far greater than the amount applied to the turf areas. If the soil is heavy or has a tendency toward poor drainage plants sentitive to waterlogged soils can be injured. To reduce the chances of this happening, water turf areas only when needed, and do not operate the system on a time clock. If you have a permanent irrigation system, be sure that the turf areas are under separate watering control from the landscape beds and annual and perennial plantings. Apply the water slowly enough to reduce runoff to a minimum. Finally, change the surface drainage pattern so that the flow is away from rather than into the landscape beds. This involves raising the soil level slightly.

FERTILIZING LAWNS

To maintain a vigorous turf area, you need a systematic fertilization program. Chapter 7 gives a fertilization schedule for a bluegrass turf. The actual timing of applications varies according to the geographic location of the site, the type of turf grass present, the type of fertilizer used, and the level of maintenance. A fine, high-quality lawn requires more frequent fertilizations.

Using a Spreader. The two basic types of fertilizer spreaders are described in Chapter 7. For most areas the impeller spreader is the fastest and most foolproof for uniform applications. When you use this piece of equipment, calibrate it to deliver the correct amount of fertilizer over a given area. Calibration means adjusting the opening on the hopper to deliver the right amount of fertilizer in accordance with your walking speed and the size of the fertilizer granules.

The manufacturer of the spreader often provides a starting setting. You achieve proper adjustment by trial and error. Set the setting at

Fig. 9.3 *Check the amount of water being applied by placing several straight-sided cans in different locations in the distribution pattern of the lawn sprinkler.*

one-half the amount to be applied: for the most uniform delivery, the application should be made in two directions at 90 degrees to each other. The time needed to cover an area with the impeller spreader is so short that you can cover the area twice and still save a large amount of time compared to using the gravity-feed spreader.

Place a measured amount of fertilizer (1 to 2 pounds) in the hopper. Carefully put a plastic bag over the distribution end of the spreader. This is difficult to do without getting the bag entangled in the workings of the spreader, but it can be done. Then walk the area just as though you were applying fertilizer, but instead collect the fertilizer in the bag. Measure and compare the area that would have been covered with the measured amount of fertilizer to determine if the setting is correct. Make any necessary adjustments in the setting, and repeat the check if necessary. Because each person walks at a different speed, the spreader should be calibrated by the person applying the fertilizer. Record the setting so that it can be used the next time. Recalibration is necessary if you change the type or brand of fertilizer.

When using the impeller spreader, never stop walking without first shutting off the spreader, to prevent fertilizer burn of small areas. Also, never stop turning the impeller of the carried model without first shutting off the hopper.

The gravity-feed spreader is also commonly used to apply fertilizer to lawns, and some fertilizer manufacturers have developed a gravity-feed spreader specifically for their products. The required settings are for their particular products. However, the spreader must be calibrated for each product; calibrate the spreader prior to use. Set the spreader

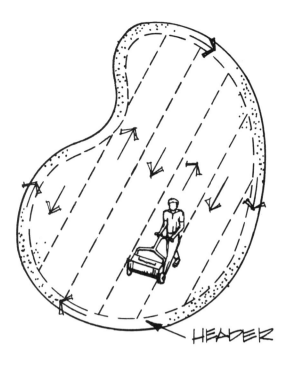

Fig. 9.4 *Application techniques when using a gravity-feed spreader. The method varies slightly with the shape of the area being fertilized.*

opening on the recommended setting. Place a measured amount of fertilizer (5 pounds) uniformly across the bottom of the hopper. Then apply the fertilizer to a driveway or sidewalk and measure the area covered. Calculate the amount delivered in relation to the total area, and determine if the recommended rate is being delivered. If it is not, reset the spreader and check again. Repeat until the spreader delivers the correct amount of fertilizer. Remember that when you are pushing the nearly empty spreader over a driveway, you might walk faster, so try to walk at the same speed as you would if you were pushing a full spreader over your lawn. Finally, sweep up and collect the fertilizer on the driveway or walk. Do not allow it to run into surrounding turf or fertilizer burn may occur along the edges of the walk or driveway.

Note that with a gravity-feed spreader the full amount of fertilizer is applied on one application, and the application pattern is different than with an impeller spreader. Across each end of the area to be fertilized, place two header strips parallel to the spreader. Push the spreader back and forth the length of the area until the area is completely covered. At the end of each strip, shut off the spreader when it reaches the header strips. Turn around and start back, opening the spreader when the turn is complete and as the spreader leaves the header strip. Always shut the spreader off when stopping or turning. To prevent striping, overlap one wheel width for each strip. Insufficient overlapping causes striping and gives a poor appearance to a lawn. For an irregularly shaped area, run a header strip completely around the area. Then complete the coverage as for a regularly shaped area.

Regardless of the spreader you use, wash it thoroughly after each use, and make certain it is completely dry before storing it. Oil mechanical parts, and leave the spreader open to its widest setting. Fertilizers are very corrosive, so leaving a little fertilizer in a spreader for even a few days can cause severe damage.

FERTILIZING TREES AND SHRUBS

A good feeding program helps keep trees and shrubs healthy and less susceptible to attacks by insects and diseases. Most landscape beds with shrubs and trees benefit from the addition of fertilizer. However, fertilizer demands of trees and shrubs, are much less rigorous than those of the lawn: once per year, or even once very 2 years if done properly, is

123

adequate fertilization for most trees and shrubs. If the trees are in a turf area which is being properly fertilized, the trees will need no additional fertilization.

There are several ways to determine whether trees and shrubs, healthy or not, are suffering from nutrient deficiences. Leaves should be full size and green or dark green, depending on the variety. Some plants have naturally light green foliage, and additional fertilizer will not darken the leaves. Young, immature trees should have a new growth of from 9 to 12 inches per year depending on the species. If they do not, they probably would benefit from fertilizer. Mature trees should have a minimum annual growth of 6 to 9 inches. The growth rate for shrubs varies so greatly between species that the need for fertilizer is indicated by the general appearance and health of the plants.

When to Fertilize. The recommended time that fertilizer should be applied varies quite a bit. In northern climates, an early spring application is recommended, but recent research has shown that the trees and shrubs will take up nutrients even late in the fall after defoliation has occurred, when the soil is warm and the roots are still active. In the early spring the soils are very cold and the roots are inactive, so it will be mid-spring or later before the roots can actively absorb nutrients. For those plants that make a spring flush of growth — such as *Euonymus alatus* (burning bush) — fertilization in the fall is probably a better choice. In southern and warmer climates, fertilize just prior to the start of growth.

For woody plants, the most important fertilizer element is nitrogen. A standard recommendation is to apply nitrogen every 1 to 3 years. Trees and shrubs show a response only to nitrogen in most instances.

How Much Fertilizer? The amount of fertilizer to apply to a landscape bed or for trees growing in open turf areas is based on the soil area to be covered. An older but infrequently used method for trees is to base the rate on a tree's trunk diameter.

If you are fertilizing a landscape bed, a ratio of 3-1-1 is best, since nitrogen is the most important ingredient. Apply an analysis of 15-5-5 at the rate of 40 pounds per 1,000 square feet. (This will result in an application of 6 pounds of nitrogen.) You can make this application at one time, unless there is turf in the area to be fertilized. Spread fertilizer uniformly over the soil surface. If some fertilizer salts are left on the

foliage, or the bed is a ground cover planting, irrigate the area to remove the fertilizer from the foliage. To apply the fertilizer you can use the gravity-feed spreader or the impeller spreader. Use the same techniques as described for applying fertilizer to turf. Use the correct amounts, and shut off the spreader when turning or stopping to avoid fertilizer burn.

Broadcasting. To fertilize trees, you can broadcast (scatter) the fertilizer on the soil's surface, or place it in holes in the root zone. The broadcast method is by far the easiest and has two advantages over the deep-root feeding method: (1) it distributes the fertilizer over the entire root area of the tree, and (2) because broadcasting can be done quickly, you can repeat applications when needed. However, there are three main disadvantages:

1. If the tree is located in a turf area, fertilizer under the tree will cause the turf to grow faster than the surrounding turf area, resulting in a "green oasis" effect. Remember, if you are following an active turf fertilization program, the tree does not need to be fertilized.

2. There are none of the benefits of root zone aeration that occurs with deep-root feeding.

3. Applying the recommended rate of 6 pounds nitrogen per 1,000 square feet in one application can, under certain conditions, seriously burn the turf. The maximum amount should be 3 pounds nitrogen per 1,000 square feet, with the application split, preferably one in the spring and one in the early fall. The following discussion tells how to determine the amount of actual nitrogen in a particular fertilizer.

Different materials are available for broadcast application; Table 9-1 lists several of the materials, their analysis and the amounts to apply to obtain various amounts of nitrogen per 1,000 square feet. There are other fertilizers with different nitrogen percentages, but by interpolating the chart you can determine the amount needed. Another way to determine the

Table 9-1 Pounds of nitrogen-source fertilizers to add to obtain two pounds actual nitrogen per 1,000 square feet.

Fertilizer	Analysis	Pounds per 1,000 sq ft
Urea	45-0-0	4
Ammonium nitrate	33.5-0-0	6
Ammonium sulfate	21-0-0	10
Sodium nitrate	16-0-0	12

From: Plants in the Landscape, 1975. Philip Carpenter, Theodore Walker and Frederick Lanphear. W.H. Freeman and Co.

amount to use is to divide the pounds of actual nitrogen needed by the percentage of nitrogen in the fertilizer. For example, if 3 pounds nitrogen per 1,000 square feet are needed, and the analysis of the fertilizer is 15-10-10, divide the 3 pounds by 0.15 (15%) to get 20 pounds of 15-10-10 fertilizer per 1,000 square feet. Remember that (1) the rate is based on the nitrogen in the fertilizer and not the other two elements and, (2) when dividing, the decimal point must be in the right place for the percentage: 5 percent = 0.05, 10 percent = 0.10, and so on.

Deep-Root Feeding. There are several ways to deep-root feed a tree; the high-pressure liquid fertilization method has to be done by professionals because of the equipment needed. Use the deep-root feeding method if you are applying phosphorus because phosphorus does not move readily downward in the soil. (Remember that mature woody plants do not normally respond to phosphorus fertilizer.) Other good reasons for using the deep-root feeding method are (1) it avoids the oasis effect, (2) it improves the aeration of the soil in the root zone, and (3) the fully recommended amount can be used without the fertilizer burning the turf. However, unless your soil is very heavy and poorly drained and thus needs aeration, the surface (broadcast) application is still the best one because then you can fertilize quickly and efficiently.

To deep-root feed, space holes 2 feet apart in a rectangular pattern beneath a tree with a few holes beyond the spread of the limbs (sometimes called the drip line). Figure 9-5 illustrates the placement of the holes. The holes should be from 1 to 2 inches in diameter and 12 to 18 inches deep. The "feeder" roots on most trees are in the top 18 inches of soil. Placing the fertilizer deeper is wasteful. Before making each

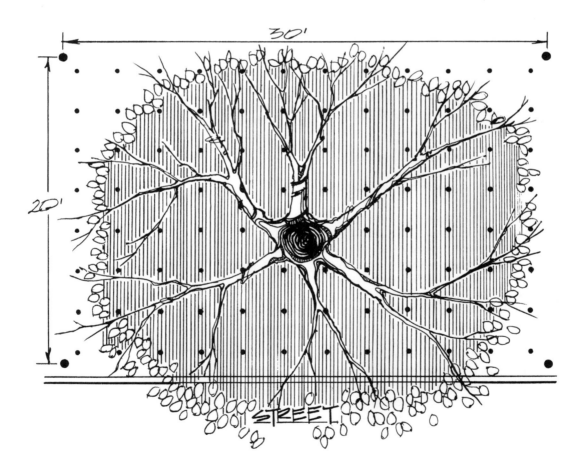

Fig. 9.5 *Using the deep root feeding method helps improve aeration around tree roots in poorly drained soils. (Source: Illinois Natural History Survey)*

hole, cut a plug of grass the same diameter as the hole; the plug will be replaced later to avoid unsightly damage to the turf. Drill the holes with a handpowered or a large electric auger. You can punch the holes in moist soil with bar, but this method does not improve soil aeration because the soil becomes compacted around the bar. Do not drill holes within 2 feet of trees with a trunk diameter of 12 to 18 inches; for tree trunks over 18 inches, do not place holes within 3 feet of the trees.

Once you prepare the holes, measure the area covered by the holes and calculate the surface area. Then compute the fertilizer needed to apply the correct amount to the trees. For instance, 10 feet by 10 feet, measures 100 square feet; the fertilizer needed, if the rate of 6 pounds actual nitrogen per 1,000 square feet is used, is 0.6 pounds nitrogen

$$\frac{(6 \text{ pounds} \times 100 = 0.6 \text{ pound})}{1,000}.$$

If the fertilizer analysis is 20-10-10 the 0.6 pound is divided by 0.20, to get 3 pounds (48 ounces). Divide the total amount of fertilizer by the number of holes, then measure out equal amounts for each hole. Once you put the fertilizer in the holes, fill the holes with sand. Add a little soil on top, and replace the grass plug. This technique minimally disturbs the appearance of the area.

Water Needles, Food Spikes. The water needles that attach to a garden hose to inject fertilizer into soil are not satisfactory for fertilizing anything but very small trees because the amount of fertilizer held in the apparatus is so small that the tree does not receive an adequate amount. However, water needles do get water into trees' root zones and help aeration. Overwatering in heavy soils is a possibility you must consider when using a water needle.

The so-called food spike can be driven into the ground around the area covered by the spread of the tree limbs. This spike is a high-nitrogen but complete fertilizer held together in the shape of a spike by a resin that eventually breaks down in the soil. The spikes can be driven into the soil rapidly and so involve less time than drilling holes: they also prevent the green oasis effect in turf. If the correct number are used, trees will receive an adequate supply of nitrogen, but the manufacturer's recommendation is totally inadequate to provide a satisfactory amount of fertilizer to a large tree. Calculate the weight of fertilizer needed based on the tree size (area of plant

spread), and then use the number of spikes required to supply the proper amount of fertilizer.

The disadvantages of food spikes are: (1) the cost is extremely high in comparison to the other methods described; (2) the spikes tend to cause fertilizer burn on the turf at points of entry, which appear as brown spots that last for several weeks; and (3) the soil is not aerated.

PLANTS REQUIRING SPECIAL FERTILIZATION

Many landscape plants require special fertilizers or corrective fertilization when specific problems occur. Rhododendrons and azaleas are among the plants that require a low soil pH for lush growth. These plants should be fertilized annually with an acid-reacting fertilizer such as ammonium sulfate, or, even better, with a fertilizer manufactured specifically for these plants.

For fertile soils prepared as recommended, for azalea and rhododendrons, apply ammonium sulfate early each spring at no more than 1/2 to 1 pound per 100 square feet; water it in. One month later, apply 1/4 to 1/2 pound per 100 square feet; water it in. A fall application in late October or in November can also be made when the plants are dormant and while the soil is still warm (above 45°F) at the same rates as noted. Apply this material after several days when the average 24-hour temperature has been under 50°F each day. Some authorities suggest that no fertilization is necessary once the plants are established and adequate organic matter is present. However,

Fig. 9.6 *Rhododendron flower production is better if the proper soil pH is maintained and if an active fertility program is carried out.*

on most sites heavy growth can be expected if an annual fertilization program is carried out. If soil tests reveal that the soil pH has increased to a level that might cause an iron deficiency in the plants, lower the pH with soil sulfur.

Some trees such as Pin Oak (*Quercus palustris*), will suffer from iron chlorosis (deficiency), and the foliage will be light yellow between the veins. In more severe cases the foliage will be stunted, the branches will die back, and overall growth will be poor. One reason for this problem is a high soil pH; the iron in the soil is not available to the tree. There are three ways to treat such a problem. If the problem is severe and the tree is in danger of limb loss because of dying back, spray the foliage with ferrous sulfate or iron chelate solution in the early spring as the new leaves grow. Follow the directions on the package as to the amounts to use in the solution. Repeat the sprays two or three times at 7- to 10-day

Fig. 9.7 *To help correct iron chlorosis in pin oak it may be necessary to inject the trunk with iron capsules.*

intervals. This temporary solution to the problem helps the tree survive until more permanent but slower-acting correcting measures can be carried out.

Another method is to inject the trunk with iron-containing capsules. These capsules are sold at most garden centers; but be sure to obtain the ones containing iron and follow installation directions carefully. The effect of this treatment last from 2 to 5 years; when iron chlorosis (yellow foliage) reappears, repeat the treatment.

The longest-lasting treatment is to treat the soil, the source of the problem. Correcting a high pH is a slow process that may not work in time to help the tree; therefore, other treatments may be needed if the problem is severe and the decline advanced. It is possible to lower the soil pH in the root zone of the pin oak tree by making surface applications of sulfur via the deep-root feeding method described in the previous section. In this case use a special iron sulfate-sulfur mixture in place of the fertilizer. See Table 9-2 for the recommended rates of the mixture to use, based on tree size.

All this indicates why you should not plant a tree or plant that requires so much attention. A soil test prior to purchasing a plant requiring an acid soil will indicate immediately whether problems will arise. If the soil pH is too high for pin oaks or other plants requiring acid soils, buy something else. If the plants are already present on your site and they are of a size that makes replacing them with another species difficult, use the corrective measures just described.

Finally, a word about foliar (leaf) feeding of landscape plants. Foliar feeding is generally a

Table 9-2 Soil applications of an iron sulfate-sulfur mixture for control of chlorosis in trees and shrubs.

Diameter of tree 4 feet above ground (inches)	Total amount of the iron sulfate-sulfur mixture per tree (pounds)	Two-inch diameter holes in ground		Total amount of the iron sulfate-sulfur mixture per hole (pounds)
		Number of holes	Depth of holes (inches)	
1	1	4	12	0.25
2	2	4	12	0.5
3	4	6	15	0.75
4	6	8	15	1.0
5	10	10	15	1.0
6	12	12	15	1.0
7	14	14	18	1.0
8	16	16	18	1.0
9	18	18	18	1.0
10	20	20	18	1.0
15	30	30	18	1.0
20	40	40	18	1.0
25	50	50	18	1.0

From: Plants in the Landscape, *1975.Philip Carpenter, Theodore Walker and Frederick Lanphear. W.H. Freeman and Co.*

waste of time and money, except for supplying some essential minor elements that might be lacking in a particular locality in the country. If minor-element deficiencies are a problem in your area, check with your county agricultural extension agent about the recommended solutions for the specific elements. Beware of "miracle" fertilizers and nutrients; there are no such things. Good environmental conditions for plant growth are the answer, and good plant nutrition with conventional fertility programs will provide optimum plant growth.

PRUNING TREES AND SHRUBS

Of all plant maintenance practices, pruning is the one that is most likely to be improperly carried out. Pruning is an essential maintenance practice that markedly increases the longevity of the plants in the landscape. In fact, proper pruning practices in countries like England and Japan have extended the useful life of some woody plants to centuries. Unfortunately, pruning is often ignored until it is too late: the plants have become very overgrown, and corrective pruning is nearly impossible. Ideally, you should do some pruning yearly to maintain plants in the form desired.

Fig. 9.8 *The leaf area on newly planted bare root trees must be reduced by pruning.*

Why Prune. Pruning maintains the size of a tree or shrub or, in some instances, reduces the size. Pruning prevents overgrowing, maintains the desired shape of the plant, and encourages vigorous new growth. Sometimes a plant has damaged or dead branches that need to be removed. Pruning newly planted trees and shrubs will reduce the leaf area; for bare root plants this may be essential to cut down water loss. The plant has a better chance of becoming established and starting to grow. In some instances corrective pruning on newly planted trees and even on older trees is necessary to remove weak branches or branches that might form weak crotches.

The removal of old flower heads and newly developing seed heads will encourage new growth and flower bud set. Rhododendrons are the classic example of plants that benefit from the prompt removal of their old flower heads for improved flower bud set for next season. If you have many rhododendrons on your site, it may be impossible to remove all the old flower heads, but those plants in key places in the site should receive this grooming.

When plants have become overgrown because of previous neglect of pruning, they may respond to rejuvenation pruning, which restores their vigor and reduces their size. This means removing many old branches; depending on the species, this should be done over a 3-year period. Some shrubs can be rejuvenated, but others cannot. Lilac, privet, forsythia, and spirea all benefit from this pruning, but be sure to check with an expert in your area before you start rejuvenation pruning on an overgrown shrub.

Another reason for pruning is to remove branches and limbs that might be hanging over walls, driveways, roads, and, sometimes, power lines. Limbs over the roof of a house can be a problem, particularly in areas of heavy snow or high winds. All of these situations constitute a danger that should be removed before injury or property damage occurs.

Pruning also enables you to form plants into a shape other than that of their natural growth habit. Hedges and screen plantings are shaped by pruning to form visual and physical barriers. Topiary is the shaping of plants in decorate forms, such as animals. This art form was popular in the past, but currently it is rarely seen except in areas such as theme parks. Evergreen globes and squares are in poor taste in most residential landscapes. Generally, for

128

Fig. 9.9   An effective, properly pruned juniper hedge that serves as a screen planting.

Table 9-3 Trees and shrubs which may be pruned both before and after bloom.

Botanical name	Common name
Cornus stolonifera	Red Osier dogwood
Cotoneaster apiculata	Cranberry cotoneaster
Cotoneaster divaricata	Spreading cotoneaster
Cotoneaster multiflora	Multiflora cotoneaster
Mahonia aquifolium	Oregon hollygrape
Spiraea bumalda	Anthony Waterer and Frobel spirea
Symphoricarpos albus	Snowberry
Symphoricarpos chenaulti	Coralberry
Weigela florida	Rose Weigela

residences, plants should be allowed to develop their natural growth habit.

When to Prune. Correct timing of the pruning operation maximizes the beauty of the landscape plants. There are eight basic rules you should follow:

1. Prune trees and shrubs that flower in the spring immediately after flowering. These plants set their next season's flower buds on the growth that is developing during the summer; the buds overwinter on this growth. Pruning anytime from the late summer until before flowering will remove many of these buds, resulting in a very disappointing flower show in the spring.

2. You can prune trees and shrubs that flower in the summer and fall during their dormant season. Their flower buds develop on the current season's growth.

3. A few plants can be lightly pruned before and after flowering. This seems to stimulate their flowering and growth. Table 9-3 lists several of these plants (note that there are only a few).

4. Plants such as some crabapples are prized both for their flower in the early spring and their fruit in the fall. Do you prune immediately after flowering, as suggested in rule 1, and lose fruit, or do you prune in the fall after fruiting and lose some of next season's flowers? The general rule is to prune these plants lightly each season after fruiting. This will maintain a steady flower- and fruit-production level.

5. Prune narrow- and broad-leaved evergreens anytime the wood is not frozen. Frozen wood is brittle, so if you try to prune, the branches may break and the plant shape may be seriously damaged. Annual pruning is important so that evergreens do not become overgrown.

6. So-called bleeder trees will lose large quantities of sap if pruned during periods of high sap flow. This is not normally injurious to the plant, but the dripping sap can be objectionable if it lands on sidewalks, cars, people, or property. Late fall pruning is best for trees in this group, which includes maples, birches, dogwood, elms, walnuts, and yellowwood.

7. In northern climates (hardiness zone 5 and north), avoid late summer and early fall pruning, which may encourage a flush of late-season growth that will not harden sufficiently before cold temperatures set in. Winter damage to the new growth can occur.

8. Remove broken or diseased branches as soon as you notice them.

The maintenance schedule in Chapter 7 is built largely around the pruning requirements of the plants. The correct timing of pruning is very important, so you should be aware of when to prune all the plants in your landscape.

Having the proper tools for pruning and keeping them in good condition is important because otherwise you cannot do a good job. The tools for pruning are described in Chapter 7 along with the use of each tool. Use only those tools suited for the particular pruning task.

Pruning Deciduous Trees and Shrubs. Always prune deciduous trees and shrubs in their natural growth habit. Not only do deciduous shrubs formed into compact globes, squares, or cones look ugly, but such pruning can also affect the plant's health. "Haircut" pruning (shearing just the edges of the plants with hedge shears) leaves a dense, thick, internal growth that will soon be weakened by a lack of light to the internal parts of the shrubs. The correct method is to thin the shrub's branches and reduce the length of the remaining branches, but not all the same length. Some of the large branches in the interior of the shrub can be removed at the ground line. Remove crossing and rubbing branches.

When making the individual cut, try to cut 1/4 inch above the active bud (an outward facing bud) so that the growth of shoots is in an outward direction from the center of the plant. Cutting higher than 1/4 inch above a bud on a stem will leave a stub that may not heal and that can be a source of decay or an entry port for disease. When removing a branch from a main branch or trunk, cut close to the branch so that no stub is left and the wound can heal rapidly.

There is controversy over the use of tree wound dressing to cover wounds 1 inch or more in diameter. Some authorities recommend the use of such a dressing to prevent the wound from becoming an entry place for disease or decay. Others say that this dressing is not necessary, that in fact it may slow the healing. Until more evidence is available, follow the recommendations of horticulturists in your area. If you do decide to use tree wound dressings, make sure you use only materials manufactured for this purpose; you can buy them at garden supply shops or any store that carries such items. Do not use tars or house paints because they may injure the tree trunk.

Pruning Evergreens. It is very tempting to shear evergreens into a square or round shape because they respond fairly well to this type of trimming. However, the evergreen generally has a very pleasing natural shape that blends in well in most residential landscapes. If you live in a French chateau, then formal pruning of evergreens is in order, but most informal American homes are complemented by the soft, natural form of the evergreen. However, this does not mean that evergreens should not be pruned to keep them in bounds. Prune them annually, but use the thinning technique described for deciduous shrubs. Cutting back the new growth by approximately one-half helps keep the plant in bounds and encourages plant vigor. Cut the branches individually at different lengths. Do not use hedge shears; use small hand pruners. The nongreen, heavy growth of many evergreen species will not produce new growth, so do not cut back to the nongreen portions. Rejuvenation of large, overgrown evergreens is often impossible.

Conifers (evergreen trees such as pines, spruces, and firs) need to be pruned in a different manner. If you want a dense, tight growth habit, such as in a Christmas tree, pinch out one-half the length of each new candle (new

Fig. 9.10 *Prune branches close to the main stems and do not leave stubs.*

Fig. 9.11 a & b *The neatly pruned evergreen globes and squares do not lend a pleasing appearance to this small home.*

Fig. 9.12 *These pine "candles" are ready to be pinched to thicken the growth of the tree.*

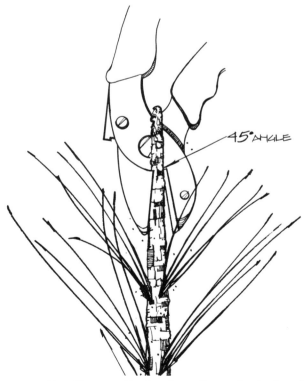

Fig. 9.13 *The central leader of a conifer may be shortened by cutting at a 45 degree angle.*

growth) when it is approximately 2 inches long. It is best not to cut the candles with shears because the needles will be damaged, causing the tips to turn brown and giving conifers an unsightly appearance during the year. However, if there are many conifers on your site, you will not have the time to pinch out each candle, in which case you should shear the candles when they have hardened (approximately 6 weeks after they start to elongate in the spring).

With some conifer species the distance between each whorl or layer of branches is too great, giving young trees a sparse, leggy appearance. To bring the whorls closer together and provide a denser growth habit, shorten (but do not remove) the central leader candle. Cut the leader at a 45 degree angle when it is hardened, at approximately midpoint in its length. This angled cut encourages a new leader to develop next year. A straight cut causes the development of a "bird nest" because several shoots develop from the cut.

Prune broad-leaved and narrow-leaved evergreens in the same manner as deciduous shrubs. Let them develop a natural growth habit. In certain sections of the country, low boxwood (*Buxus* spp.) hedges are used as garden borders and require formal pruning. American and English hollies (*Ilex* spp.) can be pruned at Christmas time. You can heavily prune every 3 years, or lightly prune annually.

Pruning Large Trees. In certain sections of the country, particularly the midwest, large trees are topped. But topping deforms a tree, ruining its shape forever. An even more serious consequence is that certain trees may actually be killed by the process. Tree topping has been promoted as a rejuvenation and safety process, but this is just not true. Numerous water sprouts develop; the interior growth is weakened by the soft dense growth of these sprouts; the large wounds can decay causing internal breakdown of the wood; and, in most instances, an ugly, weak tree results. The large leaves that often develop on the water sprouts give the illusion that the tree has new vigor, but actually the tree is just struggling to survive.

To remove branches and limbs from a large tree, hire an arborist. Supervise the work to be sure the tree is not being topped. A good arborist can drop work a tree, that is, lower its height, without destroying its shape. *Never remove limbs and trees growing near power lines.* Contact the utility company to have this done; they will do it without cost to you and safely.

On branches 1 inch or more in diameter, use the double-cut method. If you make one cut close to the trunk, the weight of the limb may break away before the cut is finished, causing tearing of bark and wood that heals very slowly. For the double-cut method, make the first cut approximately 6 inches from the tree trunk on the underside of the limb, approximately halfway through the limb. Make the second cut approximately 1 inch farther out on the limb and the top side of the limb. As the second cut approaches halfway through the limb, the limb will break away. Remove the stub so that it is flush with the trunk, and round off the edge of the wound with a sharp knife so that the wound will start to heal properly.

Rejuvenation of Overgrown Shrubs. Certain shrubs that have become overgrown can be rejuvenated by pruning. You can cut back privet hedges to 2 or 3 inches above the soil level. The new growth can be trained in the desired shape for a hedge. For other plants, such as lilac, forsythia or rhododendrons, the rejuvenation process should be done over a 3-year period, removing about one-third of the old, heavy growth each year. Cut back the new growth that occurs from the base of the plant to varying lengths to force a thickened, dense-type growth at the base of the plant. Remember that not all plants can be rejuvenated, so check with an authority before you start to drastically cut back a large plant.

Peegee Hydrangea (*Hydrangea paniculata* 'Grandiflora'), butterfly bush, ((*buddleia alternifolia*), and St. John's Wort (*Hypericum prolificum*) should all be cut back in the same manner as privet, but cut back annually. This pruning is necessary to force the plant to develop heavy, vigorous shoot growth.

Pruning Hedges. A good hedge or screen planting should be full all the way to the ground, but too often hedges are improperly pruned and the plants become leggy. The hedges are pruned with a wide top and a narrow base (vase-shaped), and this heavy top growth causes the lower portion to be shaded out. The result is an open appearance at the base. Proper hedge-pruning techniques are a wide base and narrow top so that the base will receive sunlight and the growth will remain active and vigorous. This simple technique should be used to achieve the full effectiveness of hedges and screen plantings. Prune hedges with hedge shears.

Pruning Roses. Prune bush roses in the early spring, just before new growth starts. In many

Fig. 9.14   *These trees have been ruined by topping and severe pruning.*

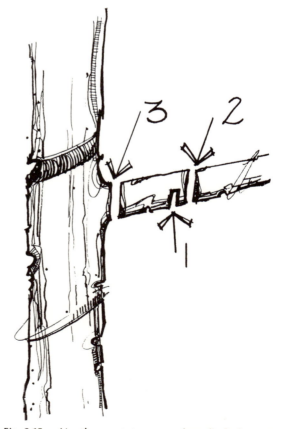

Fig. 9.15   *Use three cuts to remove large limbs from trees.*

Fig. 9.16   *Prune hedges with a narrow top and a wide base to keep the growth dense to the ground.*

sections of the country there will be considerable dieback because of winter damage. Remove all dead or damaged wood by cutting at least 1 inch into the live wood. Cut out all weak growth from the previous season by cutting close to the crown. Always remove inward-growing branches, and remove the weakest, crossing, or rubbing branches. Shape the plant by cutting back the strong canes to a nearly uniform height. Do not use hedge shears; use hand shears, and cut each cane just above an outward-facing bud.

Prune climbing or rambler roses just after their spring flowering. Remove any damaged or dead wood in the spring, but be careful because heavily pruned live wood will reduce the number of flowers. Shorten strong canes to encourage new vigorous lateral branches to develop. If you are training the roses to a trellis, loosely tie the new growth to the trellis.

Appendix A
Landscape Contractor — Homeowner Relationship

Dealing with a landscape contractor is no different than dealing with a building contractor, or electrical contractor or, for that matter, buying an automobile. In all cases a clear understanding of what is to transpire and what the product will be makes for a satisfactory deal. Timing, product guarantees, workmanship, costs, payment procedure, and overall landscape design should all be agreed to in advance. This appendix discusses in some detail the business relationship between the client and landscape contractor.

CONTRACTS

Many landscape contractors now require the signing of a contract very similar to a building contract before any work starts on a project. This contract is a two-way agreement that protects both the contractor and the client. It tells what the contractor will do and how he is to be paid, and it will probably also discuss any guarantees provided on materials and workmanship. In other words, it establishes a clear understanding of what is to happen during the construction and planting of the landscape site. Various contracts and part of contracts are discussed below.

In most instances of residential landscape construction, the design is often prepared by a landscape architect or designer in the employ of the landscape contractor. In this case the contract that is to define the work to be done is prepared by the contractor. Figure A-1 is an example of such a contract.

The first part of this contract is merely the owner's name and location. The letterhead identifies the landscape contracting firm and in this manner both parties involved on the projects are identified. The formal definition of the parties involved used in the previous contract is necessary. The next part is a brief description of the work to be done, and the total price for completion of the project. The description will only list the work to be done and there is no set of specifications describing in detail *how* the work is to be done. If a landscape plan (it probably will be) is supplied it should be considered one of the contract documents.

A payment plan is also defined and it should be made clear to the owner if partial payments are to be made as the project progresses and just how much of the work will be done at each stage when payment is due.

Under the Miscellaneous section it should be noted that this contract supercedes all others signed with the company and the attachments are considered a part of the contract. This means a set of specifications could be included as well as a landscape plan. Again, make absolutely certain that you read completely and understand the terms on all the documents involved in the contract.

The last statement on *Acceptance* is included so that the owner has the option of thinking about the contract prior to returning it to the Contractor. It is a means of taking the pressure off the owner and represents sound business practices by the landscape contractor. He does not want the customer to feel pressured into signing any contract and then having second thoughts. The contract can be returned within a few days after the sale presentation has been made. The number of days is given on the

WAL-CAR CONSTRUCTION CORPORATION
1220 Midtown Road
Mesa, Arizona 85201

_____   _____
Owner's Name   Date

_____   _____
Address

_____   _____
City   State   Zip Code   Phone

The contractor will furnish all labor, materials and equipment necessary to complete the following described work.

```
To install the lawns, landscape plant materials
deck, fence, and sprinkling system as described
on the landscape plan.
```

The work to be completed for the sum of:

Seven thousand three hundred _____ Dollars ($ 7,300)

Payments will be made in Mesa, Arizona as follows:

1/3 prior to starting work and 2/3 upon completion.

If method of payment is not stated, Owner shall make payment in full within ten (10) days of receipt of invoice. Contractor will be paid for partial completion of job, and stoppage of work for the convenience of owner shall be considered as partial completion and full payment shall be due for all work done.

Miscellaneous: This contract is made before any work is begun, and all prior arrangements are part of this contract. All landscape plans are part of this contract. No change in this contract shall be valid unless approved by both parties to this agreement.

Acceptance: Your acceptance of this proposal by signing and returning one copy to us within _____ days will constitute a contract.

Accepted: WAL-CAR CONSTRUCTION CORP.
(Owner)

_____   By: _____
                                        President

Fig. A.1 _Example of a sample contract._

contract, but if you return the contract with the sales representative the contract is binding to both parties concerned.

OTHER DOCUMENTS

Besides the formal contract for the work to be done, there are several other documents that are often part of the contract. Such as the landscape plan. In some instances when money is to be owed to the landscape contractor for any period of time after completion of the work, he will ask for the owners to sign a note guaranteeing payment and usually interest on the amount to be paid will also be included (Fig. A-2).

Also, there may be a *Conditions of Contract* which lists some factors relating to the contract. There are several points that should be noted on this set of conditions (Fig. A-3). Under Item 2, *Materials,* the contractor may substitute materials unless forbidden by the plan or specifications. The owner should make absolutely certain that they want the contractor to have this right. Item 3, *Changes,* means that changes in the work once materials have been purchased may result in additional charges if the materials cannot be used on the job. This is only fair since the materials may have been purchased specifically for your project and their use elsewhere may present a problem to the contractor.

Item 5, *Drainage.* The contractor is not responsible for any drainage changes, therefore, the owner should be absolutely certain that there is no change in drainage

State of _____ _____ 19 _____

after date, I, we, or either of us, the undersigned,

promise to pay to   or order, the

sum of   DOLLARS,

with interest thereon from date until maturity at the rate of   per centum per annum, the interest

payable   as it accrues, both principal and interest payable at

This note is given in   payment for the construction of certain improvements upon that

lot or parcel of land situated in

this day contracted to be erected by

for   and to secure

the payment thereof, an express Contract and Mechanic's Lien is given by said contract upon said lands and improvements.

All past due principal and interest on this Note shall bear interest from maturity until paid at the rate of ten per cent per annum.

It is understood and agreed that failure to pay this Note or any installment of interest thereon, when due, or failure to insure and keep said improvements insured, for the benefit of the holder of this note, or failure to pay taxes now due, if any, and keep the taxes paid, as they accrue, upon said premises, or a total or partial destruction of said improvements, shall, at the option of the holder of same, mature the entire indebtedness evidenced by the note this day given by the undersigned for erection of said improvements.

And it is hereby specially agreed that if this Note is placed in the hands of an attorney for collection, or if collected by suit, or through Probate or Bankruptcy proceedings, the undersigned agree to pay ten per cent additional on the amount of principal and interest then owing thereon as attorney's fees.

Due   day of   19   _____

Address   _____

Fig. A.2 *Sample note guaranteeing payment.*

CONDITIONS OF CONTRACT

1. **Acceptance:**   This bid is based on the current price of labor and materials.

2. **Materials:**   Unless otherwise specified in the plans and specifications, the contractor shall have the right to substitute other materials of equal or better quality.

3. **Charges:**   Alterations, additions or deviations shall be charged to the owner at the contractor's normal selling price. If contracted materials had been purchased prior to the change in work, then the owner must pay all cost necessary to dispose of materials in the change.

4. **Unavoidable Interruptions:**   It is hereby mutually agreed that the contractor shall not be held responsible or liable for any loss, damage or delay caused by fire, acts of God, civil or military authority, or by any other cause beyond the contractor's control.

5. **Drainage:**   The contractor will not be responsible for the drainage of water onto, across or from the owner's property or from any roof.

6. The owner shall be responsible for location of all *property lines and corners.*

7. **Responsibility:**   Owner shall locate and the contractor will not assume responsibility for damage done to any type of underground object including but not limited to cesspools, septic tanks, water lines, gas lines, electrical conduit, *sprinkler systems,* or to sidewalk and approach aprons or any other objects unless designated prior to the beginning of work on appropriate blueprints, copies of which shall be furnished contractor and form a part hereof. Theft of plants or materials after they are placed on the job site will be the owner's responsibility, unless set forth in writing herein.

8. **Guarantee:**   All plantings as indicated will be guaranteed as follows: shrubs and vines for 90 days and trees for one year, unless otherwise specified. Where plants die, replacements will be made with plants of the original size and quality as previously installed, at no cost to the owner, provided only, one replacement for each plant that dies. No guarantee shall be given for bulbs, roses, annuals, grass, potted or tubbed plants or bedding plants. While reasonable efforts will be made to assure that transplanted plants will continue to live, we cannot guarantee their life. The above guarantee will not apply where plants die because of animal damage, vandalism, injury by fire, drowning, storms, hail, drought, insects, disease, exceptional or untimely heat or freeze, acts of God or any casualty. The owner hereby agrees that for the guarantee to be effective, he will water thoroughly at least twice a week during dry periods and cultivate beds lightly and weed beds at least twice a month as a minimum, and follow any written instructions furnished by contractor, violation of which will void this guarantee. Delinquent payment voids guarantee.

9. **Grading:**   The landscape contractor will receive the site at finished grade unless otherwise specified. An extra charge will be made if rock interrupts work and or special equipment is required.

10. **Terminations:**   Both parties agree that this contract may not be cancelled after acceptance without written consent of contractor, unless at the time of cancellation a sum equal to the greater of (i) the value of all services rendered and materials furnished to the date of cancellation or (ii) 20% of the contract price, as liquidated damages, is paid to the contractor by the owner.

11. **Penalties:**   This account shall be due and payable in full within ten (10) days from the date of invoice, and purchaser agrees to pay interest on the unpaid balance from the due date until paid at the maximum lawful contract rate. In the event the account is turned over to an attorney for collection, owner will pay landscape contractor's reasonable attorney's fees.

12. **Pay Rates:**   The landscape contractor's price is based on their normal pay rate schedule. If union or F.H.A. pay rates are required, then the owner will pay the difference plus the mark-up in pay rates, which shall apply to the prices quoted accordingly.

Fig. A.3 *Sample conditions of contract.*

patterns caused by the design of the project. It should be noted in Item 7, *Responsibility*, that it is the owner's responsibility to locate and make available a blueprint locating all utilities and other underground objects that might be damaged during the installation of the landscape. Also of interest is that security is the owner's responsibility once materials are placed on the site. It would be wise to carry insurance to protect against theft or check to see if the homeowner's policy covers such events.

The guarantee provided on the plantings is given in Item 8, *Guarantee*. It also spells out the owner's maintenance obligation during the guarantee period as well as the Acts of God clause that voids the guarantee. It should be noted that extreme temperatures voids the guarantee so that plant loss due to extremely cold winters are considered an Act of God and the owner is not protected by the guarantee. Also, if you do not make proper contracted payments for the project, the guarantee is void.

Both Items 10, *Termination*, and 11 *Penalties*, define the owner's obligation to the contractor in the event a decision is made not to start or not to complete the project once it is started and the penalties for not making payment as specified in the contract. If for some reason the contractor must pay a higher wage rate to his workers than is normally paid, it is the responsibility of the owner to pay the increased costs. This is covered in Item 12, *Pay Rates*.

Sometimes a subcontractor will be used. A subcontractor is one who contracts to do a special part of the project and the actual work is not done by the landscape contractor. For example, if the landscape project calls for a swimming pool, in most instances the landscape contractor does not install swimming pools. But since the pool is part of this project he will be responsible for its installation. Therefore, he must hire another firm (a subcontractor) to do the installation. The cost will be part of the total price for the landscape project and it will be the responsibility of the landscape contractor to make certain that the pool is of the quality desired and the installation is carried out in a satisfactory manner. Also, the landscape contractor will pay the subcontractor, but it is important that the owner receive a certification that the subcontractor has been paid. This protects the owner from the possibility of being sued or have a mechanic's lien placed against his property for nonpayment for work done. This could occur if the landscape contractor went bankrupt and did not pay his subcontractors. In many states the subcontractor then can require the owner of the project to pay for the work

even though the owner has already paid the bankrupt landscape contractor. This is true for all phases of contracting work, not just landscape construction.

A subcontractor might be hired by a landscape contractor to install cement work such as drives, walks, etc.; to build fences, decks, and other wood landscape features; to install masonry features and outdoor electrical and plumbing parts of the project, as well as any unusual construction items that he, the landscape contractor, is not equipped to do.

CHANGE ORDER

Often, after a project has started, more or less work might be desired by the owner. This requires a change to be made in the original contract and this is handled by issuing a change order. If the owner is represented by a landscape architect, the landscape architect issues a change order to the landscape contractor for the changes to be made in the project. If the owner is dealing directly with the contractor, it is the contractor who prepares a change order based on the requests of the owner. Regardless, there is, or should be, a form called the change order which becomes part of the contract documents. Figure A-4 is a typical change order document. The first part of the

---

CHANGE ORDER

Date: _____ Change order no.: _____
To WAL-CAR Construction Corp.: _____
_____
Project: _____
_____
You are authorized to make the following changes in this contract:

Previous contract total: _____ $ _____
Contract shall be (increased)
(decreased) by the sum of _____ $ _____
Contract total including
this change order _____ $ _____
Contractor acceptance: _____ Date: _____
Owner approval: _____ Date: _____

Fig. A.4 *Example of a change order.*

change order is the identification of the change order by project and contractor as well as date. Then the changes are listed as well as the changes in the cost of the project. Finally all parties concerned sign the order which makes it a part of the legal contract for the project. Do not request changes to be made on the project without having a change order prepared including the changes in the price of the project.

GUARANTEES

Guarantees vary greatly with the individual landscape contractor and the individual nurseryman where you might buy your landscape plants. If there is to be a contract signed, the guarantee should be included in these documents. it will tell how long the plant material will be guaranteed. For example, a small shade tree might be guaranteed for one year from the date of planting, while a large tree (over 4 inch trunk diameter) might have a 2 year guarantee period. Evergreens might be guaranteed for 1 growing season. In some northern climates exceptionally harsh winters might void the guarantee. Also, the guarantee will describe the owner's obligation to care for the plant material during the guarantee period. Failure to provide adequate care will probably void the guarantee. Construction materials are usually guaranteed for a period that is commonly used in the trade.

The important thing to remember is that each firm will have its own guarantee policy. It is your obligation to find out what the policy is and to check with other customers to determine if a firm backs its work. In the landscape industry all reputable firms back their guarantees, and the only time a problem will occur is if there is a question concerning whether the owner maintained the site properly.

These are the contract documents that might be prepared for a project. Often no contracts, plans or specifications are used for smaller landscape projects, but the author of this book believes that unless it is a single plant installation a plan should always be prepared. Regardless of whether many contract documents are prepared or whether there is a simple agreement between the owner and the landscape contractor, there are certain steps and procedures that should be followed prior to and during the development of the landscape project.

1. Always ask to see some of the other projects of the landscape contractor. Examine the site to determine if the installation methods used and the quality of materials including the plant are satisfactory.

2. If at all possible, talk to at least one and preferably more owners of other projects that have been completed by the contractor. Ask them if they were satisfied with the work performed, the appearance and attitude of the work force used, and the project dealings with the contractor, including payment procedures. Many would say it is none of the owner's business of how the crew of the contractor looks or their attitude, but remember, if the project is at a residence, your family or guests may be present when the work is being done and the crew reflects on you as well as the contractor.

3. Talk to the contractor and try to determine if you and he will have a reasonable working relationship.

4. Remember the landscape contractor is a businessman whose time is valuable and who must purchase all his materials for the project. Be fair in what you expect. Main changes cannot be made in the project without affecting the price. Do not make unreasonable requests for such changes.

5. Before signing any contracts make certain that you have read and approved all the documents that constitute the contract. If you have questions concerning the terms of the contract, consult with your attorney if it is of a legal nature. And if the questions concern the execution of the project discuss them with the landscape contractor.

6. Make absolutely certain that you and the contractor have a written agreement as to when and how the project will be done.

PHOTOGRAPHER CREDITS

Unless otherwise credited below all photographs are by the author.

Preface

vii, viii Theodore D. Walker

Chapter 1
Fig. 1.1 A.E. Bye
Figures 1.2, 1.3, 1.7, 1.17 Theodore D. Walker
Fig. 1.8 Audio-Visual Department, Purdue University

Chapter 2
Fig. 2.1A Harrison Flint
Figures 2.1b, 2.2—2.4 Theodore D. Walker
Figures 2.6, 2.9 David Hamilton
Figures 2.7, 2.8, 2.11 Audio-Visual Department, Purdue University

Chapter 3
Figures 3.1, 3.5, 3.6 Audio-Visual Department, Purdue University
Fig. 3.2 I. Didrichsons, Nebraska Department of Roads
Figures 3.3, 3.14 Theodore D. Walker
Fig. 3.15 Richard Hayden

Chapter 4
Fig. 4.1 Pan American Seed Co.
Figures 4.2a—4.2c All-America Selections
Fig. 4.3 Theodore Brickman Co.
Fig. 4.5 E.R. Honeywell
Figures 4.6, 4.7 Walters Gardens
Figures 4.8—4.10 Netherlands Flower-Bulb Institute
Figures 4.11, 4.13, 4.14 Theodore D. Walker
Fig. 4.12 A.E. Bye

Chapter 5
Fig. 5.1 Edward L. Carpenter
Figures 5.3a—5.5, 5.8, 5.14 William Daniel
Figures 5.6, 5.7 Theodore D. Walker
Figure 5.9—5.13 Ford Motor Company
Fig. 5.15 Reinco Equipment
Fig. 5.16 Audio-Visual Department, Purdue University

Chapter 6
Figures 6.4—6.9 Agricutural Communications Department, Purdue University
Fig. 6.11 Audio-Visual Department, Purdue University

Chapter 7
Fig. 7.1 Theodore Brickman Co.
Fig. 7.2 Thomas Weiler
Fig. 7.3 A.E. Bye
Fig. 7.4 Theodore D. Walker
Figure 7.6a,b William Daniel

Chapter 8
Figures 8.1, 8.8 William Daniel
Figures 8.3, 8.5—8.7a Theodore D. Walker
Fig. 8.7b A.E. Bye

Chapter 9
Figures 9.1a,b, 9.6, 9.11—9.12 Theodore D. Walker
Figures 9.3, 9.8, 9.10, 9.14, 9.16 Audio-Visual Department, Purdue University
Fig. 9.9 Edward L. Carpenter

Index